# SUETONIUS

## VESPASIAN

# SUETONIUS
# VESPASIAN

Edited with Introduction,
Commentary and Bibliography by
**Brian W. Jones**

**Bristol Classical Press**

First published in 2000 by
Bristol Classical Press
an imprint of
Gerald Duckworth & Co. Ltd
61 Frith Street
London W1V 5TA
e-mail: inquiries@duckworth-publishers.co.uk
Website: www.ducknet.co.uk

A catalogue record for this book is available
from the British Library

ISBN 1-85399-584-3

Printed in Great Britain by
Booksprint

# Contents

# Preface

In this edition of Suetonius' *Diuus Vespasianus*, my aim has been to examine the political, social and, to a lesser extent, the literary, textual and grammatical questions posed by the *Life*. I hope that it will be of value not only to students of Latin but also to those historians interested in the Flavian period.

The debt I owe to previous scholars is obvious – Birley, Eck, Syme to mention but a few. I have also found much of value in previous commentaries on the *Diuus Vespasianus*, especially those of Braithwaite (1927) and Mooney (1930). I am indebted to the many colleagues who have helped me over the years in my work on the Flavians. They are too numerous to mention here, but I must thank Dr Jim Stewart for commenting on an early version of the text, Penny Peel for her untiring assistance in preparing my manuscript for publication, and Professor Bob Milns for having read and carefully dissected sections of the work. I need hardly add that any errors or misconceptions that remain are entirely my own.

Unfortunately, Levick's long-awaited biography of Vespasian arrived when the commentary was in its final form and only brief references could be made to it.

All dates are AD unless otherwise indicated; references to modern works are made by surname of the author(s) and date of publication; and the *Diuus Vespasianus* is cited by chapter and section only, e.g. 1.3 and not Suetonius, *Vesp.* 1.3.

B.W.J.
Brisbane, November 1999

# Abbreviations

The abbreviations are those of *L'Année Philologique* and *The Oxford Classical Dictionary* (3rd edn 1996), with the following additions:

AE      *L'Année Epigraphique* (Paris, 1888-)

ANRW      *Aufstieg und Niedergang der Römischen Welt*, ed. H. Temporini (Berlin and New York, 1972-)

Atti      *Atti del Congresso Internazionale di Studi Vespasianei: Rieti, Settembre 1979* (Rieti, 1981)

BMC      *Coins of the Roman Empire in the British Museum*, ed. H. Mattingly (London, 1923-40)

CAH      *Cambridge Ancient History* (Cambridge, 1923-)

CIL      *Corpus Inscriptionum Latinarum* (Berlin, 1869-)

ILS      *Inscriptiones Latinae Selectae* (Berlin, 1882-1916)

MW      McCrum, M. and A.G. Woodhead, *Select Documents of the Principates of the Flavian Emperors including the Year of Revolution AD 68-96* (Cambridge, 1966)

OCD      *Oxford Classical Dictionary*, 3rd edn (Oxford, 1996)

OLD      *Oxford Latin Dictionary* (Oxford, 1982)

PIR¹      *Prosopographia Imperii Romani Saec. I,II,III*, 1st edn (Berlin, 1897-8)

PIR²      *Prosopographia Imperii Romani Saec. I,II,III*, 2nd edn (Berlin and Leipzig, 1933-)

RE      *Realencyclopädie der Classischen Altertumswissenschaft* (Stuttgart, 1894-1980)

RP      Syme, R., *Roman Papers* (Oxford, 1979-91)

Str      Mommen, Th., *Römische Staatsrecht* (Berlin, 1886-7)

# Introduction

Not so long ago Suetonius was described as a 'literary man with the muck-rake, too keen upon petty and prurient detail to produce a scientific account of his subjects' (Duff, 1964: 508). Now he is seen as a courtier and as the author of a 'long list of scholarly, antiquarian and biographical works' (Millar, 1977: 91); and Wallace-Hadrill devotes over twenty pages to Suetonius the 'Scholarly Biographer'. This change of attitude has not occurred overnight, but the impetus for it has undoubtedly been the discovery of an inscription from Hippo Regius (= Annaba) with hitherto unknown details of Suetonius' career (*AE* 1953, 73). A series of articles by Townend appeared not long after, as did monographs by Anna (1954), della Corte (1967), Mouchova (1968), Gugel (1977) and Cizek (1977); then came De Coninck (1983) and Gascou (1984). The lack of major works in English was remedied in 1983 by both Wallace-Hadrill and Baldwin, with Lounsbury following in 1987. At around the same time appeared articles by Syme and Bradley, whilst this decade saw the (belated) publication of *ANRW* 2.33.5 (1991) with articles by Galand-Hallyn (3576-622), Lewis (3623-74), De Coninck (3675-700) and Bradley (3701-32).

So, too, there had been a dearth of up-to-date commentaries in English on the *Caesares*: Shuckburg's *Diuus Augustus*, published in 1896, was reprinted seventy-four years later and Mooney's *Galba to Domitian* of 1930 was reprinted in 1979. Once more, the remedy has been comparatively recent, with the Bristol Classical Press' series of commentaries by Warmington (*Nero*: 1977 – new edition in 1999), Carter (*Augustus*: 1982), Mottershead (*Claudius*: 1986), Murison (*Galba, Otho and Vitellius*: 1992), Lindsay (*Gaius*: 1993 and *Tiberius*: 1995) and Jones (*Domitianus*: 1996). There are two commentaries in English on the *Diuus Vespasianus*, those of Braithwaite (1927) and Mooney (1930).

## Suetonius' Career

Debate on his official career has been intense of late (see above) though somewhat inconclusive. Four distinct sources of information about him survive from antiquity, viz. (a) what he tells us himself (*Calig.* 19.3; *Claud.* 15.3; *Nero* 57.2; *Otho* 10.1; *Dom.* 12.2; *De Gramm.* 4 and *Vita Lucani*); (b) what emerges from the letters written to him by Pliny (*Ep.* 1.18, 3.8, 5.10, 9.34) and from references to him in Pliny's letters to Baebius Hispanus and the emperor Trajan (*Ep.* 1.24, 10.94, 10.95); what can be learned from (c) the Hippo Regius inscription and from (d) three late sources (*SHA*, Lydus and the Suda). Such variety is unusual: few literary figures are so well documented.

Son of Suetonius Laetus who had fought for Otho as an equestrian military tribune in Legio XIII during the civil war of 69, Suetonius Tranquillus was probably born in Hippo Regius (Annaba) in North Africa (see Birley, 1998: 203; but compare Brunt, 1990: 490) soon after the war ended and hence, so it is argued by Syme (*RP* 3.1053), acquired the *cognomen* Tranquillus. On the other hand, some have suggested that he was born as early as 62, others as late as 77 (for the details, see Wallace-Hadrill, 1995: 3 n.4). Far more secure evidence shows that he was brought up in the capital and educated there. One of his teachers seems to have been the aptly named Princeps (*me quidem adulescentulo, repeto quendam Principem nomine alternis diebus declamare, alternis disputare, nonnullis mane uero disserere*: *De Gramm.* 4). He describes himself as *adulescens* in 88 (*Nero* 57.2) and as *adulescentulus* during Domitian's reign, when he witnessed the physical examination in Rome of a Jewish man aged ninety (*Dom.* 12.2).

A slightly older Suetonius appears in Pliny's letters. In their first exchange, from the last years of the first century AD, the theme is the effect a bad dream had on Suetonius (*Ep.* 1.18). The next (3.8: ca 101-3) clarifies their relationship: for Pliny had obtained a military tribunate for Suetonius with L. Neratius Marcellus (attested as consular legate of Britain in 103: *CIL* 16.48), but Suetonius wanted to transfer it to one of his relatives. In 5.10 (?after 106), Pliny urges him to publish, i.e. *perfectum opus absolutumque est...patere (me) audire describi legi uenire uolumina Tranquilli mei*; and in 9.34 (105-8) Pliny asks him about a suitable *lector* for a *recitatio* of one of Pliny's works. By 110, Suetonius had secured the exceedingly valuable patronage of Pliny, an *amicus* of Trajan, and influential enough to obtain for him the *ius trium liberorum* (*Ep.* 10.94 and 95). One other letter remains (1.24; of uncertain date but probably very early – see Bradley, 1998: 3), and in some ways it is the most important, for it has given rise to the belief that Suetonius was little more than a retiring, timid scholar. Writing to Baebius Hispanus, Pliny begins *Tranquillus contubernalis meus uult emere agellum*, points out that amongst the property's advantages is its *uicinitas urbis* and adds that *scholasticis porro dominis, ut hic est, sufficit abunde tantum soli ut releuare caput, reficere oculos...* (1.24.1-4). The words *agellum* and *scholasticus* have been stressed rather than Pliny's comment that one of the property's advantages was the fact that it was close to Rome. The emphasis on Suetonius' desire for seclusion was misplaced. He was well aware of the real world and was not seeking *otium*.

Pliny's letter to Trajan, probably written in 110 not long before his death, begins with a useful summary of Suetonius at the age of forty: *Suetonium Tranquillum, probissimum honestissimum eruditissimum uirum, et mores secutus et studia iam pridem, domine, in contubernium adsumpsi, tantoque magis diligere coepi quanto nunc propius inspexi* (10.94.1). The last words could be interpreted to mean that Suetonius had accompanied Pliny to Bithynia, a not-unexpected development in view of the close relationship between literary studies and public careers in the Rome of this time (see below). Whether or not Suetonius went to Bithynia, his reputation as a scholar was not irrelevant to his subsequent appointments and was now vouched for (in *Ep.* 10.94) by an imperial *amicus*. Not long after the death of Pliny ca 111, Suetonius was to be found in Rome, not in search of a new patron but rather (it may be surmised) to take up some sort of official post. Even though the preface to the *De Vita Caesarum* contained a dedication to the praetorian prefect Septicius Clarus (Lydus, *De Mag.* 2.6: see Bradley, 1998: 5), appointed to that post in 119 with Turbo (*SHA Hadr.* 9.4), such action hardly proves that Septicius replaced Pliny as a patron of Suetonius, the timid *scholasticus* anxiously seeking new means of support.

More precise information is provided by the inscription from Hippo Regius (discussed most recently by Lindsay, 1993: 1-2, 15-17 and by Bradley, 1998: 4). In brief, it indicates that he held two priesthoods (*flamen, pontifex Volcanalis*) and was probably adlected (by Trajan) to the equestrian jury panel (*iudices selecti*, if that is the correct restoration: neither word appears on the stone). Perhaps he maintained some of the interest in the law hinted at in *Ep.* 1.18.6, where he had appeared with Pliny in a case before the Centumviral court. The inscription finally reveals that Suetonius held three senior administrative posts within the Palace, i.e. *a studiis, a bibliothecis* and *ab epistulis* (Cultural Secretary, Director of Imperial Libraries and Director of Chancery – see Birley, 1998: 138 and 142).

As *a studiis*, he would have been responsible for advising and assisting the emperor on literary matters. Many of the *Vitae* refer to the emperor's *liberalia studia* (e.g. *Dom.* 20), for Suetonius believed that 'an emperor ought to interest himself in literary matters...(and) the range of the literary interests he documents...is astonishing' (Wallace-Hadrill, 1995: 83-4). Subsequently, he was appointed *a bibliothecis*. As the *bibliotheca Ulpia* within Trajan's Forum was finished ca 112, this would provide a suitable moment to assign another senior administrative post to an equestrian official such as Suetonius (Lindsay, 1993: 2-3). So, after a brief stint as *a studiis*, he became *a bibliothecis* and then *ab epistulis*, presumably after the accession of Hadrian (some, however, argue that he held all his senior posts under Hadrian; see below and Vacher, 1993: xvii-xviii). This was the most prestigious post of all. It was a an onerous office, a *molem immensam,...et uix tractabile pondus;...nec enim numerosior altera sacra/cura domo* (if one cares to believe Statius, *Siluae* 5.1.84-6); and the incumbent had to deal with a multitude of issues, from the river heights in Egypt to candidates suitable for military appointments (*ibid.*, 95-9). For a more measured discussion of his duties, see Millar (1977) 83-110 and Lindsay, *Historia* 43 (1994) 454-68.

When he held these posts is less clear: much depends on the date of his dismissal from the highly influential post of imperial *ab epistulis*. That he was dismissed is stated in the *Vita Hadriani*, in a passage usually assigned to the year 122, viz. *Septicio Claro praefecto praetorii et Suetonio Tranquillo epistularum magistro multisque aliis, quod apud Sabinam uxorem iniussu eius familiarius se tunc egerant quam reuerentia domus aulicae postulabat, successores dedit* (*SHA Hadr.* 11.3). However, the *Vita Hadriani*'s chronological accuracy is often impugned and a case has been made for assigning this passage (and Suetonius' dismissal) to 128 (Lindsay, 1993: 4-5 and 1994: 454-68; rejected by Birley, 1998: 313 n. 5. See also Birley's discussion of the dismissal, 1998: 138-40). The problem is exacerbated by the lacuna in the Hippo inscription immediately after the Trajanic *adlectio inter iudices selectos* and before his three senior appointments. If he was dismissed in 122, then it is possible that some of the latter were made by Trajan; on the other hand, a date of 128 would imply that they were all Hadrianic. Scholars generally if not universally favour the earlier date.

What sort of people were appointed to these positions? Despite the *SHA*, it was not Hadrian who first used an equestrian instead of a freedmen as an *a libellis* or *ab epistulis*. The innovation had occurred far earlier, possibly under Claudius (Millar, 1977: 85-6) and certainly under Vitellius (*Hist.* 1.58; *ILS* 1447 = *MW 338*, i.e. Sex. Caesius Propertianus). Domitian, in a sense, went further. He seems not to have looked for administrative experience in his *ab epistulis*, if we are to judge by C. Octavius Titinius Capito. Pliny lauds Capito as *inter praecipua saeculi ornamenta numerandus*, (because) *colit studia, studiosos amat fauet prouehit...denique litterarum iam senescentium reductor ac reformator...scribit exitus inlustrium uirorum* (*Ep.* 8.12.1, 4). Particularly striking is the difference between Propertianus and Capito. The latter's career may have been military in name only. Whereas Propertianus had been *tr. mil. IIII Macedonic., praef. coh. III His(pa)nor...*(*MW* 338), Titinius appears as *praef. cohortis trib. milit. donat. hasta pura corona uallari proc. ab epistulis...*(*MW* 347). No units are named, an unusual omission perhaps suggesting that the posts were assigned to him *honoris causa* (see Millar, 1977: 89). One wonders, too, about those decorations. Capito was an intellectual, a poet and a scholar, and appointed for those very qualities. Millar refers to these appointees as 'intellectuals from the Latin world' (1977: 89) and that is an apt description of Capito and of Suetonius as well. So, if Suetonius' *perfectum opus* (*Ep.* 5.10) earned for him the reputation of being an *eruditissimum uirum* (*Ep.* 10.94.1), it may well be that, soon after 111, he was appointed by Trajan (and promoted by Hadrian) to prestigious posts in the imperial service on the strength of his literary reputation. But these were not the sort of tasks to be assigned to a timid, retiring *scholasticus*: that image of Suetonius should be rejected. As Wallace-Hadrill has observed:

> ...it was his scholarship that made Suetonius and others like him useful to emperors. Because the society in which they operated placed a high value on literary culture of the hellenistic type, emperors played an important role in the world of culture.... They liked to be seen themselves as men of education, in their conversation and their public letters and pronouncements. For this reason learned men had a place in their entourage. There is no gulf between Suetonius the secretary and Tranquillus the philologist.
>
> (1995: 95-6)

## His Sources

How much assistance did Suetonius the secretary give Tranquillus the biographer is still debated. Scholars have often regarded the timing of Suetonius' dismissal as relevant to the date of composition of the *Caesares* on the assumption that the less detailed lives were probably written after the dismissal, because he no longer had access to the imperial archives (see Townend, 1959: 286; compare Wallace-Hadrill, 1995: 89-95 and Baldwin, 1983: 48). That may well be, yet if we accept the evidence of Lydus (*De Mag.* 2.6), it is highly likely that the *Caesares* as a whole were dedicated to Septicius before he and Suetonius fell from grace (but see Murison, 1992: vii).

The archival question does not really get us very far, especially with regard to the *Vespasianus*. In the first place, it does not follow that the longer the *Vita*, the greater the author's access to the archives; the more detailed treatment of Julius Caesar and Augustus can reasonably be explained by the fact that Suetonius' area of expertise was the Ciceronian and Augustan period (see Wallace-Hadrill, 1995: 56-7). Again, whilst access to such evidence may well be a *sine qua non* for a modern historian, we have no reason to believe that it was so for his ancient counterpart. Suetonius is one ancient author who at least does make occasional use of archival material (see below), but does it in a way that today seems fairly casual and haphazard.

On the other hand, he obviously made a careful investigation into Vespasian's background. Commenting on certain activities of Vespasian's grandfather (Flavius Petro), he states that *ipse ne uestigium quidem de hoc, quamuis satis curiose inquirerem, inueni* (1.4); he probably visited the town of Vespasiae, *ubi Vespasiorum complura monumenta exstant* (1.3) and the house where Titus was born (*sordidis aedibus, cubiculo uero perparuo et obscuro, nam manet adhuc et ostenditur: Titus* 1.1). He had also read of Vespasian's formidable mother who *eum [Vespasianum] identidem per contumeliam anteambulonem fratris appellat* (2.2).

There were written sources aplenty. Tacitus' *Historiae*, published at least a decade before the *Caesares* (unfortunately, the books dealing with the period of Vespasian's reign have not survived), and Plutarch's *Lives of Galba and Otho* (written not long after 96; see Murison, 1992: xiii) were available to him, as were various other works; but, as they have not survived, we cannot assess whether or to what extent Suetonius made use of them: no doubt they would have contained material relevant to Vespasian's career as *priuatus*. Apart from the writings of Tacitus and Plutarch, useful information could have been gleaned from the Elder Pliny's *Continuation of the History of Aufidius Bassus* (*Ep.* 3.5.6), praised by Quintilian (*Inst. Or.* 10.1.103) but possibly pro-Flavian (see the criticism of such writers by Tacitus, *Hist.* 2.101); from Ti. Claudius Pollio's *(Liber) de uita eius* (of Annius Bassus: *Ep.* 7.31.5); as well as from the works of Fabius Rusticus (*Liuius ueterum, Fabius Rusticus recentium eloquentissimi auctores: Agr.* 10.3), Pompeius Planta (*Ep.* 9.1.1), Cluvius Rufus (*Ann.* 13.20, 14.2) and Vipstanus Messalla (*Hist.* 3.25, 28). More useful would have been the *exitus* literature of Titinius Capito (*exitus inlustrium uirorum: Ep.* 8.12.4) and, perhaps, C. Fannius (*exitus occisorum aut relegatorum a Nerone: Ep.* 5.5.3). Fannius was, in effect, a pre-Suetonian Suetonius, 'writing by categories' (Sherwin-White, 1966: 321), i.e. *primum librum quem de sceleribus eius [Neronis] ediderat* (*Ep.* 5.5.5). Material favourable to one of Vespasian's victims, Helvidius Priscus, could have been obtained from both Herennius Senecio's *de uita Heluidi Libri* (*Ep.* 7.19.5) and from Helvidius Priscus' own diaries (*commentarii*) given to Senecio by Helvidius' widow, Fannia (*Ep.* 7.19.5-6), whilst M. Aquillius Regulus' work *in quo Rusticum insectatur (et in quo)...lacerat Herennium Senecionem* (*Ep.* 1.5.2-3) would have supplied more hostile details. However, in view of the fact that Suetonius names Arulenus Rusticus rather than Senecio as Helvidius' biographer (*Dom.* 10.3), it is to be presumed that the role of the philosophic opposition held minimal interest for him.

Oral testimony was available in abundance. Suetonius all but ignored it. He lived in Rome during the reign of Vespasian's son, Domitian, although it is far from obvious in the *De Vita Caesarum* – he mentions only one incident that he witnessed personally (*Dom.* 12.2). Of course, it would have been unwise to refer to the activities of Flavian officials still alive in the early years of Hadrian's reign. Perhaps he had (?also) lost interest in the entire project and was determined to complete it with all possible speed (see Wallace-Hadrill, 1995: 61-2).

## Suetonius' Works

Apart from the *De Vita Caesarum* and the *De Viris Illustribus*, he wrote in Latin and Greek on a vast range of topics. A list of them appears in the Suda and some are vouched for by Aulus Gellius, Lydus and other late writers (see Mooney, 1930: 39-44; Duff [1964] 505). He had earned Pliny's *encomium* (*eruditissimus*: *Ep.* 10.94.1), for his works include *Names and Types of Clothes, Physical Defects, Insults, Weather-Signs, Names of Seas and Rivers, Names of Winds, Greek Games, Roman Spectacles and Games, The Roman Year, Rome and its Customs and Manners, The Institution of Offices, Famous Prostitutes, Kings* and *Cicero's Republic.* Unfortunately, only a few small fragments of them have survived.

The *De Viris Illustribus* must have been a fairly substantial work with biographies of poets, orators, historians, philosophers, grammarians and rhetoricians. We have some of his *De Grammaticis et Rhetoribus*, with (very brief) lives of Terence, Vergil, Horace, Tibullus, Persius, Lucan, Pliny the Elder and Passienus Crispus.

## Suetonius and the Biographical Tradition

There has been considerable speculation about Suetonius' place in the biographical tradition and most of it is beyond the scope of a commentary on one *Vita.* The area of disputation lies in the models Suetonius used or at least were available to him, and the extent of his dependence on them; but as few examples of Greek and Roman biography have survived from antiquity, any attempt to assess the influence upon him of such models (whichever they were) is extremely hazardous. No doubt the genre was Greek-based, yet it could well be that there were Latin (rather than Greek) models for the general structure of the *Caesares.* The topic is treated in some detail by Wallace-Hadrill, 1995: 10-25 and 66-72, with a list of earlier discussions at 67 n.17.

Suetonius himself explained the biographical form he proposed to use, i.e. *proposita uitae eius (Augusti) uelut summa partes singillatim neque per tempora sed per species exsequar, quo distinctius demonstrari cognoscique possint (Aug.* 9). Avoiding a strictly chronological or annalistic approach, he composed his *Vitae* under various headings (*per species*). In general, he begins with an account of an emperor's birth and early life until his accession, follows it with a number of chapters on specific areas of his government (games, legislation, public works, wars, physical description and so on) and ends with the events (including omens and prodigies) leading up to his death. Often there is a definite break or *diuisio* between imperial *acta* that are commendable and non-commendable.

Within that framework, there is a secondary theme that Wallace-Hadrill calls 'the ethical dimension to (Suetonius') portrayal of a Caesar in his public capacity. Was he virtuous or vicious?.... Was he clement or cruel? Liberal, or mean and grasping? Civil or arrogant? Continent, or self-indulgent, luxurious and lustful? These are the polarities in terms of which emperor after emperor is judged' (1995: 142). For Suetonius, then, there was an imperial 'ideal'. He had a clear image of just what constituted an emperor's obligations, duties and general behaviour, both private and public. So his 'categories' are significant: they represent the criteria by which an emperor is to be assessed. For a detailed discussion, see Bradley, 1998: 18-22.

## Suetonius' *Vespasian*

According to Suetonius, Vespasian met many of these criteria. He rated the emperor highly (as he did Titus) and deliberately omitted any 'controversial' items (such as the execution of Julius Sabinus and his family; see Dio 66.16.1-2 for their fate) or else tried to mitigate their effect on the reader (hence the claim that Vespasian *neque caede cuiusquam umquam laetatus iustis suppliciis inlacrimauit etiam et ingemuit: Vesp.* 15).

There are a number of other omissions and also some inaccuracies in the *Life*. Incorrect statements include his description of Petro as a *municeps* (see the discussion at 1.2); his reference to Florus as *caeso* (4.5); his figures for the military establishment in Judaea (*additis...ad copias duabus legionibus* and *octo alis, cohortibus decem* – 4.6); the implication in *aduenere litterae* (7.1) that there was little or no interval between the second battle of Bedriacum and Vitellius' death and his reference to Commagene as being *dicionis regiae usque ad id tempus* (8.4).

Other misleading statements include his downplaying of Claudius' role in the invasion of Britain (see below at 4.1: *Claudi[i] ipsius ductu*); his exaggeration of the nature of Vespasian's *secessus* (4.2: *medium tempus...in otio secessuque*); his incomplete explanation of the circumstances surrounding Nero's offer of the Judaean command to Vespasian late in 66 (4.4: *latenti...extrema metuenti*); his assessment of the attitude of the Syrian legions in 67 (4.6: *correcta...disciplina*); his over-generous interpretation of the *lutum in toga* incident (5.3: *luto...oppleri*); his explanation of just when Vespasian determined on civil war (7.1: *suscepto igitur ciuili bello*); his assessment of the reasons for army reform (8.2: *milites...processerant*); his too brief comment on the disbanding of the Vitellian legions (8.2: *Vitellianorum...exauctorauit plurimos*); his deficient summary of

Vespasian's provincial arrangements (8.4: *Achaiam...equite Romano*); and his failure to note that Vespasian's *uectigalia noua* were imposed for a limited time only (16.1: *noua et grauia addidisse*). At times, his chronology is misleading, e.g. at 2.2 (with his use of *diu*) and at 4.1 (*in breui spatio*); at others, it is almost certainly wrong, e.g. at 5.4 (*arbor...resurrexit*), 5.6 (*Carmeli dei oraculum*), 5.7 (*statua...*conuersa) and 10 (*sorte elegit...restituerentur*).

Sometimes, and especially in reference to the events of 1 July 69 and to Vespasian's performance in Alexandria, it is clear that Suetonius used the same source as Tacitus. Compare, on the one hand, *Hist.* 2.79 and, on the other, *primus... legiones adegit, principatus dies in posterum obseruatus est* and *apud ipsum iurauit* (6.3). Again, *summotis omnibus solus* at 7.1, *statim* at 7.1, *e plebe quidam* at 7.2, *debili crure* at 7.2, *per quietem* at 7.2 and *hortantibus amicis* at 7.3 all are closely paralleled in *Hist.* 4.81.

On at least six occasions they differ on matters of some importance. Suetonius' assessment of Vespasian's proconsular performance in Africa (*integerrime...administrauit* at 4.3 contradicts Tacitus at *Hist.* 2.97; Tacitus at *Ann.* 16.5 assigns Vespasian's famous 'lapse' (see below at 4.4: *praesens obdormisceret*) to a different time and place; they differ on the date when the Judaean legions swore allegiance to Vespasian (*V Idus Iul.* at 6.3 but Tacitus prefers 3 July: see *Hist.* 2.79); they disagree on the timing of Vespasian's visit to the Serapeum (*Alexandriam transiit* at 7.1); and Suetonius' reference to Helvidius Priscus (*altercationibus insolentissimis* at 15) is at considerable variance with Tacitus' *encomium* of him at *Hist.* 4.5. Finally, there is Suetonius' claim at 6.2 (s.u. *Moesiaci...milia*) that a number of Danubian vexillations declared for Vespasian well before 1 July – contradicted by Tacitus at *Hist.* 2.46 and 2.85.

The only substantial account of the reign itself apart from Suetonius' is that provided by Dio Cassius (or, rather, his epitomators). Whilst it seems that he and Suetonius had access to a common source, the few additional pieces of information to be found in Dio suggest that either he included items from Tacitus that did not fit into a Suetonian category (e.g. the reference to Vespasian's astrologer Barbillus in 66.9.2) or else that he had access to a source other than Tacitus. Dio's additional items include Vespasian's quip (on his arrival in Rome ca Oct 70) to the effect that he thanked Domitian for permitting him to hold office and for not dethroning him (66.4.3); his problems with the people of Alexandria including the tax of six obols and the fact that some of their taunts were addressed to Titus (66.8.4-7); his banishment of the astrologers, even though he consulted one himself, i.e. Barbillus (66.9.2); an anecdote illustrating his *auaritia*, not included in Suetonius' extensive list (66.10.3a – the people laughed 'at every time he used to say, when spending money "I am paying for this out of my own purse"'); his preference for the *Horti Sallustiani* over the palace (9.4); his reply to Vologaesus, omitting the royal titles as he had been addressed simply as 'Flavius Vespasianus' (10.3); Mucianus' attacks on the Stoics and the subsequent expulsion of philosophers apart from Musonius (10.1-11.2); Caenis' role in the downfall of Sejanus (14.2); the fact that the temple of Peace was dedicated in 75 (15.1); Titus' sham fight with Caecina Alienus (15.2); the punishment of Diogenes and Heras (15.4-5) and the fate of Julius Sabinus and his family (16.1-2). The only significant difference is Suetonius' omission of the last two items: see above.

Aurelius Victor and his epitomator usually repeat Suetonius' version of events precisely, but in this *Life* they occasionally provide extra information, e.g. on Vespasian's policy towards the Parthians (though the details are inconsistent; see 6.4, s.u. *e regibus Vologaesus Parthus*), on the number of new senators enrolled by Vespasian (see 9.2, s.u. *exhaustos caede...equite*), on Suetonius' use of the word *auaritia* to describe Vespasian's financial policy (which Victor virtually rejects, referring to it as *prudentia magis quam auaritia*: see 16.1, s.u. *sola...merito culpetur*), on the fact that some of Vespasian's 'new' taxes were imposed for a limited time only (see 16.1, s.u. *noua et grauia addidisse*), on work connected with the Via Flaminia (see 17, s.u. *plurimas...restituit in melius*) and, in the epitome alone, on the reason for Titus' execution of Caecina Alienus (see 25, s.u. *assiduas in se coniurationes*).

In preparing this commentary, I have made frequent use of Braithwaite (1927) and Mooney (1930). The text is essentially that of Ihm (1908: but see below) and I have, for convenience, used the Loeb translations of Josephus and Dio Cassius.

# Textual Variants

Apart from a number of alterations in punctuation, spelling and paragraphing as well as the expansion of abbreviations, the following are the only variants from the Teubner text of M. Ihm (Leipzig, 1908):

| Reference | Ihm | This Edition |
|---|---|---|
| 1.2 | manebantque | manebuntque |
| 2.3 | tribunatum | tribunus |
| 4.2 | amici | amicos |
| 18 | plebiculam | plebeculam |
| 19 | Appellari | Apellae |
| 23.1 | et de | ut et de |
| 23.3 | poneret | ponere |

# C. Svetoni Tranqvilli De Vita Caesarvm
# Divvs Vespasianvs

## Text

**1.**1 rebellione trium principum et caede incertum diu et quasi uagum imperium suscepit firmauitque tandem gens Flauia, obscura illa quidem ac sine ullis maiorum imaginibus, sed tamen rei publicae nequaquam paenitenda, constet licet Domitianum cupiditatis ac saeuitiae merito poenas luisse. **1.2** T. Flauius Petro, municeps Reatinus, bello ciuili Pompeianarum partium centurio an euocatus, profugit ex Pharsalica acie domumque se contulit, ubi deinde uenia et missione impetrata coactiones argentarias factitauit. huius filius, cognomine Sabinus, expers militiae – etsi quidam eum primipilarem, nonnulli, cum adhuc ordines duceret, sacramento solutum per causam ualetudinis tradunt – publicum quadragesimae in Asia egit; manebuntque imagines a ciuitatibus ei positae sub hoc titulo: ΚΑΛΩΣ ΤΕΛΩΝΗΣΑΝΤΙ. **1.3** postea faenus apud Heluetios exercuit ibique diem obiit superstitibus uxore Vespasia Polla et duobus ex ea liberis, quorum maior Sabinus ad praefecturam urbis, minor Vespasianus ad principatum usque processit. Polla Nursiae honesto genere orta patrem habuit Vespasium Pollionem, ter tribunum militum praefectumque castrorum, fratrem senatorem praetoriae dignitatis. locus etiam ad sextum miliarium a Nursia Spoletium euntibus in monte summo appellatur Vespasiae, ubi Vespasiorum complura monumenta exstant, magnum indicium splendoris familiae et uetustatis. **1.4** non negauerim iactatum a quibusdam Petronis patrem e regione Transpadana fuisse mancipem operarum, quae ex Vmbria in Sabinos ad culturam agrorum quotannis commeare soleant; subsedisse autem in oppido Reatino uxore ibidem ducta. ipse ne uestigium quidem de hoc, quamuis satis curiose inquirerem, inueni.

**2.**1 Vespasianus natus est in Sabinis ultra Reate uico modico, cui nomen est Falacrinae, XV Kal. Decb. uesperi, Q. Sulpicio Camerino C. Poppaeo Sabino cons., quinquennio ante quam Augustus excederet; educatus sub paterna auia Tertulla in praediis Cosanis. quare princeps quoque et locum incunabulorum assidue frequentauit, manente uilla qualis fuerat olim, ne quid scilicet oculorum consuetudini deperiret; et auiae memoriam tanto opere dilexit ut sollemnibus ac festis diebus pocillo quoque eius argenteo potare perseuerauerit. **2.2** sumpta uirili toga latum clauum, quamquam fratre adepto, diu auersatus est, nec ut tandem appeteret compelli nisi a matre potuit. ea demum extudit magis conuicio quam precibus uel auctoritate, dum eum identidem per contumeliam anteambulonem fratris appellat. **2.3** tribunus militum in Thracia meruit; quaestor Cretam et Cyrenas prouinciam sorte cepit; aedilitatis ac mox praeturae candidatus, illam non sine repulsa sextoque uix adeptus est loco, ha c prima statim petitione et in primis. praetor infensum senatui Gaium ne quo non genere demereretur, ludos extraordinarios pro uictoria eius Germanica depoposcit poenaeque coniuratorum addendum censuit ut insepulti proicerentur. egit et gratias ei apud amplissimum ordinem quod se honore cenae dignatus esset.

**3** inter haec Flauiam Domitillam duxit uxorem, Statili Capellae equitis Romani Sabratensis ex Africa delicatam olim Latinaeque condicionis, sed mox ingenuam et ciuem Romanam reciperatorio iudicio pronuntiatam, patre asserente Flauio Liberale Ferenti genito nec quicquam amplius quam quaestorio scriba. ex hac liberos tulit Titum et Domitianum et Domitillam. uxori ac filiae superstes fuit atque utramque adhuc priuatus amisit. post uxoris excessum Caenidem, Antoniae libertam et a manu, dilectam quondam sibi reuocauit in contubernium habuitque etiam imperator paene iustae uxoris loco.

**4.1** Claudio principe Narcissi gratia legatus legionis in Germaniam missus est; inde in Britanniam translatus tricies cum hoste conflixit. duas ualidissimas gentes superque uiginti oppida et insulam Vectem Britanniae proximam in dicionem redegit partim Auli Plauti legati consularis partim Claudi[i] ipsius ductu. **4.2** quare triumphalia ornamenta et in breui spatio duplex sacerdotium accepit, praeterea consulatum, quem gessit per duos nouissimos anni menses. medium tempus ad proconsulatum usque in otio secessuque egit, Agrippinam timens potentem adhuc apud filium et defuncti quoque Narcissi amicos perosam. **4.3** exim sortitus Africam integerrime nec sine magna dignatione administrauit, nisi quod Hadrumeti seditione quadam rapa in eum iacta sunt. rediit certe nihilo opulentior, ut qui prope labefactata iam fide omnia praedia fratri obligaret necessarioque ad mangonicos quaestus sustinendae dignitatis causa descenderit; propter quod uulgo *mulio* uocabatur. conuictus quoque dicitur ducenta sestertia expressisse iuueni, cui latum clauum aduersus patris uoluntatem impetrarat, eoque nomine grauiter increpitus. **4.4** peregrinatione Achaica inter comites Neronis cum cantante eo aut discederet saepius aut praesens obdormisceret, grauissimam contraxit offensam, prohibitusque non contubernio modo sed etiam publica salutatione secessit in paruam ac deuiam ciuitatem, quoad latenti etiamque extrema metuenti prouincia cum exercitu oblata est. **4.5** percrebruerat Oriente toto uetus et constans opinio esse in fatis ut eo tempore Iudaea profecti rerum potirentur. id de imperatore Romano, quantum postea euentu paruit, praedictum Iudaei ad se trahentes rebellarunt caesoque praeposito legatum insuper Syriae consularem suppetias ferentem rapta aquila fugauerunt. ad hunc motum comprimendum cum exercitu ampliore et non instrenuo duce, cui tamen tuto tanta res committeretur, opus esset, ipse potissimum delectus est ut et industriae expertae nec metuendus ullo modo ob humilitatem generis ac nominis. **4.6** additis igitur ad copias duabus legionibus, octo alis, cohortibus decem, atque inter legatos maiore filio assumpto, ut primum prouinciam attigit, proximas quoque conuertit in se, correcta statim castrorum disciplina, unoque et altero proelio tam constanter inito ut in oppugnatione castelli lapidis ictum genu scutoque sagittas aliquot exceperit.

**5.1** post Neronem Galbamque Othone ac Vitellio de principatu certantibus in spem imperii uenit iam pridem sibi per haec ostenta conceptam. **5.2** in suburbano Flauiorum quercus antiqua, quae erat Marti sacra, per tres Vespasiae partus singulos repente ramos a frutice dedit, haud dubia signa futuri cuiusque fati: primum exilem et cito arefactum, ideoque puella nata non perannauit, secundum praeualidum ac prolixum et qui magnam felicitatem portenderet, tertium uero instar arboris. quare patrem Sabinum ferunt, haruspicio insuper confirmatum, renuntiasse matri, nepotem ei Caesarem genitum; nec illam quicquam aliud quam cachinnasse, mirantem *quod adhuc se mentis compote deliraret iam filius suus.* **5.3** mox, cum aedilem eum C. Caesar, succensens curam uerrendis uiis non adhibitam, luto iussisset oppleri congesto per milites in praetextae sinum, non defuerunt qui interpretarentur, quandoque proculcatam desertamque rem publicam ciuili aliqua perturbatione in tutelam eius ac uelut in gremium deuenturam. **5.4** prandente eo quondam canis extrarius e triuio manum humanam intulit mensaeque subiecit. cenante rursus bos arator decusso iugo triclinium irrupit ac fugatis ministris quasi repente defessus procidit ad ipsos accumbentis pedes ceruicemque summisit. arbor quoque cupressus in agro auito sine ulla ui tempestatis euulsa radicitus atque prostrata insequenti die uiridior ac firmior resurrexit. **5.5** at in Achaia somniauit initium sibi suisque felicitatis futurum, simul ac dens Neroni exemptus esset; euenitque ut sequenti die progressus in atrium medicus dentem ei ostenderet tantumque quod exemptum. **5.6** apud Iudaeam Carmeli dei oraculum consulentem ita confirmauere sortes ut, quidquid cogitaret uolueretque animo quamlibet magnum, id esse prouenturum pollicerentur; et unus ex nobilibus captiuis Iosephus, cum coiceretur in uincula, constantissime asseuerauit fore ut ab eodem breui solueretur, uerum iam imperatore. **5.7** nuntiabantur et ex urbe praesagia: Neronem diebus ultimis monitum per quietem ut tensam Iouis Optimi Maximi e sacrario in domum Vespasiani et inde in circum deduceret; ac non multo post comitia secundi consulatus ineunte Galba statua Diui Iuli ad Orientem sponte conuersa, acieque Betriacensi, prius quam committeretur, duas aquilas in conspectu omnium conflixisse uictaque altera superuenisse tertiam ab solis exortu ac uictricem abegisse.

**6.1** nec tamen quicquam ante temptauit, promptissimis atque etiam instantibus suis, quam sollicitatus quorundam et ignotorum et absentium fortuito fauore. **6.2** Moesiaci exercitus bina e tribus legionibus milia missa auxilio Othoni, postquam ingressis iter nuntiatum est uictum eum ac uim uitae suae attulisse, nihilo setius Aquileiam usque perseuerauerunt, quasi rumori minus crederent. ibi per occasionem ac licentiam omni rapinarum genere grassati, cum timerent ne sibi reuersis reddenda ratio ac subeunda poena esset, consilium inierunt eligendi creandique imperatoris; neque enim deteriores esse aut Hispaniensi exercitu qui Galbam, aut praetoriano qui Othonem, aut Germaniciano qui Vitellium fecissent. **6.3** propositis itaque nominibus legatorum consularium, quot ubique tunc erant, cum ceteros alium alia de causa improbarent et quidam e legione tertia, quae sub exitu Neronis translata ex Syria in Moesiam fuerat, Vespasianum laudibus ferrent, assensere cuncti nomenque eius uexillis omnibus sine mora inscripserunt. et tunc quidem compressa res est reuocatis ad officium numeris parumper. ceterum diuulgato facto Tiberius Alexander praefectus Aegypti primus in uerba Vespasiani legiones adegit Kal. Iul., qui principatus dies in posterum obseruatus est; Iudaicus deinde exercitus V Idus Iul. apud ipsum iurauit. **6.4** plurimum coeptis contulerunt iactatum exemplar epistulae uerae siue falsae defuncti Othonis ad Vespasianum extrema obtestatione ultionem mandantis et ut rei publicae subueniret optantis, simul rumor dissipatus destinasse uictorem Vitellium permutare hiberna legionum et Germanicas transferre in Orientem ad securiorem mollioremque militiam, praeterea ex praesidibus prouinciarum Licinius Mucianus et e regibus Vologaesus Parthus; ille deposita simultate, quam in id tempus ex aemulatione non obscure gerebat, Syriacum promisit exercitum, hic quadraginta milia sagittariorum.

**7.1** suscepto igitur ciuili bello ac ducibus copiisque in Italiam praemissis interim Alexandriam transiit ut claustra Aegypti obtineret. hic cum de firmitate imperii capturus auspicium aedem Serapidis summotis omnibus solus intrasset ac propitiato multum deo tandem se conuertisset, uerbenas coronasque et panificia, ut illic assolet, Basilides libertus obtulisse ei uisus est; quem neque admissum a quoquam et iam pridem propter neruorum ualetudinem uix ingredi longeque abesse constabat. ac statim aduenere litterae fusas apud Cremonam Vitelli copias, ipsum in urbe interemptum nuntiantes. **7.2** auctoritas et quasi maiestas quaedam ut scilicet inopinato et adhuc nouo principi deerat; haec quoque accessit. e plebe quidam luminibus orbatus, item alius debili crure sedentem pro tribunali pariter adierunt orantes opem ualetudini demonstratam a Serapide per quietem: restituturum oculos si inspuisset; confirmaturum crus si dignaretur calce contingere. **7.3** cum uix fides esset ullo modo rem successuram ideoque ne experiri quidem auderet, extremo hortantibus amicis palam pro contione utrumque temptauit, nec euentus defuit. per idem tempus Tegeae in Arc[h]adia instinctu uaticinantium effossa sunt sacrato loco uasa operis antiqui

4

atque in iis assimilis Vespasiano imago.

**8.**1 talis tantaque cum fama in urbem reuersus acto de Iudaeis triumpho consulatus octo ueteri addidit; suscepit et censuram ac per totum imperii tempus nihil habuit antiquius quam prope afflictam nutantemque rem publicam stabilire primo, deinde et ornare. **8.**2 milites pars uictoriae fiducia, pars ignominiae dolore ad omnem licentiam audaciamque processerant; sed et prouinciae ciuitatesque liberae, nec non et regna quaedam tumultuosius inter se agebant. quare Vitellianorum quidem et exauctorauit plurimos et coercuit, participibus autem uictoriae adeo nihil extra ordinem indulsit ut etiam legitima praemia sero persoluerit. **8.**3 ac ne quam occasionem corrigendi disciplinam praetermitteret, adulescentulum fragrantem unguento, cum sibi pro impetrata praefectura gratias ageret, nutu aspernatus, uoce etiam grauissima increpuit: *maluissem alium oboluisses*, litterasque reuocauit. classiarios uero, qui ab Ostia et Puteolis Romam pedibus per uices commeant, petentes constitui aliquid sibi calciarii nomine, quasi parum esset sine responso abegisse, iussit posthac excalciatos cursitare; et ex eo ita cursitant. **8.**4 Achaiam, Lyciam, Rhodum, Byzantium, Samum libertate adempta, item Trachiam Ciliciam et Commagenen dicionis regiae usque ad id tempus, in prouinciarum formam redegit. Cappadociae propter adsiduos barbarorum incursus legiones addidit consularemque rectorem imposuit pro equite Romano. **8.**5 deformis urbs ueteribus incendiis ac ruinis erat; uacuas areas occupare et aedificare, si possessores cessarent, cuicumque permisit. ipse restitutionem Capitolii adgressus ruderibus purgandis manus primus admouit ac suo collo quaedam extulit; aerearumque tabularum tria milia, quae simul conflagrauerant, restituenda suscepit undique inuestigatis exemplaribus: instrumentum imperii pulcherrimum ac uetustissimum, quo continebantur paene ab exordio urbis senatus consulta, plebi[s] scita de societate et foedere ac priuilegio cuicumque concessis.

**9.**1 fecit et noua opera templum Pacis foro proximum Diuique Claudi in Caelio monte coeptum quidem ab Agrippina, sed a Nerone prope funditus destructum; item amphitheatrum urbe media ut destinasse compererat Augustum. **9.**2 amplissimos ordines et exhaustos caede uaria et contaminatos ueteri neglegentia purgauit suppleuitque recenso senatu et equite, summotis indignissimis et honestissimo quoque Italicorum ac prouincialium allecto. atque uti notum esset utrumque ordinem non tam libertate inter se quam dignitate differre, de iurgio quodam senatoris equitisque Romani ita pronuntiauit, *non oportere maledici senatoribus, remaledici ciuile fasque esse.*

**10** litium series ubique maiorem in modum excreuerant, manentibus antiquis intercapedine iuris dictionis, accedentibus nouis ex condicione tumultuque temporum; sorte elegit per quos rapta bello restituerentur quique iudicia centumuiralia, quibus peragendis uix suffectura litigatorum uidebatur aetas, extra ordinem diiudicarent redigerentque ad breuissimum numerum.

**11** libido atque luxuria coercente nullo inualuerat; auctor senatui fuit decernendi ut quae se alieno seruo iunxisset ancilla haberetur; neue filiorum familiarum faeneratoribus exigendi crediti ius umquam esset, hoc est ne post patrum quidem mortem.

**12** ceteris in rebus statim ab initio principatus usque ad exitum ciuilis et clemens, mediocritatem pristinam neque dissimulauit umquam ac frequenter etiam prae se tulit. quin et conantis quosdam originem Flauii generis ad conditores Reatinos comitemque Herculis, cuius monimentum exstat Salaria uia, referre irrisit ultro. adeoque nihil ornamentorum extrinsecus cupide appetiuit ut triumphi die fatigatus tarditate et taedio pompae non reticuerit, *merito se plecti, qui triumphum, quasi aut debitum maioribus suis aut speratum umquam sibi, tam inepte senex concupisset.* ac ne tribuniciam quidem potestatem...patris patriae appellationem nisi sero recepit. nam consuetudinem scrutandi salutantes manente adhuc bello ciuili omiserat.

**13** amicorum libertatem, causidicorum figuras ac philosophorum contumaciam lenissime tulit. Licinium Mucianum notae impudicitiae, sed meritorum fiducia minus sui reuerentem, numquam nisi clam et hactenus retaxare sustinuit ut apud communem aliquem amicum querens adderet clausulam: *ego tamen uir sum.* Saluium Liberalem in defensione diuitis rei ausum dicere: *quid ad Caesarem, si Hipparchus sestertium milies habet?* et ipse laudauit. Demetrium Cynicum in itinere obuium sibi post damnationem ac neque assurgere neque salutare se dignantem, oblatrantem etiam nescio quid, satis habuit *canem* appellare.

**14** offensarum inimicitiarumque minime memor executorue Vitelli[i] hostis sui filiam splendidissime maritauit, dotauit etiam et instruxit. trepidum eum interdicta aula sub Nerone quaerentemque quidnam ageret aut quo abiret, quidam ex officio admissionis simul expellens *abire Morbouiam* iusserat. in hunc postea deprecantem non ultra uerba excanduit, et quidem totidem fere atque eadem. nam ut suspicione aliqua uel metu ad perniciem cuiusquam compelleretur tantum afuit ut monentibus amicis cauendum esse Mettium Pompusianum, quod uulgo crederetur genesim habere imperatoriam, insuper consulem fecerit, spondens quandoque beneficii memorem futurum.

**15** non temere quis punitus insons reperi[r]etur nisi absente eo et ignaro aut certe inuito atque decepto. Heluidio Prisco, qui et reuersum se ex Syria solus priuato nomine Vespasianum salutauerat et in praetura omnibus edictis sine honore ac mentione ulla transmiserat, non ante succensuit quam altercationibus insolentissimis paene in ordinem redactus. hunc quoque, quamuis relegatum primo, deinde et interfici iussum, magni aestimauit seruare quoquo modo, missis qui percussores reuocarent; et seruasset, nisi iam perisse falso renuntiatum esset. ceterum neque caede cuiusquam umquam <......> iustis suppliciis inlacrimauit etiam et ingemuit.

**16.**1 sola est, in qua merito culpetur, pecuniae cupiditas. non enim contentus omissa sub Galba uectigalia reuocasse, noua et grauia addidisse, auxisse tributa prouinciis, nonnullis et duplicasse, negotiationes quoque uel priuato pudendas propalam exercuit, coemendo quaedam tantum ut pluris postea distraheret. **16.**2 ne candidatis quidem honores reisue tam innoxiis quam nocentibus absolutiones uenditare cunctatus est. creditur etiam procuratorum rapacissimum quemque ad ampliora officia ex industria solitus promouere quo locupletiores mox condemnaret; quibus quidem uolgo pro spongiis dicebatur uti, quod quasi et siccos madefaceret et exprimeret umentis. **16.**3 quidam natura cupidissimum tradunt, idque exprobratum ei a sene bubulco, qui negata[m] sibi gratuita[m] libertate[m], quam imperium ade[m]ptum suppliciter orabat, proclamauerit *uulpem pilum mutare, non mores.* sunt contra qui opinentur ad manubias et rapinas necessitate compulsum summa aerarii fiscique inopia, de qua testificatus sit initio statim principatus, professus *quadringenties milies opus esse ut res publica stare posset.* quod et ueri similius uidetur, quando et male partis optime usus est.

**17** in omne hominum genus liberalissimus expleuit censum senatorium, consulares inopes quingenis sestertiis annuis sustentauit, plurimas per totum orbem ciuitates terrae motu aut incendio afflictas restituit in melius, ingenia et artes uel maxime fouit.

**18** primus e fisco Latinis Graecisque rhetoribus annua centena constituit; praestantis poetas, nec non et artifices, Coae Veneris, item Colossi refectorem insigni congiario magnaque mercede donauit; mechanico quoque grandis columnas exigua impensa perducturum in Capitolium pollicenti praemium pro commento non mediocre obtulit, operam remisit praefatus *sineret se plebeculam pascere.*

**19.**1 ludis, per quos scaena Marcelliani theatri restituta dedicabatur, uetera quoque acroamata reuocauerat. Apellae tragoedo quadringenta, Terpno Diodoroque citharoedis ducena, nonnullis centena, quibus minimum, quadragena sestertia super plurimas coronas aureas dedit. sed et conuiuabatur assidue ac saepius recta et dapsile ut macellarios adiuuaret. dabat sicut Saturnalibus uiris apophoreta, ita per Kal. Mart. feminis. et tamen ne sic quidem pristina cupiditatis infamia caruit. **19.**2 Alexandrini Cybiosacten eum uocare perseuerauerunt, cognomine unius e regibus suis turpissimarum sordium. sed et in funere Fauor archimimus personam eius ferens imitansque, ut est mos, facta ac dicta uiui, interrogatis palam procuratoribus quanti funus et pompa constaret, ut audit *sestertium centiens,* exclamauit, *centum sibi sestertia darent ac se uel in Tiberim proicerent.*

**20** statura fuit quadrata, compactis firmisque membris, uultu ueluti nitentis; de quo quidam urbanorum non infacete, siquidem petenti ut et in se aliquid diceret: *dicam,* inquit, *cum uentrem exonerare desieris.* ualetudine prosperrima usus est, quamuis ad tuendam eam nihil amplius quam fauces ceteraque membra sibimet ad numerum in sphaeristerio defricaret inediamque unius diei per singulos menses interponeret.

**21** ordinem uitae hunc fere tenuit. in principatu maturius semper ac de nocte uigilabat; dein perlectis epistulis officiorumque omnium breuiariis, amicos admittebat, ac dum salutabatur, et calciabat ipse se et amiciebat; postque decisa quaecumque obuenissent negotia gestationi et inde quieti uacabat, accubante aliqua pallacarum, quas in locum defunctae Caenidis plurimas constituerat; a secreto in balineum tricliniumque transibat. nec ullo tempore facilior aut indulgentior traditur, eaque momenta domestici ad aliquid petendum magno <o>pere captabant.

**22** et super cenam autem et semper alias comissimus multa ioco transigebat; erat enim dicacitatis plurimae, esti scurrilis et sordidae ut ne praetextatis quidem uerbis abstineret. et tamen nonnulla eius facetissima exstant, in quibus et haec. Mestrium Florum consularem, admonitus ab eo *plaustra* potius quam *plostra* dicenda, postero die *Flaurum* salutauit. expugnatus autem a quadam, quasi amore suo deperiret, cum perductae pro concubitu sestertia quadringenta donasset, admonente dispensatore, quem ad modum summam rationibus uellet inferri: *Vespasiano*, inquit, *adamato*.

**23.1** utebatur et uersibus Graecis tempestiue satis ut et de quodam procerae staturae improbiusque nato:

Μακρὰ βιβάς, κραδάων δολιχόσκιν γχος,

et de Cerylo liberto, qui diues admodum ob subterfugiendum quandoque ius fisci ingenuum se et Lachetem mutato nomine coeperat ferre:

ὦ Λάχης Λάχης,
πὰν ἀποθάνῃς, αὖθις ξ ἀρχῆς σι
σὺ Κηρύλος.

maxime tamen dicacitatem adfectabat in deformibus lucris ut inuidiam aliqua cauillatione dilueret transferretque ad sales. **23.2** quendam e caris ministris dispensationem cuidam quasi fratri petentem cum distulisset, ipsum candidatum ad se uocauit; exactaque pecunia, quantam is cum suffragatore suo pepigerat, sine mora ordinauit; interpellanti mox ministro: *alium tibi*, ait, *quaere fratrem; hic, quem tuum putas, meus est.* mulionem in itinere quodam suspicatus ad calciandas mulas desiluisse ut adeunti litigatori spatium moramque praeberet, interrogauit *quanti calciasset*, <et> pactus est lucri partem. **23.3** reprehendenti filio Tito, quod etiam urinae uectigal commentus esset, pecuniam ex prima pensione admouit ad nares, sciscitans *num odore offenderetur*; et illo negante: *atquin*, inquit, *e lotio est*. nuntiantis legatos decretam ei publice non mediocris summae statuam colosseam, iussit uel continuo ponere, cauam manum ostentans et *paratam basim* dicens. **23.4** ac ne in metu quidem ac periculo mortis extremo abstinuit iocis. nam cum inter cetera prodigia Mausoleum derepente patuisset et stella crinita in caelo apparuisset, alterum ad Iuniam Caluinam e gente Augusti pertinere dicebat, alterum ad Parthorum regem qui capillatus esset; prima quoque morbi accessione: *uae*, inquit, *puto deus fio*.

**24** consulatu suo nono temptatus in Campania motiunculis leuibus protinusque urbe repetita, Cutilias ac Reatina rura, ubi aestiuare quotannis solebat, petit. hic cum super urgentem ualetudinem creberrimo frigidae aquae usu etiam intestina uitiasset nec eo minus muneribus imperatoriis ex consuetudine fungeretur ut etiam legationes audiret cubans, aluo repente usque ad defectionem soluta, *imperatorem* ait *stantem mori oportere*; dumque consurgit ac nititur, inter manus subleuantium extinctus est VIIII Kal. Iul. annum agens aetatis sexagensimum ac nonum superque mensem ac diem septimum.

**25** conuenit inter omnis, tam certum eum de sua suorumque genitura semper fuisse ut post assiduas in se coniurationes ausus sit adfirmare senatui *aut filios sibi successuros aut neminem*. dicitur etiam uidisse quondam per quietem stateram media parte uestibuli Palatinae domus positam examine aequo, cum in altera lance Claudius et Nero starent, in altera ipse ac filii. nec res fefellit, quando totidem annis parique temporis spatio utrique imperauerunt.

# Commentary

**1.1**

This section is designed as an introduction to the eighth and last book of Suetonius' *De Vita Caesarum* and so offers a brief review of the three Flavians – Vespasian, Titus and Domitian.

**trium principum:** Galba, Otho and Vitellius. Orosius calls them *tyranni: breui illa quidem sed turbida tyrannorum tempestate* (7.9.1).

**imperium suscepit firmauitque:** Suetonius provides an accurate summary of the Flavians' achievement. Aurelius Victor, less precise, assigns the credit to Vespasian alone, i.e. *Vespasianus...exsanguem diu fessumque terrarum orbem breui refecit* (*De Caes.* 9.1).

**gens Flavia:** The name was not a rare one. During the Republic, Flavii could be found not only in the Sabine territory but elsewhere in Italy as well. The family itself was plebeian and remained so until at least 47: see 4.1 below, s.u. *Claudio principe...missus est.*

**sine ullis maiorum imaginibus:** i.e., unlike Augustus, with *multis in familia senatoriis imaginibus* (*Aug.* 4.1), none of Vespasian's ancestors in the male line (or female; see Badian in *OCD* 749) had held a curule office. According to Mommsen (*Str* 1.442), the right to display waxen masks of one's ancestors (*maiorum imagines*) was limited to the descendants of those who had held curule magistracies, a definition rejected by Hopkins, 1983: 255-6. Cicero, as aedile, was to receive [*inter alia*] *sellam curulem, ius imaginis ad memoriam posteritatemque prodendae* (*Verr.* 2.5.36).

**cupiditatis ac saeuitiae:** Suetonius maintains and develops the theme. At *Dom.* 3.2, Domitian is described as *inopia rapax, metu saeuus*: despite hints of *abstinentia* and *liberalitas* and hardly any signs of *cupiditas* or *auaritia* (*Dom.* 9.1), the last of the Flavians *aliquanto celerius ad saeuitiam desciuit quam ad cupiditatem* (*Dom.* 10.1).

1.2

**T. Flauius Petro:** This section contains the only information we have about Vespasian's paternal grandfather.

**municeps Reatinus:** Reate (Rieti) was a Sabine town on the Avens (Velino), where the Via Salaria crossed the river. Suetonius' description of Petro as *municeps* is not strictly accurate, as Reate remained a *praefectura* throughout the *bellum ciuile* and became a *municipium* only in the early empire (*CIL* 6.4686, 27 BC). Vespasian settled a number of his veterans there, e.g. C. Julius Longinus of *ILS* 2460 = *MW* 378.

**centurio an euocatus:** *Euocati* were veterans retained for further service under improved conditions; they were always senior to private soldiers and could even be given positions of authority. According to Dio, Augustus was the first to use them and, by Dio's time, they constituted 'a special corps, carrying rods like centurions' (55.24.8). Maxfield has argued that the term came to be used 'almost exclusively' of former praetorians, retained for service as centurions after completing their sixteen years in the guard (1981: 210); for their pay, see below, s.u. *ordines duceret*. But, of the 280 *euocati* in E. Birley's files, only 35 were commissioned as centurions (1981: 29) and Birley also rejected the argument that the *euocati* undertook provincial service at a higher rank since sixty percent of his 280 never left Italy (1981: 25, 29). Here, though, as Braithwaite suggests (1927: 19), it may simply be that Suetonius was uncertain of Petro's precise rank.

**ex Pharsalica acie:** In 48 BC, Caesar defeated Pompey at Pharsalus in Thessaly.

**uenia:** Suetonius refers elsewhere to Caesar's clemency *in uictoria belli ciuilis*, i.e. *moderationem clementiamque...admirabilem exhibuit (Caesar)*: *Iul.* 75.1. For Vespasian's, see 12 below, s.u. *clemens*.

**missione impetrata:** There were three categories of discharge, i.e. *honesta missio* (after the appropriate term of service was completed: for some examples, see the military diplomas listed in *MW* 396-404), *causaria* (through illness: see below, s.u. *per causam ualetudinis*) and *ignominiosa* (dishonourable). So Petro must have gained an honourable discharge (*honesta missio*) unless he had retired through ill health.

**coactiones argentarias:** He collected debts on commission. The *argentarii* (bankers) conducted sales and auctions and employed their staff as collectors (*coac- tores*). One famous *exactionum coactor* was Horace's father (Suet., *Vit. Horat.* 1).

**Sabinus:** T. Flavius Sabinus, Vespasian's father. Four Flavians of that name are known to us – Vespasian's father and brother (*praef. urb.* 69), the latter's son (*cos.* II 72) and grandson (*cos. ord.* 82); see Townend, 1961: 54-62.

**primipilarem:** If Sabinus really was a *primipilaris*, the consequences are important. Under Augustus (and later emperors), a former *primus pilus* (chief centurion) received a substantial gratuity, considerable social prestige and a new honorary title, *primipilaris* (Dobson, 1974: 396). The size (and existence) of Sabinus' gratuity together with his precise social status are, of course, matters of conjecture; but he may already have been of equestrian rank, and, if so, was clearly a *promagister* in Asia, and not a *uilicus* (see below, s.u. *publicum...egit*).

**ordines duceret:** He was a centurion. Some idea of the relative importance of the posts Sabinus may have held emerges from their relative pay scales. Under Augustus, the annual pay for a *miles legionis* was 900 sesterces with 9,000 for an *euocatus Augusti* of the praetorian guard; a *centurio legionis* received 13,500 *per annum* (M.A. Speidel, 1992: 102, 106) but a *primus pilus* 54,000 (or 60,000, according to Duncan-Jones, 1974: 3 n.4).

**sacramento solutum:** On the military oath, see Watson, 1969: 44-50; for some examples of it, see Lewis and Reinhold, 1966: 85-9.

**per causam ualetudinis:** According to Ulpian (*Digest* 3.2.2), *missio est causaria quae propter ualetudinem laboribus militiae [militem] soluit.*

**publicum quadragesimae in Asia egit:** The *publicum* ('state-tax') referred to is the *portorium* (*OCD* 1228; *AE* 1991, 1501 and Gordon, 1997: 221-2) or import duty which in Asia and Gaul was 2.5% (*quadragesima*), in Spain 2% (*quinquagesima*) and in Sicily 5% (*uicesima*); see De Laet, 1949: 104-6, 371 and *AE* 1989, 681 (a document of 62 from Ephesus providing details of the *portoria*). Magie cites *CIL* 3.7153, which describes a tax-collecting agent as a *ser[uus] uil[icus]*, and suggests that Sabinus may have been a similar agent (1950: 1424 n.4). But, whether or not Sabinus was a *primipilaris*, the fact that statues were set up to him in various cites of Asia indicates that he was, at the very least, of very senior social status, a director or *promagister*, presumably, and stationed at Ephesus (van Berchem, 1978: 269) – but hardly a *seruus uilicus*.

**manebuntque:** The imperfect (*manebant*) of the manuscripts is difficult to explain; the future *manebunt* or even Casaubon's *manent hodieque* would make more sense. For a detailed discussion, see Mooney, 1930: 375.

ΚΑΛΩΣ ΤΕΛΩΝΗΣΑΝΤΙ: In Latin, we find *teloniarius* 'a collector of customs' (*CIL* 3.13677) and *teloneum* 'a customs-post' (*CIL* 8.12314).

1.3

**Heluetios:** The territory of the Helvetii, forming part of Gallia Belgica under Augustus and part of Germania Superior under Domitian, was more or less equivalent to Switzerland. See Caesar, *BGall.* 1.1-6 and Tacitus, *Germ.* 28.2. Their *civitas* capital was Aventicum (Avenches).

**diem obiit:** i.e. *mortuus est.*

**faenus...exercuit:** He was a moneylender. The theory that Sabinus discharged the same sort of office in Gaul (*quadragesima Galliarum*) as he had in Asia (proposed by Stein, *RE* 6.2610, then accepted by Mooney, 1930: 376 and De Laet, 1949: 153, 377) must be rejected, as he would either have been stationed at Lyons or else the post he was holding would have been one normally assigned to freedmen (van Berchem, 1978: 269). But Sabinus was definitely not a freedman; he had decided to move from Ephesus to Aventicum (Avenches) in Switzerland in order to become a banker or moneylender, a role in which he must have been remarkably successful (described as the 'first gnome of Zurich' by A.R. Birley, 1986: 64), for he was able to provide both his sons with the senatorial census. During the latter part of Tiberius' reign, so it seems, Sabinus settled at Aventicum which had become the centre of a prosperous and rapidly developing area (van Berchem, 1978: 269-70). That he operated from there is very likely in view of *CIL* 13.5138, from the tombstone of a Pompeia Gemella, the *educatrix* of *Augustus noster*. Van Berchem has argued that Pompeia was the *educatrix* of Titus (not of Vespasian as has usually been assumed) and that Titus had been sent to live with his grandfather Sabinus at Aventicum in the early years of Claudius' reign when Vespasian was serving under Aulus Plautius in Britain. So, too, when Sabinus was in Ephesus, unwilling to expose the young Vespasian 'aux dangers d'une éducation à la grecque' (van Berchem, 1978: 269), he had arranged for him to be raised by his grandmother Tertulla, at Cosa, *in praediis Cosanis* (2.1 below).

**Vespasia Polla:** Vespasian's mother came from an equestrian family (see below, s.u. *honesto genere orta*) that was wealthy enough to ensure that her brother could attain senatorial status.

**Sabinus:** Before Vespasian's accession to the empire, Titus Flavius Sabinus was the senior member of the *gens Flavia* in age, status and reputation – *quod inter* *omnes constiterit, ante principatum Vespasiani decus domus penes Sabinum erat* (*Hist* 3.75). His was a very distinguished career, hinted at in *ILS* 984 (= *MW* 97) and set out in more detail by Tacitus in *Hist*. 3.75, i.e. *quinque et triginta stipendia in re publica fecerat, domi militiaeque clarus. innocentiam iustitiamque eius non argueres; sermonis nimius erat: id unum septem annis quibus Moesiam, duodecim quibus praefecturam urbis obtinuit, calumniatus est rumor*. But it was one that has generated much discussion thanks to Tacitus' text which assigns him a city prefecture of twelve years: *ILS* 984 merely reads *praef. urb.* – with *iterum* as a restoration. That much is, at best, difficult to explain since L. Pedanius Secundus held that post when he was killed in 61 (*Ann*. 14.42). Of the more recent accounts, Nicols' is vitiated by his claim (i) that Sabinus was consul in 44 and (ii) that he was *praefectus urbi* on three separate occasions (1978: 26-30). A more likely version is that of Griffin (1976: 456-7) and A.R. Birley (1981: 224-5), i.e. Sabinus probably entered the senate in 34, when he was over the minimum age (Chastagnol, 1976: 255) and was consul almost certainly in 47 (A.R. Birley, 1981: 225), after serving as legionary legate (of *legio* IX or XIV or XX) in the invasion of Britain, together with his younger brother Vespasian, who commanded the *II Augusta*. Thereafter, he governed Moesia, perhaps from 53 to 60 and then became *praefectus urbi* on two occasions, from 61 to 68 and again in 69 (from ?16 Jan. until his death). Despite Braithwaite (1927: 21) and many others, he was the grandfather, and not the father, of Flavius Sabinus, *cos. ord.* 82 and of Flavius Clemens, *cos. ord.* 95. For a less than flattering account of his actions in 69, see Wallace who laments his 'passive, wait-and-see, do-nothing behaviour' (1987: 357).

**praefecturam urbis:** For its early history, see *Ann*. 6.11. In the empire, the *praefectus urbi* was always a senior senator with *imperium*; he served for a number of years, commanded the urban cohorts and was responsible for maintaining law and order in the city, presiding over his own court of justice that, with time, became increasingly more powerful. In Juvenal's fourth satire, the City Prefect ([Plo]tius Pegasus: *OCD* 1131) was the first member of Domitian's *consilium* to be admitted to the meeting and was described as *optimus atque/interpres legum sanctissimus* (*Sat*. 4.78-79). According to Syme, the post 'stood at the peak of the senatorial career' (*RP* 5.608). See Cadoux, 1959: 152-60; Syme, *RP* 5. 608-21 and the bibliography in *OCD* 1239.

**Nursiae:** Nursia (Norcia) was a Sabine mountain-town at the foot of the Apennines, the birthplace of Sertorius – and Saint Benedict. Its cold climate was legendary, e.g. *frigida Nurcia* (*Aen*. 7.716).

**honesto genere orta:** References by the equestrian Suetonius to a family's status are quite precise: hence *honestus* is used of Polla's equestrian family, whereas Titus' second wife, the 'senatorial' Marcia Furnilla, was *splendidi generis* (*Titus* 4.2).

**Vespasium Pollionem:** Apart from Suetonius' comments here, nothing else is known of him. See Saddington, 1996: 247 No. 11.

**tribunum militum:** In the Republic, the tribunes (six in number) were the senior officers of a legion, usually with at least five years of previous military experience, but their significance diminished with the creation of the post of *legatus*; see A.R. Birley, 1981: 8-12. So it was that, during the empire, the post was held early in one's career; see 2.3. below, s.u. *tribunus militum in Thracia*.

**praefectum castrorum:** This officer is first attested in the early empire, with the establishment of permanent camps. His duties were administrative – he was, for instance, responsible for the construction of camps, transport, garrison duties etc. Next in seniority after the senatorial *legatus legionis* and the *tribunus laticlauius*, he was 'the only senior officer with more than a few years' experience of the military life' (Dobson, 1974: 396-7). According to Vegetius, he was *peritissimus omnium*, chosen *post longam probatamque militiam* (2.10): so he was a *primipilaris*, though the earliest *praefecti* (such as Pollio and the L. Arrius Salanus of *ILS* 6285) may not have been so qualified. In the later empire, the *praefectus castrorum* replaced the *legatus legionis*. For his pay and *dona*, see Maxfield, 1981: 179 and 204-5.

**fratrem senatorem praetoriae dignitatis:** Vespasian's maternal uncle (Vespasius) was the first of his ancestors to attain senatorial rank and would have done so in Augustus' reign: the shrewd Sabinus married well.

**Spoletium:** Spoleto (in Umbria, some 30 km from Nursia) became a *municipium* in 45 BC; see *OCD* 1436.

**Vespasiae:** Nothing else is known of it.

1.4

**Petronis patrem e regione Transpadana:** That Petro's father came from the area north of the Po – so was not even an 'Italian'! – was a rumour without apparent foundation according to Suetonius' careful investigation.

15

**mancipem operarum:** He imported labourers and then hired them out to local farmers, apparently another unfounded rumour, neatly described as 'predictable invective' by Wallace-Hadrill (1995: 106). Perhaps the efforts of the pro-Flavian historians to stress (i.e. invent) the family's loss of influence and status under the 'bad' Julio-Claudian emperors inspired even greater inventiveness.

**quamuis satis curiose inquirerem:** This section provides ample evidence that Suetonius was capable of careful, independent research, hardly surprising in one who reached the highest office in the imperial bureaucracy and who was described by Pliny as *scholasticus* (*Ep.* 1.24) and as *eruditissimus* (*Ep.* 10.94). See the discussion of Wallace-Hadrill, 1995: *passim* but especially 50-72.

2.1

**Falacrinae:** Falacrina (the manuscripts have *Phalacrinae* and *Phalacrine*; on the spelling, see *RE* 6.1968) was near the modern Città Reale, some 30 km from Reate on the Via Salaria. The name is preserved in the church of S. Silvestro in Falacrino.

**XV Kal. Decb.:** i.e. 17 November.

**Q. Sulpicio Camerino...Sabino:** Q. Sulpicius Camerinus and C. Poppaeus Sabinus were ordinary consuls in 9. Grandfather of Nero's Poppaea Sabina, the latter was somewhat unkindly but no doubt accurately described by Tacitus as *maximis prouinciis per quattuor et uiginti annos impositus, nullam ob eximiam artem sed quod par negotiis neque supra erat* (*Ann.* 6.39).

**quinquennio...excederet:** Augustus died on 19 August 14 (*Aug.* 100.1).

**Tertulla:** Wife of T. Flavius Petro (1.2).

**in praediis Cosanis:** On the Etrurian coastal town of Cosa with its harbour, the *portus Cosanus*, see *RE* 6.2627 (but compare *RE* 4.1667 where Hülsen thinks that the reference is to Cossa, a town of the Hirpini); Brown, 1951: 73-5; Brunt, 1971: 84-5; Fentress, 1994: 209-22 and *OCD* 404. Vespasian was brought up there whilst Sabinus was in Ephesus, not (as, e.g., Braithwaite, 1927: 23) when he was in Aventicum; see above, s.u. *faenus...exercuit*.

**sollemnibus ac festis diebus:** The reference, presumably, is not to official, public *dies festi*, but rather to family occasions such as weddings, birthdays etc.

2.2

**sumpta uirili toga:** As he was born in 9, he replaced his *toga praetexta* (on which, see next item) with the *toga uirilis* at the festival of the *Liberalia* on 17 March ca 27; see Millar, 1977: 291 n.7.

**fratre adepto:** According to Chastagnol (1976: 255), Sabinus received the *latus clauus* (i.e. the broad purple stripe on the toga indicating that the wearer belonged to the senatorial order) at the time of his quaestorship in 34, and not before. He accepts the statement of Dio (59.9.5) that, until the accession of Gaius in 37, only the sons of senators could 'assume the *latus clauus* immediately after the *toga uirilis*' (*Aug.* 38.2); see the discussion below.

**latum clauum:** The senatorial 'broad stripe' has to be distinguished from the equestrian narrow (*angustus clauus*) one. Moreover, the stripes were on the undertunic and ran vertically over the shoulders and down the front; they could not be confused with the purple border of the *toga praetexta*.

Scholars from Mooney (1930: 380) to Levick (1999: 8-9) believe that, once this was conferred on Vespasian, he became eligible for the vigintivirate, a view rejected by Chastagnol (1976: 253-4) who bases his argument on *Aug.* 38.2 (*liberis senatorum, quo celerius rei publicae assuescerent, protinus a uirili toga latum clauum induere et curiae interesse permisit militiamque auspicantibus non tribunatum modo legionum sed et praefecturas alarum dedit*) and Dio 59.9.5 ('Gaius even permitted some [members of the equestrian order] to wear the senatorial dress before they had held any office through which we gain admission to the senate, on the strength of their prospects of becoming members later, whereas previously only those, it appears, who had been born into the senatorial order were allowed to do this'). According to Chastagnol (1976: 253-6, although a number of scholars have questioned his views; see the list of those supporting and opposing Chastagnol's thesis in Barrett, 1989: 312 n.86), Vespasian must have remained an equestrian until he was of an age to sue for the quaestorship, i.e. very late in Tiberius' reign and so, despite Braithwaite (1927: 23) and Mooney (1930: 380), he could never have held a post in the vigintivirate but would have served in Thrace – as a *tribunus angusticlauius*. For the standard view, see Millar, 1977: 290-3.

**diu auersatus est:** Both before and after his period of service in Thrace (*diu*), he must have expressed a desire to pursue a career similar to his father's and not seek the *latus clauus* once he became eligible to do so (ca 34). If Chastagnol (1976: 253-6) is correct, Suetonius' account is slightly misleading as Vespasian was quaestor only a year later than his brother (see below); on the other hand,

Sabinus may for some time have made it clear that he would try for senatorial status once this was legally possible, whilst Vespasian, with his well-attested interest in monetary matters (see 16 below), may well have taken precisely the opposite point of view, preferring to emulate those his father and grandfather. See also Nicols, 1978: 19-20.

**nec ut tandem...nisi a matre:** A number of scholars have accepted Suetonius' statement that Vespasian's change of heart was due to the formidable Vespasia (e.g. Braithwaite, 1927: 23; Graf, 1937: 11-12 and Homo, 1949: 16-17), but Morgan (1996: 47) has suggested that it may have been linked to the omen of the cypress (see 5.4 below, s.u. *arbor...resurrexit*) which, according to Tacitus, occurred when Vespasian was *admodum iuuenis*, i.e. *cupressus arbor in agris eius conspicua altitudine repente prociderat ac postero die...resurgens procera et latior uirebat. grande id prosperumque consensu haruspicum et summa claritudo iuueni admodum Vespasiano promissa* (*Hist*.2.78) – and Vespasian *nec erat intactus tali superstitione* (ibid.). If then it was the omen and not (or perhaps as well as) Vespasia that prompted Vespasian's decision, one is forced to consider the claim that the cypress *repente prociderat*; presumably it should be linked with some unexpected change in Vespasian's circumstances and just possibly with the sudden death of his father Sabinus. There is no evidence however.

**anteambulonem:** An *anteambulo* was a slave who walked in front of his master to clear the way; the term then came to be used of a *cliens* who performed a similar service for his *patronus*. Vespasia's verbal attack on her younger son recalls Martial's description of himself as a *tumidi anteambulo regis* (2.18.5).

2.3
**tribunus militum in Thracia:** The majority of scholars (including Ihm) accept the reading of the better manuscripts, *tribunatum militum...meruit*; yet Suetonius' usage is clearly in favour of *tribunus...meruit* (the reading of Torrentius). In *Titus* 4.1, we have *tribunus militum et in Germania et in Britannia meruit*; similarly, *Tib*. 9.1 and *Vit. Horat*. 1; and, on the other hand, no parallel is cited for *tribunatum...meruit* in the sense of 'he served as a tribune'; see the full discussion in Mooney, 1930: 380.

If *tribunatum...meruit* were to be translated as 'Vespasian earned a tribunate' by his valour in Thrace, the sense would at least be consistent with Chastagnol's theory mentioned above (2.2, s.u. *latum clauum*), that (before Gaius' reform) it was only *tribuni laticlauii* who could begin their careers as military tribunes (*militiam auspicantibus* [i.e. *liberis senatorum*] *tribunatum legionum...dedit*: *Aug*. 38.2); if so, it was by his military prowess that Vespasian would have shown

18

that he deserved his tribunate and was therefore subsequently given the *latus clauus* with the concomitant right to sue for the quaestorship.

This office was held before the quaestorship. Each legion had one senatorial *tribunus laticlauius* and (in theory) five equestrian *tribuni angusticlauii*. It was perhaps ca 29-31 that Vespasian served in Thrace as *tribunus angusticlauius* (according to Chastagnol, 1976: 255) in either the IV Scythica or V Macedonica (for an argument in favour of the former, see Nicols, 1978: 2 n.9). There had been problems in that province during the last years of Augustus' reign and for much of Tiberius' (*Ann.* 2.64-7, 3.38), with, for example, Poppaeus Sabinus (see above 2.1) earning *ornamenta triumphalia* for his actions there (*Ann.* 4.46-51). See also A.R. Birley, 1981: 8-9, 226-7.

**quaestor Cretam et Cyrenas:** The date of Vespasian's tenure is disputed, e.g. Graf (1937: 12) prefers 34, Braithwaite (1927: 23-4) 35 and Homo (1949: 20) is uncertain. The likeliest time is the period from July 35 until June 36: as Vespasian became aedile in 38 at his second attempt, he must have first tried in 36 – and his brother Sabinus was quaestor in 34 – see Nicols, 1978: 3 and A.R. Birley, 1981: 227 n.6. Cyrenaica in North Africa with its capital Cyrene (*Cyrenae*) was willed to Rome in 95 BC, became a province some twenty years later and was united with Crete in 67 BC. *Creta et Cyrenae*, as it then came to be known, was made a senatorial province by Augustus and so was entitled to a quaestor who usually helped with matters financial.

**prouinciam sorte cepit:** Every year, a quaestor selected by lot was sent to one of the senatorial provinces, e.g. *sors quaesturae prouinciam Asiam [Agricolae] ...dedit* (*Agr.* 6.2).

**aedilitatis:** For the aedile's duties, including the *cura urbis*, see *OCD* 15-16. Vespasian held the post in 38, despite Graf (1937: 13) who argues for 37 and Syme (1958: 652) who prefers 39 (but 38 in *RP* 2: 808). The date is fixed by Dio who, after a reference to Vespasian's aedileship (59.12.3), continues 'Gaius now became consul again [i.e. *Cos. II* in 39]...' (59.13.1). See Chastagnol (1976: 254), Nicols (1978: 3) and A.R. Birley (1981: 226). Gaius' reaction to Vespasian's alleged neglect of his duties is discussed at 5.3, s.u. *luto...oppleri*.

**mox praeturae candidatus:** Here *mox* means 'next in the order of relevant events' and so Vespasian was not necessarily aedile and praetor in successive years; see Nicols, 1978: 5.

**repulsa:** Vespasian's defeat (*repulsa*) may have been due to the lack of time to campaign between his return from Crete and the elections; see Nicols, 1978: 4.

**sextoque...loco:** i.e. in the last place.

**in primis:** Not *primus*, as is clear from Cicero – *me cum quaestorem in primis... praetorem primum cunctis suffragiis populus Romanus faciebat (Pis.* 1).

**praetor:** He was probably praetor in 40. It is often held that he held the post in 39, e.g. by Braithwaite (1927: 24), Mooney (1930: 381) and Graf (1937: 13-14). A.R. Birley (1981: 227) suggests 39 or 40, while Nicols argues at length (1978: 4-7) for 40, the date preferred by Levick (1999: 11); he rejects the possibility of a *uictoria Germanica* (see below) in 39, on the grounds that the reference is to Gaius' northern campaign, which resulted in his absence from Rome during the period September 39 - May 40.

**infensum senatui Gaium:** For Gaius' hostility towards the senate, see *Calig.* 48.2-49.1, i.e. *urbem petit, deflexa omni acerbitate in senatum, cui...palam minabatur ... "ueniam" inquit, "ueniam, et hic mecum," capulum gladii crebro uerberans...* together with the comments of Lindsay, 1993: 115-16.

**ne quo non genere demereretur:** Vespasian's two speeches (noted by Suetonius) show that he never let slip an opportunity to curry favour with Gaius.

**ludos extraordinarios:** i.e. apart from those regularly celebrated each year. Augustus had transferred the *cura ludorum* from the aediles to the praetors in 22 BC (Dio 54.2.3).

**pro uictoria eius Germanica:** The reference is to Gaius' much discussed but little understood 'German' campaign (Barrett, 1989: 132-9) that began in September 39 and was described by Tacitus as the *Gaianarum expeditionum ludibrium* (*Hist.* 4.15) and as the *ingentes Gai Caesaris minae in ludibrium uersae (Germ.* 37). See also *Calig.* 43-7, Dio 59.21.1-4 and 25.1-5a together with the comments of Lindsay, 1993: 138-44.

**coniuratorum:** Cn. Cornelius Lentulus Gaetulicus (*cos. ord.* 26 and commander of the Upper German legions for a decade: his mild discipline was famous – *mirum amorem adsecutus erat, effusae clementiae, modicus seueritate: Ann.* 6.30: see Syme, 1989: 481) and L. Aemilius Lepidus (the last of the Aemilii Lepidi and married to Drusilla, Gaius' sister: Syme, 1989: 136, 283) were implicated in a conspiracy, if such it was, to kill Gaius and seize the throne; compare the arguments of Simpson

(1980: 347-66), Barrett (1989: 105-13), Syme (1989: 179-80) and Lindsay (1993: 110-11). Apparently, the emperor's other sisters (Julia and Agrippina) were also involved. It was suppressed in person by Gaius at Mogontiacum and word of what had happened reached Rome by 27 October 39: on that day, the Arval Brethren offered sacrifice *ob detecta nefaria con[silia in C. Germani]cum Cn. Lentuli Gae[tulici]* (*CIL* 6.2029). Gaetulicus and Lepidus were executed, Julia and Agrippina exiled: see Dio 59.22.5-6; *Claud.* 9.1 and *Calig.* 24.3.

**insepulti:** This was part of the standard penalty for treason, e.g. Tiberius Gracchus – *hostis iudicatus, ultimo supplicio affectus, sepulturae honore spoliatus* (Val. Max. 4.7). Those found guilty also suffered *damnatio memoriae* and their relatives were forbidden to wear mourning. If Vespasian's proposal coincided with Agrippina's return to Rome with Lepidus' ashes, then the hostility she showed towards him (noted by Suetonius at 4.2 below, s.u. *Agrippinam timens*) may well have had its origins at this time; see Jones, 1984a: 581-3. Moreover, her return journey would have taken at least 70 days (Nicols, 1978: 7); so, if she left Mogontiacum in October 39, she would have arrived back in January 40, when the new praetors (Vespasian included) had just taken up office. Her welcome was Vespasian's speech – no wonder she hated him.

**egit gratias:** Vespasian's speech of thanks in the senate to Gaius was his third as praetor (so the invitation to dinner was a reward for the first two). An *actio gratiarum* that has survived is Pliny's *Panegyricus*.

**amplissimum ordinem:** i.e. the Senate; so, in *Aug.* 26.2, the *amplissimus magistratus* is the consulship. In 9.2. below (*q.u.*), Suetonius uses *amplissimos ordines* of the senatorial and equestrian orders.

**honore cenae:** A wealthy provincial paid 200,000 sesterces for an invitation to dine with Gaius (see the anecdote in *Calig.*39) and a similar invitation issued by Domitian was much prized by Statius (*Silu.* 4.2) and by Martial (*Palatinae... conuiuia mensae/ambrosiasque dapes*: 8.39.1-2) – but less so by those invited to the macabre *cena* when he alone spoke and then only on 'topics relating to death and slaughter', where the name tags were gravestones...' (Dio 67.9.1-5).

**3**
**inter haec:** i.e. in Gaius' reign.

**Flauiam Domitillam:** Vespasian's wife, daughter and granddaughter bore this name (the fourth Domitilla should be retired to oblivion) but only his daughter

21

(so it seems, yet see Kienast, 1989: 141-7) was deified; on all this, see below, s.u. *Domitillam*. As Vespasian's wife was not deified, it is usually assumed (e.g. by Stein in *RE* 6.2732) that she did not receive the title *Augusta* either and so scholars have assigned to her the inscription *Flaviae Domitillae [Imp.] Vespasian[i C]aesar[is] Aug.* (*ILS* 257 = *MW* 98). See also Castritius, 1969: 492-502.

**Statili Capellae equitis Romani:** During the early empire, there were many provincials in the *ordo equester*, e.g. 500 at Gades according to Strabo (169, 213C), and Vespasian adlected more: see 9.2 below, i.e. *honestissimo quoque...prouincialium adlecto*. So Seneca described himself to Nero as *equestri et prouinciali loco ortus* (*Ann*. 14.53).

**Sabratensis ex Africa:** Lying to the west of modern Tripoli, Sabratha (Sabart or Tripoli Vecchio) was probably founded by the Phoenicians (Sil. Ital., *Pun*. 3.256); it became one of the three *ciuitates* (with Oea and Leptis Magna) of Tripolis Africana and, later, a Roman colony. See *OCD* 1342.

**Latinaeque condicionis, sed mox ingenuam et ciuem Romanam:** She had been a Junian Latin. Suetonius' choice of words (*mox ingenuam*) may well justify the use of *liberta* in the *Epit. de Caes.* to describe this Domitilla, i.e. *Titus...matre liberta Domitilla nomine genitus* (*Epit. de Caes.* 10.1) and *Domitianus Vespasiani et Domitillae libertae filius* (ibid., 11.1). Levick argues that 'she either was or had been deemed an ex-slave' and believes that it is likely that 'her mother was (Liberalis') freedwoman and concubine, freed without good cause shown, contrary to the *lex Aelia Sentia*, so acquiring only Latin status' (1999: 12 – but see also p. 212). See also Ritter, 1972: 759-61; Evans, 1979: 201; Raepsaet-Charlier, 1987: 319-21; Kienast, 1989: 141-7 and Weaver, 1990: 275-305.

**reciperatorio iudicio** The word *reciperatores* means 'regainers' or 'recoverers' and they were arbiters (usually three or five in number and appointed by the praetor) employed instead of a single judge in certain cases, e.g. (as here) of disputed legal status, debt or extortion. Domitian repeatedly warned these 'investigators of status' to be on their guard against false claims for freedom (*Dom*. 8.1) and Dio mentions the case of Claudius Pacatus, an ex-centurion restored to his master by Domitian because he was proven to be a slave (Dio 67.13.1). As they could operate even on *dies nefasti*, it is not surprising that their proceedings seem to have been conducted more rapidly than those of the other courts. See *OCD* 1296.

**patre asserente:** In cases of disputed legal status, those whose status was under investigation could not act for themselves but only through an agent called an *assertor*. The latter could even make a claim despite the wishes of the person involved: Suetonius (*De Gramm.* 21) cites the case of Gaius Melissus who, *quamquam asserente matre, permansit tamen in statu seruitutis praesentemque condicionem uerae origini anteposuit*. Again, the word appears frequently in the propaganda of the civil war and later, e.g. *adsertor libertatis* (on a denarius of 69-70: *MW* 39), *adsertor ille a Nerone libertatis* (of Vindex: *NH* 20.160), *imperium adseruit non sibi sed patriae* (Pliny, *Ep.* 6.10.4: of Verginius Rufus, on his epitaph) and *adsertor libertatis publicae* (of Vespasian: see Watson, 1973: 127-8) – the claim, in each case, being that as the human race had been enslaved by Nero, it was necessary for X to act as *assertor* in the 'legal' action aimed at restoring its *libertas*.

**Flauio Liberale:** Even though the *gens Flavia* was found throughout Italy, Flavia Domitilla was just possibly related to Vespasian by blood; one is also reminded of the eminent Flavian senators, L. *Flavius* Silva Nonius Bassus (the conqueror of Masada, *cos.ord.* 81) and C. Salvius *Liberalis* Nonius Bassus (discussed in 13 below). See also Salomies, 1992: 80, 132-3.

**Ferenti:** Ferentium (Ferentino), a small *municipium* in southern Etruria, was Otho's home town (*Otho* 1; *Hist.* 2.50); see Murison, 1992: 89 and *OCD* 592.

**quaestorio scriba:** Since the time of Sulla, there were thirty-six quaestors' clerks, some being freedmen, while others later gained senatorial rank. They worked in the *aerarium*, with two being attached to the staff of each provincial governor; see *Dom.* 9.3. As Mooney (1930: 385) points out, Suetonius' scornful tone (*nec quicquam amplius quam*) derives from the fact that they were *mercenarii*, unlike other officials and magistrates who were not paid. Nepos says of the post *multo apud Graios honorificentius est quam apud Romanos: namque apud nos re uera, sic ut sunt, mercenarii scribae existimantur* (*Eum.* 1).

**Titum:** Titus was born in Rome on 30 December 39 (McGuire, 1980: 24-5; Martinet, 1981: 6-7), *prope Septizonium, sordidis aedibus, cubiculo uero perparuo et obscuro* (*Titus* 1).

**Domitianum:** Domitian was born in Rome almost twelve years after Titus (24 October 51), *regione urbis sexta ad Malum Punicum* (*Dom.* 1.1).

**Domitillam:** This Domitilla (*PIR*² F 417), Domitian's sister, is the *diua Domitilla* appearing on coins and inscriptions, as is clear from Statius' lines on the Flavian relatives who will greet Domitian in heaven, i.e. *ibit in amplexus natus fraterque paterque/et soror...(Silu.* 1.1.97-8) – but compare Kienast, 1989: 141-7. Townend's suggestion (1961: 62) that she was born in 45 (i.e. after Titus and before Domitian) has been rejected by Nicols (1978: 8-9) since it would mean that either Vespasian's wife was with him in Britain during a war or else that he had returned to Rome in 44; furthermore, it would be necessary to disrupt the chronological order given by Suetonius. It seems that she married Q. Petillius Cerialis Caesius Rufus (*PIR*² P 260: *cos. II suff.* 74) who had at least one son by an earlier marriage (C. Petillius Firmus, P 261; see the reconstruction of his career by Bosworth, 1980: 267-77) and perhaps a second (Q. Petillius Rufus, *cos. II ord.* 83: but he may have been Cerialis' brother = P 263). Her daughter, presumably by Petillius, was also called Domitilla and she married T. Flavius Clemens, grandson of Flavius Sabinus (Vespasian's brother). Her relationship with Clemens (wife or niece?) and her fate (her place of exile) have provoked much discussion. In brief, Dio (67.14.1-2) claims that, in 95, she was accused of atheism, found guilty and banished to Pandateria. In the *Acta* of Saints Nereus and Achilleus), she (now Clemens' niece) was exiled to Terracina and later burned to death. Eusebius, however, states that Domitian had 'banished Clemens's niece, Domitilla, to Pontia' (3.17). The legend then grew apace. In the *Acta*, Domitilla was not only Clemens' niece, but also niece to the father of bishop Clement (author of *1 Clement*) and had also been assigned a mother, Plautilla. Finally, Cardinal Caesar Baronius (author of the *Annales Ecclesiastici* written between 1588 and 1607) was the first to believe in the existence of two Domitianic victims named Domitilla (4.586), a version still accepted by some scholars (e.g. Sordi, 1994: 50-51).

**adhuc priuatus:** Before 1 July 69.

**excessum:** i.e. *mortem*.

**Caenidem:** (Antonia) Caenis (*PIR*² A 888) was the secretary and freedwoman of Antonia, mother of Germanicus and Claudius [so she is described as *Antonia Aug(ustae) l(iberta) Caenis: CIL* 6.12037 = *MW* 210], thereby giving Vespasian a direct link with the imperial family when she became his mistress. She was eminently capable and trustworthy; it was to her that Antonia dictated the letter to Tiberius about Sejanus (see Dio 60.14.1-2). Another member of Antonia's *familia* was Narcissus, who became Claudius' *ab epistulis* and a supporter of Vespasian; perhaps it was she who provided the link between him and Vespasian (McDermott-Orentzel, 1979: 28). After Vespasian's accession to the throne, she amassed great wealth by selling 'procuratorships, generalships, priesthoods and, in some instances, even imperial decisions' (Dio 67.14.3). Domitian's attitude towards her is revealed by Suetonius, i.e. *Caenidi patris concubinae ex Histria reuersae osculumque, ut assuerat, offerenti manum praebuit (Dom.* 12.3). She died in the early seventies (Dio 67.14.1) and was replaced by *(pallacas) quas in locum defunctae Caenidis plurimas constituerat* (21 below). We know of property she owned near the Porta Pia, where an altar to her (with surviving inscription) was erected by her freedman Aglaus and his children (Kokkinos, 1992: 57-9). See the reconstruction of her career by McDermott-Orentzel, 1979: 27-31.

**Antoniae:** Sometimes referred to as Antonia minor (36 BC-AD 37), she was the younger daughter of Marcus Antonius, the triumvir. She married Tiberius' brother Drusus and bore him three children, Germanicus, Claudius and Livia Julia (Livilla). She exerted considerable influence through her circle whose members included not only such eminent senatorial families as the Vitellii, Plautii and Petronii but also wealthy and influential Jews (Agrippa I, Agrippa II and Tiberius Julius Alexander's family). For the assistance she provided to the Flavii, see the previous item.

4.1

**Claudio principe...missus est:** Vespasian's first praetorian posting occurred not long after the accession of Claudius in January 41, when, through the influence of L. Vitellius, Narcissus and other members of Antonia's circle (see below), he was sent to Strassburg as legionary legate of the II Augusta – *secundae legioni a Claudio praepositus (Hist.* 3.44) – no doubt to prepare the legion for its part in the invasion of Britain.

**Narcissi gratia:** Narcissus (*PIR*[2] N 23) and Pallas (A 858), 'the most trustworthy of Antonia's slaves' (*AJ* 18.182), were the all-powerful freedmen of Claudius' court *(ante omnes...[suspexit]: Claud.* 28) and even L. Vitellius *Narcissi...et Pallantis imagines aureas inter Lares coluit (Vit.* 2.5). Another influential member of Antonia's *familia* was Vespasian's mistress, Caenis; see 3 above.

Narcissus was the imperial *ab epistulis* and his influence was legendary. When, for instance, Plautius' army refused to leave Gaul for Britain, it was Narcissus who was sent to Boulogne to pacify the mutineers (Dio 60.19.2-3). Possibly, too, he was responsible for Titus being admitted to the court as a companion for Claudius' son, Britannicus (see *Titus* 2). In 49, after the death of his third wife, Messalina, Claudius married his niece Agrippina (Germanicus' daughter) who already had a son (the future emperor Nero) by an earlier husband, Domitius Ahenobarbus: *uersa ex eo ciuitas et cuncta feminae oboediebant...adductum et quasi uirile seruitium: palam seueritas ac saepius superbia: nihil domi impu-dicum nisi dominationi expediret (Ann.* 12.7).

Narcissus, moreover, made two fatal mistakes: not only had he opposed Clau-dius' marriage to Agrippina (his 'candidate' was Claudius' former wife Aelia Paetina), but he also favoured Britannicus rather than Nero. With the removal of Claudius in 54 and the accession of Nero, he was forced to commit suicide (*ad mortem agitur: Ann.* 13.1). Until Claudius and Agrippina married in 49, both Vespasian and his brother had prospered. It is even possible that, in 47, they were granted patrician status. This has been argued by McAlindon (1957: 260); rejected by Hammond (1959: 275 n.45); and, whilst an award of this nature to Vespasian or Sabinus (or both) is not mentioned by Suetonius or by any other ancient author, Suetonius does refer specifically to Claudius' grant of patrician status to Otho's father, i.e. *prosecutus est eum [L. Othonem] et Claudius adlectum inter patricios conlaudans amplissimis uerbis (Otho* 1.3). In the period following Narcissus' death, Sabinus advanced to greater honours, becoming governor of Moesia and City Prefect. Barrett (1996: 105) has argued that there is no evidence to show that Agrippina tried to block Vespasian's career; however, the fact remains that he seems to have received no consular appointment until after her death.

**legatus legionis:** For a discussion of this post during the empire, see A.R. Birley, 1981: 17-20. Vespasian's legion, the II Augusta, remained permanently in Britain; its *praefectus castrorum* (see 1.3 above) at this time was P. Anicius Maximus (*ILS* 2696).

**in Germaniam:** Similarly Eutropius – *a Claudio in Germaniam...missus* (7.19.1). The governor of Upper Germany after the execution of Gaetulicus (see 2.3 above, s.u. *coniuratorum*, for the laxity of his discipline) and during the first years of Claudius' reign was the future emperor Galba (Syme, 1989: 180-1): as the soldiers put it in their jingle, the metre being the standard trochaic septenarius, *disce miles militare, Galba est, non Gaetulicus* (*Galba* 6.2). Exaggerated accounts of Vespasian's activities there are given by Josephus ('Vespasian pacified and restored to Roman rule the West when convulsed by the Germans': *BJ* 3.4) and by Silius Italicus (*compescet ripis Rhenum: Pun.* 3.599). So, as well as (or as part of) preparing his troops for the on-coming invasion, Vespasian had perhaps led them in raids across the Rhine; see Nicols, 1978: 8 and Levick, 1999: 16.

**in Britanniam translatus:** Inevitably, Flavian writers exaggerated Vespasian's role in the Claudian invasion. A more sober and detailed account of what he did and may have done is provided by Branigan, 1970: 50-7. Hind, however, rejects the traditional version of events (i.e. landings at Dover, Lympne and Richborough) and offers an 'alternative strategy', arguing that the Romans came to shore on 'the coast and harbours of the Atrebatic kingdom behind and just to the east of the Isle of Wight' (1989: 12; see his map, 1989: 19).

According to Josephus, Vespasian 'had by his military genius added Britain to the Empire, till then almost unknown, and thus afforded Claudius...the honours of a triumph which cost him no personal exertion' (*BJ* 3.5-6). Valerius Flaccus is even more enthusiastic and far less accurate (*tuos o pelagi cui maior aperti/Fama, Caledonius postquam tua carbasa uexit/Oceanus Phrygios prius indignatus Iulos/...sancte pater*: *Argon*. 1. 7-11), as is Silius Italicus (*Hinc pater ignotam donabit uincere Thulen,/inque Caledonios primus trahet agmina lucos*: *Pun*. 3.597-8). Tacitus' assessment (*adsumpto in partem rerum Vespasiano quod initium uenturae mox fortunae fuit: domitae gentes, capti reges et monstratus fatis Vespasianus*: *Agr*. 13.3) and (*Britanniae inditus erga Vespasianum fauor, quod illic secundae legioni a Claudio praepositus et bello clarus egerat*: *Hist*. 3.44) seems more realistic.

Before the emperor's arrival, Vespasian and his elder brother Sabinus, commanding two (A.R. Birley, 1981: 224) of the four legions (II Augusta and XIV Gemina [from Upper Germany], XX Valeria Victrix [from Lower Germany] and IX Hispana [from Pannonia]), sent to Britain, had 'crossed the river [? Medway – or the Arun according to Hind, 1989: 17]...and killed many of the foe' (Dio 60.20.3). By 47, Vespasian and the II Augusta had probably advanced as far as the Fosse Way, somewhat to the north of Cirencester; see Branigan and Fowler, 1976: 17-19. For detailed accounts of the Claudian invasion, see Frere (1987: 48-69), Hind (1989: 1-21), Levick (1990: 137-48 and 1999: 14-20) and Salway (1993: 49-72).

**tricies cum hoste conflixit:** Eutropius (7.19.1) repeats Suetonius' account exactly apart from adding *et bis* to his *tricies*.

**duas ualidissimas gentes:** Their identity is disputed: most commentators agree that the Durotriges were one of them, with the other being either the Belgae (Nicols, 1978: 8), or the Dumnonii (Frere, 1987: 58; Dilke, 1981: 395), or the Dobunni (Salway, 1993: 70; Shotter, 1998: 16 – rejected by Branigan and Fowler, 1976: 26). Far less likely is the suggestion of both Braithwaite (1927: 28) and Mooney (1930: 387) that the *gentes* in question were the Belgae and the Atrebates.

**uiginti oppida:** According to Frere (1987: 58-9), the *oppida* may well have included Maiden Castle, Hod Hill, South Cadbury, Waddon Hill, Ham Hill, Wiveliscombe, Hembury, Tiverton, Okehampton, Cullompton, Bury Barton,

Killerton and North Tawton. Hind (1989: 4 and 3 n.15) proposes Pilsden Pen as well and argues that the Isle of Wight was one of the first *oppida* to fall to Vespasian (1989: 20). See also Webster (1980:108-11) and the map in Branigan (1970: 51). The expertise in siege-warfare gained here served Vespasian some two decades later in the war against the Jews.

**insulam Vectem:** Isle of Wight. Dilke (1981: 394) argues that Vespasian would have used Portchester and Bitterne as bases for the invasion of the Isle of Wight; he also suggests that, whilst the expedition itself landed at Richborough (rejected by Hind, 1989: 12 – see 4.1 above, s.u. *in Britanniam translatus*), the Romans used Fishbourne as the military harbour for the entire operation.

**Auli Plauti:** Aulus Plautius (*PIR²* P 457), with an invasion force numbering some 45,000 (see Shotter, 1998: 16), probably established Roman ascendancy in Britain over the area south of the Exe/Humber line. Dio refers to his 'skilful and successful conduct of the war in Britain (for which) he obtained an ovation' (60.30.2). Suetonius also notes that Claudius *Aulo Plautio...ouationem decreuit* (*Claud.* 24.3), as does Tacitus (*Ann.* 13.32) who describes Plautius as *bello egregius* (*Agr.* 14.1); but he was also one of the 'élite brokers of patronage' (Wallace-Hadrill, 1996: 302). He was closely related to Claudius' first wife Plautia Urgulanilla, his mother was a Vitellia, his wife a Pomponia and his sister had married P. Petronius, a *uetus conuictor* of Claudius (Seneca, *Apoc.* 14.2): these families, forming part of Antonia's circle and closely linked by a number of marriage ties, were in effect 'an influential group and nexus at the core of which (stood) the great L. Vitellius' (Syme, *RP* 2.823) – and Vespasian was *Vitellii cliens cum Vitellius collega Claudio foret* (*Hist.* 3.66), with Antonia's freed-woman, Caenis, as his mistress. See also Levick, 1999: 14-15. A detailed discussion of Plautius' career is provided by A.R. Birley, 1981: 37-40 and, for a revised version of his strategy, see Hind, 1989: 1-21.

**legati consularis:** Suffect consul in 29, he governed Pannonia from 41 to 43 and then became Britain's first (*primus praepositus: Agr.* 14.1) consular governor (from 43 to 47).

**Claudi[i] ipsius ductu:** Dio reports that, on arriving in Britain, 'Claudius, took over command (of the legions that were waiting for him), crossed the Thames, ...defeated (the enemy) in battle and captured Camulodunum [Colchester], the capital of Cunobelinus (Cymbeline). Thereupon he won over numerous tribes... and was saluted as *imperator* several times. [He then returned to Rome]...after an absence of six months, of which he had spent only sixteen days in Britain, and celebrated his triumph' (60.21.2-5, 23.1).

However, as Gascou (1984: 383) points out, Suetonius, seeing Vespasian as one of the greatest emperors, deliberately downplays Claudius' role ('dénué de tout éclat'). The emperor was not the only one to suffer. Apart from a brief comment in Dio (60.20.3, cited above, s.u. *in Britanniam translatus*), we are told nothing of the achievements in Britain of Vespasian's elder brother: Suetonius does not even refer to his presence. Yet his subsequent appointment as governor of Moesia as early as ca 53 (1.3 above), which compares more than favourably with Vespasian's posting to Judaea almost twenty years after he left Britain, suggests that Sabinus was far from inactive at that time – but compare 1.3 above, s.u. *Sabinus*.

## 4.2

**triumphalia ornamenta:** After the triumph awarded to L. Cornelius Balbus in 19 BC, only members of the imperial family could receive that honour, as generals were legally *legati* of the emperor and so were not under their own auspices (*sua auspicia*). However, the appropriate insignia (*ornamenta*, such as the right to carry the *scipio eburnus* and to wear the *toga picta, tunica palmata* and *aurea corona* together, often, with the honour of a statua triumphalis; see *RE* 18.1121-2 and Maxfield, 1981: 105-9) could still be conferred on successful commanders. According to Dio, Claudius awarded *ornamenta* to 'the senators who had taken part in the campaign with him,...a thing he was accustomed to do most lavishly on other occasions on the slightest excuse' (60.23.2). It is unlikely that Vespasian returned to Rome in 44 to receive his award. He probably remained in Britain until 47 (A.R. Birley, 1981: 227) and his comparatively long period commanding the II Augusta stood him in good stead in 69 (*Hist.* 3.44 and Wellesley, 1972: 137) – E. Birley argues that it took the lead in convincing the other British legions to support Vespasian (1978: 243-5). For the differences between a triumph, an *ouatio* and triumphal *ornamenta*, see *OCD* 1077, 1084 and 1554.

**in breui spatio:** Suetonius is a little misleading as the *ornamenta* were awarded in 47, the consulship at the end of 51 and it would be hazardous to attempt to assign a date to the two priesthoods (discussed in the next item). See also Talbert, 1984: 513.

**duplex sacerdotium:** Before his accession to the throne, he was probably a *sacerdos* in a major college (Levick suggests that he may have been one of the *septemuiri epulonum*: 1999: 19) and also a *sodalis*; see Hoffman-Lewis, 1955: 63, 143. That he was augur and *pontifex* (so Homo, 1949: 24) is highly unlikely, for no private citizen at that time belonged to more than one major college, not even Ti. Plautius Silvanus, Pompeius Silvanus or A. Vitellius: see Hoffman-Lewis, 1955: 157 n.5. That he was augur and chief priest (Mooney, 1930: 388) is impossible since Suetonius' reference is to the period when Vespasian was still a *priuatus*.

**consulatum...menses:** Vespasian was suffect consul with Claudius for the last two months of 51, despite Suetonius' statement in *Claud.* 14 that the emperor relinquished his office after six months; see Gallivan, 1978: 409. Whilst consul *suo anno*, he nonetheless received no remission for his son Titus; see A.R. Birley, 1981: 228.

**medium tempus...in otio secessuque:** Suetonius exaggerates: Titus was *educatus in aula cum Britannico* and was with him (early in 55) when he was poisoned (*Titus* 2). No doubt Vespasian was less welcome *in aula*, at least until 59 when Nero had Agrippina murdered. At this same period, the future emperor Galba also *prope ad medium Neronis principatum in secessu plurimum uixit* (*Galba* 8.1); for the details, see Murison, 1992: 49.

**Agrippinam timens:** Vespasian had reason to fear her: see 2.3 above, s.u. *insepulti* and 4.1, s.u. *Narcissi gratia*. However, at a time when she was extremely influential (*cuncta feminae oboediebant: Ann.* 12.7), he became consul and his son's education at court continued – though he received no consular appointment until after her death.

**potentem adhuc apud filium:** Tacitus twice uses *potentia* in reference to her, i.e. *cupientibus cunctis infringi potentiam matris* (*Ann.* 14.1) and *infracta paulatim potentia matris delapso Nerone in amorem libertae* (*Ann.* 13.12), for it was greatest in the first years of Nero's reign, but gradually declined.

**Narcissi amicos perosam:** Read *amicos* rather than *amici*. The better manuscripts have *amici*, preferred by Ihm, but editors before him read *amicos* on the grounds that the genitive with *perosam* is not found before Prudentius and Boethius. Narcissus had made the mistake of urging Claudius to marry Aelia Paetina instead of Agrippina and of favouring Britannicus over Nero; see 4.1 above, s.u. *Narcissi gratia*.

4.3

**sortitus Africam:** At this period, the interval between the consulship and the proconsulship of Asia and Africa varied from eight to twelve years; so his proconsulship is probably to be assigned to the early sixties (A.R. Birley, 1981: 228).

**integerrime...administrauit:** Silius Italicus' encomium is brief (*reget impiger Afros*: *Pun.* 3.599) and, like Suetonius' assessment, seemingly at odds with Tacitus' statement that Vespasian's proconsulship was *famosus inuisusque* (*Hist.* 2.97) and that he was unpopular there in 69 (*nec ambigitur prouinciam* [i.e. *Africam*] *et militem alienato erga Vespasianum animo fuisse*: Hist. 4.49). But, if he had returned home *nihilo opulentior* (below), then it was his severity and parsimony that earned him his unfavourable reputation; see Chilver, 1979: 258.

**Hadrumeti:** Hadrumetum (modern Sousse), a city of Phoenician origin south of Carthage. Under Trajan, it became a Roman colony, *Colonia Concordia Ulpia Traiana Augusta Frugifera Hadrumetina*; Justinian renamed it Justinianopolis. See *OCD* 663-4.

**rapa in eum iacta sunt:** Similarly, Claudius had pieces of bread thrown at him in the Forum because of a grain shortage.

**rediit certe...nihilo opulentior:** This is consistent with Suetonius' reference to the 'poverty' experienced by Domitian in his youth, i.e. *tanta inopia...ut nullum argenteum uas in usu haberet* (*Dom.* 1.1). Nicols believes (1978: 10) that Suetonius' use of *certe* suggests that he was not vouching for the accuracy of the Hadrumetum incident – presumably taking *certe* in the sense of 'without any doubt' (*OLD* 303).

**omnia praedia fratri obligaret:** On his brother Flavius Sabinus, see 1.3. Tacitus' version of the incident (*credebatur adfectam eius fidem parce iuuisse domo agrisque pignori acceptis*: Hist. 3.65) implies that he had some doubts about the accuracy of the rumour and, in comparing the brothers, he merely states that *auctoritate pecuniaque Vespasianum (Sabinus) anteibat*: Hist. 3.65) – but he adds *unde, quamquam manente in speciem concordia, offensarum operta metuebantur* (ibid.).

Suetonius is presumably influenced by the Flavian version of events that downplayed the family's successes under the Julio-Claudians and emphasised their misfortunes, i.e. Vespasian was covered with 'mud' by Gaius (5.3), twice officially rebuked by Nero (*Vesp.* 4.3 and 4.4) and Domitian was brought up in poverty, for the family had *nullum argenteum uas in usu* (*Dom.* 1.1).

**ad mangonicos quaestus:** A *mango* (hence English 'monger') was a trader who used every possible device to dispose of his goods; and the word was often used of a slave trader (e.g. *Dom.* 7.1).

***mulio***: Various explanations have been offered. As Reate was known for its mules (*NH* 8.167), Vespasian may have supplied the famous mules of Nero's court: Poppaea Sabina had 'gilded shoes put on the mules that drew her' (Dio 62.28.1: similarly, *NH* 33.140) whilst Nero *numquam minus mille carrucis fecisse iter traditur, soleis mularum argenteis, canusinatis mulionibus* (*Nero* 30.3). Selling mules was inappropriate behaviour for a senator but it must have been profitable; and we know that both Cicero (*NH* 7.135) and Plancus (*ad Fam.* 10.18) referred to Ventidius Bassus (who was granted a triumph in 38 BC for his victory over the Parthians) as *mulio* for the same reason. Another explanation was offered by Lipsius. On the basis of Seneca's description of Hercules as having travelled over *plura loca quam ullus mulio perpetuarius* (*Apoc.* 6), he suggested that Vespasian was an itinerant merchant and Wellesley (1975: 116) describes him as a 'transport contractor, whence his nickname "muledriver", suitable enough, too, for one who...brooked no indiscipline from Marius' mules, the legionaries of Rome'.

**conuictus...dicitur:** If *conuictus* implies some sort of judicial process – the *OLD* (441) gives the meaning 'to find guilty, convict (of a punishable offence or, with weakened sense, of a vice or fault') – it is odd that Suetonius uses the word *dicitur*.

**latum clauum:** See 2.2 above. Vespasian's *auaritia* (discussed in 16.1 below) was legendary: *si auaritia abesset, antiquis ducibus par* (*Hist.* 2.5).

**eo nomine...crepitus:** The criticism he received for this sort of behaviour in his early years did little to enhance his reputation, as later writers continued to observe, e.g. *olim qui dubiam priuato in tempore famam,/rarum aliis, princeps transtulit in melius* (Ausonius, *De XII Caes., Tetrasticha* 43-44). If, as seems likely, this chapter is arranged in chronological order, then the incident must have occurred just after his return from Africa, when he was *nihilo opulentior*. Suetonius, then, is using *nomen* in the sense of 'a ground of accusation or complaint, score' (*OLD* 1186).

4.4

**peregrinatione Achaica:** During his tour in Greece that lasted from September 66 to the early part of 68, Nero sang publicly at all the *musici agones*; see *Nero* 22.3-24. He insisted that the regular cycle of contests be rearranged to suit his timetable, i.e. *quae [certamina] diuersissimorum temporum sunt, cogi in unum annum, quibusdam etiam iteratis, iussit et Olympiae quoque praeter consuetudinem musicum agona commisit* (*Nero* 23.1). His triumphal return to Rome with his 1,808 victorious crowns is described by Dio 63.20.1 – 21.1. As Dio put it, he had overcome 'Terpnus and Diodorus and Pammenes, instead of Philip or Perseus or Antiochus' (63.8.4). According to Juvenal, *haec opera atque hae sunt generosi principis artes/gaudentis foedo peregrina ad pulpita cantu/prostitui Graiaeque apium meruisse coronae* (8. 22-6). For the chronology of the *peregrinatio*, see Bradley, 1978: 61-72.

**inter comites Neronis:** Emperors travelling beyond Rome and Italy were accompanied, in the first instance, by selected *amici* (*cohors amicorum: Galba* 7.1) who were usually assigned specific tasks and paid a *salarium* – though Tiberius *pecuniae parcus ac tenax comites peregrinationum expeditionumque numquam salario, cibariis tantum sustentauit* (*Tib.* 46). For imperial journeys and *comites* in general, see Friedländer, 1968: 75-6; Bérard, 1984: 259-324 and *OCD* 372.

Nero's entourage was enormous and included Statilia Messalina (his wife), Calvia Crispinilla (wardrobe mistress and chaperone of Sporus), Sporus himself and Pythagoras (Nero's homosexual partners), Cluvius Rufus (senior senator and imperial herald), Vespasian (together with other *comites*, both senators and equestrians), Ofonius Tigellinus (praetorian prefect), Terpnus, Diodorus and Pammenes (musicians), Phoebus and other freedmen (including, presumably, the *ab epistulis* and *a libellis* Epaphroditus), Nero's cheerleaders (the Augustiani who were said to number five thousand), members of the praetorian guard and perhaps the German imperial bodyguard. With reference to the latter section of Nero's entourage, Dio states that 'a multitude not only of the Augustiani but of other persons as well were taken with him, large enough, if it had been a hostile host, to have subdued both Parthians and all other nations. But they were the kind you would have expected Nero's soldiers to be, and the arms they carried were lyres and plectra, masks and buskins' (63.8.3). See Bradley, 1979: 152-7.

**cum cantante eo...discederet saepius:** Nero was seriously offended by such behaviour and Vespasian apparently dared to repeat the offence. For the fate awaiting those who were inattentive or who left during the performance, see *Nero* 23.2, i.e. *cantante eo ne necessaria quidem causa excedere theatro licitum est* and, in more detail, *Ann.* 16.5.

**praesens obdormisceret:** The sources differ in their accounts of Vespasian's lapse. Tacitus sets it during the Quinquennial Games of 65 in Rome (*ferebantque Vespasianum, tamquam somno coniueret, a Phoebo liberto increpitum aegreque meliorum precibus obtectum, mox imminentem perniciem maiore fato effugisse*: Tac. *Ann.* 16.5). Dio/Xiphilinus agrees with Suetonius and places it in Greece, with Vespasian being reprimanded (? once again) by Phoebus, not for sleeping, but for frowning at Nero's behaviour (66.11.2: see 14, s.u. *quidam*); Petrus

Patricius has the same story but does not identify the 'certain man who frowned and was not over-lavish with his praises [of Nero's performance]' (Dio 63.10.1a). In Josephus' account, Nero 'lavishes soothing and flattering compliments' (*BJ* 3.7) on Vespasian when giving him the Judaean command, in an effort, presumably, to repair their relationship.

Weynand (*RE* 6.2629) and later scholars have argued that Vespasian erred once and once only: if we accept a major lapse on his part in 65 (as Tacitus), then he may have been considered guilty of a less serious offence in Greece that resulted in a brief (see below, s.u. *secessit...deuiam ciuitatem*) estrangement, quickly settled by Nero (*BJ* 3.7), but 'enhanced' by pro-Flavian historians. The extraordinary nature of the command offered Vespasian at that time (see 4.6 below, s.u. *inter legatos...assumpto*) could be regarded as a form of recompense.

A final point. Whilst it is difficult to accept that someone as sycophantic as Vespasian would have risked offending Nero twice, it is worth noting that Suetonius relates the exchange with *quidam ex officio admissionis* (he nowhere mentions Phoebus by name), not in the context of the *peregrinatio Achaica* (as does Dio), but in a later chapter (14 below) and with no indication of the setting. See Wallace-Hadrill, 1996: 283-4 with n.3.

**prohibitus:** Thrasea Paetus took such a prohibition as a *praenuntiam imminentis caedis* (*Ann.* 15.23); for its effect on Vespasian, see 14 below.

**contubernio:** *Contubernium* is used of the close relationship between the emperor and those *amici* admitted to his inner circle. It was not permanent: so Tiberius *Seleucum grammaticum...primum a contubernio remouit, deinde etiam ad mortem compulit* (*Tib.* 56).

**publica salutatione:** This was distinct from the private *salutatio* of the sort referred to by Pliny when he noted that his uncle *ante lucem ibat ad Vespasianum imperatorem, nam ille quoque noctibus utebatur* (*Ep.* 3.5.9). On the other hand, Claudius admitted *feminae praetextatique pueri et puellae* to his public *salutationes* (*Claud.* 35.2) and Galba *Pisonem...e media salutantium turba adprehendit* (*Galba* 17). Augustus went even further and *promiscuis salutationibus admittebat et plebem* (*Aug.* 53.2). So Vespasian (according to Suetonius) 'was banned not only from the inner circle but even from the general audience' (Wallace-Hadrill, 1996: 283; see also 289-90). For a discussion of the *salutationes*, see Friedländer, 1968: 86-93; Crook, 1955: 23 and *OCD 1350*.

**secessit...deuiam ciuitatem:** The *secessus*, whatever its nature, must have been of extremely short duration, since Nero left Rome late in September 66 (Smallwood,

1967: No. 26) and Vespasian was fighting in Judaea early the following year; see also *latenti...extrema metuenti* below and *dens...die* in 5.5. That he was in Greece when Nero's offer was made is confirmed by Josephus, i.e. 'From Achaia, where he was in attendance on Nero, Vespasian...proceeded to Syria' (*BJ* 3.8).

**prouincia cum exercitu oblata:** The precise extent of his *prouincia* is uncertain. It is worth noting that, from the spring to the autumn of 67, Vespasian's base was not in Judaea at all, but in the Syrian city of Ptolemais. So, during the initial period, i.e. until the appointment of Mucianus to Syria to replace its consular legate, Cestius Gallus, who had just died, his official *prouincia* probably included Syria (argued by Nicols, 1978: 48, 114). Thus Josephus' comment that Nero 'sent (Vespasian) to take command of the armies in Syria' (*BJ* 3.7) ought not to be rejected outright.

**latenti...extrema metuenti:** Suetonius fails to explain fully the unusual circumstances surrounding Nero's offer. At one moment, Vespasian was in hiding (*latenti*) and in fear of his life (*extrema metuenti*), at the next, he was being offered command of three legions with, so it seems, the unprecedented privilege of choosing his legionary commanders, one of whom was his own son; see 4.6 below, s.u. *inter legatos...assumpto*. Josephus' comment that Nero lavished 'soothing and flattering compliments' on Vespasian (*BJ* 3.7) is certainly relevant, as is Suetonius' reference to Vespasian's military ability (see 4.5 below, s.u. *non instrenuo duce* and *industriae expertae*). It is only part of the story however, and there remains the distinct impression that both the seriousness and the effect of Vespasian's 'offence' has been grossly exaggerated. Once again, the Flavian historians on whom Suetonius relied strained the truth to and beyond its limits in disguising the slavish adulation lavished by Vespasian on the emperor of the day and exaggerated (or invented) any loss of influence the family suffered.

4.5
**uetus et constans opinio:** Tacitus (*Hist.* 5.13), Josephus (*BJ* 6.312) and Orosius (7.9.2) report the prediction in much the same terms; see the following items.

**Iudaea profecti rerum potirentur:** Tacitus (*Hist.* 5.13) uses precisely the same words, but, unlike Suetonius and Orosius (7.9.2: see below), explains that the plural *profecti* refers to both Vespasian and Titus, i.e. *pluribus persuasio inerat antiquis sacerdotum litteris contineri eo ipso tempore fore ut ualesceret Oriens profectique Iudaea rerum potirentur. quae ambages Vespasianum ac Titum praedixerat, sed uulgus more humanae cupidinis sibi tantam fatorum magnitudinem interpretati ne aduersis quidem ad uera mutabantur* (*Hist.* 5.13). Josephus, however, prefers the singular, i.e. 'the oracle...signified Vespasian' (*BJ* 6.312).

**de imperatore Romano:** This explanation, accepted by Josephus (*BJ* 6.312), was rejected by Christian writers such as Eusebius (*Hist. Eccl.* 3.8).

**Iudaei ad se trahentes:** Josephus' report is similar: 'An ambiguous oracle, likewise found in their sacred scriptures, to the effect that one from their country would become ruler of the world. This they understood to mean someone of their own race, and many of their wise men went astray in their interpretation of it. The oracle, however, in reality, signified Vespasian who was proclaimed emperor on Jewish soil' (*BJ* 6.312). Orosius, though, wrongly assigns it to the occasion when Vespasian visited Mt Carmel (5.6 below), i.e. *Iudaei...quibusdam in Carmelo monte seducti sortibus, quae portenderent exortos a Iudaea duces rerum potituros fore, praedictumque ad se trahentes in rebellionem exarserunt* (7.9.2).

**caeso praeposito:** The reference is to Gessius Florus (*PIR*² G 170; Cohen, 1979: 251; Goodman, 1987: 152-5, 170-2 and Price, 1992: 9), a Greek from Clazomenae on the central coast of Asia Minor, who, thanks to the influence of Poppaea Sabina (*AJ* 20.252), was appointed procurator of Judaea in 64. His repressive régime ('He abstained from no form of robbery or violence...he stripped whole cities and ruined entire populations' *BJ* 2.277-78) led to the outbreak of insurrection in 66. Suetonius' *caeso* is incorrect: Florus withdrew to Caesarea (*BJ* 2.331) and was still alive when Cestius Gallus lay siege to Jerusalem (*BJ* 2.531). The error was noted by Orosius who, though usually copying Suetonius precisely, substituted *extinctisque Romanis praesidiis* for *caeso praeposito*. On the other hand, Suetonius may, just possibly, be referring to either Metilius, commander of the garrison in Jerusalem, who may have been executed some time after the rest of his men perished (*BJ* 2.450-4) or even to the unnamed commander of the Antonia's garrison, presumably killed with the rest of his colleagues (*BJ* 2.430).

**legatum...Syriae consularem:** C. Cestius Gallus (*PIR*² C 691; Gichon, 1981: 39-62; Shatzman, 1989: 471; Price, 1992: 10-11 and Millar, 1993: 71), suffect consul in 42 and governor of Syria in 66 (so 'a man who had passed his prime': *RP* 3.1382). Tacitus sums up his military 'prowess' in unflattering terms: *uaria proelia ac saepius aduersa excepere* (*Hist.* 5.10). He had left Antioch with a large force – the XII Fulminata, vexillations from the IV Scythica, VI Ferrata, III Gallica and X Fretensis (and, less probably, from the V Macedonica and XV Apollinaris as well – Campbell, 1986: 124), six auxiliary cohorts and four *alae* (*BJ* 2.500). He took Joppa, marched on Jerusalem but, presumably because it was late in the season (November), abandoned the siege and was defeated at Beth

Commentary

Horon with the loss of nearly 6,000 men (*BJ* 2.513-56). Soon after, he died – *fato aut taedio occidit* (*Hist.* 5.10).

**rapta aquila:** The legion must have been the XII Fulminata as only vexillations of the others were present. It was certainly humiliated (*BJ* 5.41), although Ritterling (*RE* 12.1706) and other scholars have doubted that it actually lost its eagle, while Campbell suggests that the loss was only temporary (*OCD* 841). The XII Fulminata was not used by Vespasian in any of the sieges during 67, 68 or 69, but was assigned to Titus for the assault on Jerusalem; afterwards, it was banished to Melitene (*BJ* 7.18).

**exercitu ampliore:** Vespasian's 'rather large' army consisted of three complete legions (V Macedonica, X Fretensis and XV Apollinaris: *BJ* 3.65) and other forces amounting to some 60,000 men (*BJ* 3.69); see 4.6 below, s.u. *octo alis*.

**non instrenuo duce:** Tacitus confirms – *Vespasianus acer militiae anteire agmen, locum castris capere, noctu diuque consilio ac, si res posceret, manu hostibus obniti...prorsus, si auaritia abesset, antiquis ducibus par* (*Hist.* 2.5); he was also a *senex triumphalis* (4.8).

**tuto tanta res:** Right to the end, Nero seems to have regarded Vespasian as *tutus* – and correctly so. See below, s.u. *nec metuendus...nominis*.

**industriae expertae:** Josephus not unexpectedly agrees with Suetonius' assessment – '(Vespasian was) a man with the steadiness resulting from years and experience' (*BJ* 3.3), as does Aurelius Victor, who also praises Vespasian's *industria*: *industria rebusque pacis ac militiae longe nobilis habebatur* (*De Caes.* 8.4).

**nec metuendus...ob humilitatem generis ac nominis:** This was not the whole story. The urgency of the situation (the loss of 6,000 men) and the time of year (midwinter) would have reduced the number of acceptable candidates present *inter comites Neronis*. Another factor may have been Vespasian's past connection with Antonia's circle, two former members of which were the pro-Roman Jews Agrippa II and Ti. Julius Alexander; see Nicols, 1978: 25-6. Vitellius, too, when appointed to the Lower German command was regarded as *non metuendus*, but for a different reason – *Galba prae se tulit nullos minus metuendos quam qui de solo uictu cogitarent* (*Vit.* 7.1).

4.6
**additis...ad copias duabus legionibus:** It is not easy to make sense of this

37

statement since, in the winter of 66/67, there were practically no Roman forces in Judaea and Vespasian was assigned not two, but three (see 4.5 above, s.u. *exercitu ampliore*) legions. Just possibly Suetonius is referring to the fact that, when Vespasian arrived in Ptolemais (situated in Syria, not in Judaea), he was in effective command of the forces in Syria until Mucianus took up his appointment later in the year: the X Fretensis was a Syrian legion, whereas the V Macedonica (from Moesia) and the XV Apollinaris (from Pannonia) were still in Asia after Corbulo's Armenian campaign and so were 'added' to the X Fretensis.

**octo alis, cohortibus decem:** Suetonius' figures differ substantially from those of Josephus who states that Vespasian added five *alae* and eighteen cohorts to the one *ala* and five cohorts already in Judaea (*BJ* 3.66) – and Josephus is more likely to be correct. In addition, the client kings (Antiochus IV of Commagene, Agrippa II, Sohaemus of Emesa and Malchus II of Nabataea) provided a further 18,000 men (*BJ* 3.68), making a total of sixty thousand (*BJ* 3.69).

**inter legatos maiore filio assumpto:** Titus' appointment was unusual. Aged about 27 at this time, he was still of quaestorian rank; moreover, this was the only recorded occasion when the leader of an expeditionary force had his own son in control of one of his legions. Nero seems to have given Vespasian a completely free hand in choosing the commanders of his three legions, viz. XV Apollinaris (with Titus as legate: *BJ* 3.8), X Fretensis (with Trajan's father as legate [*BJ* 3.289; for his career, see Dabrowa, 1993: 23-5]; he and Titus may well have married sisters [Champlin, 1983: 257-64] or half-sisters [Bennett, 1997: 11-12]) and V Macedonica (under Sex. Vettulenus Cerialis [*BJ* 3.310; for his career, see Dabrowa, 1993: 27-8], almost certainly from Vespasian's home town of Reate).

**prouinciam:** Judaea (so Hist. 2.5, i.e. *hic (Mucianus) Syriae, ille (Vespasianus) Iudaeae praepositus*), even though Vespasian based himself for a time at Ptolemais (in Syria); see 6.4 below, s.u. *ille deposita simultate*. From 53 to 40 BC, Judaea was part of Syria and from then until 4 BC was ruled by Herod. In 4 BC, it was divided into three sections: (a) Judaea, including Samaria and Idumaea, under Archelaus; when he was banished in 6, this became a Roman province governed by a procurator; (b) Batanaea and the nearby regions under the tetrarch Philip; and (c) Galilee and Peraea with Herod Antipas as tetrarch. Between 37 and 41, these three sections were united and given to Agrippa I but, on his death in 44, Judaea became a procuratorial province and remained so until 70. Around 55, Agrippa II was given Batanaea, Auranitis, Trachonitis, Gaulonitis and Abilene together with Tiberias and Tarichea in Galilee and Julias in Peraea. Once Jerusalem fell in 70, Judaea became an imperial province governed by the legate of the X Fretensis; for the early governors, see Dabrowa, 1993: 53.

**proximas...conuertit in se:** Vespasian had long cherished the hope of becoming emperor (*spem imperii iam pridem...conceptam*: see 5.1 below), and now, according to Suetonius, gained the support of the *proximas prouincias*, i.e. Egypt and Syria.

**correcta...disciplina:** Suetonius implies that the standard of discipline and training among the Syrian legions was low, despite the standards that had been demanded by Corbulo over a considerable period of time; yet how could this have occurred in the brief interval between Corbulo's death (mid 66) and Vespasian's arrival (early 67)? The real problem facing the Syrian legions was not lack of discipline but loss of the patronage that Corbulo had been expected to provide. What Vespasian (or Mucianus) had to 'correct' was the soldiers' disappointment and hostile attitude, for Vespasian, after all, was Nero's representative. Moreover, apart from their annoyance at the loss of their prospects, they had to face a commander who had just severed his own friendship (i.e., according to Helvidius Priscus, *fuisse Vespasiano amicitiam cum Thrasea, Sorano, Sentio*: *Hist.* 4.7) and his son's marital connection (*cum qua* [i.e. *Marcia Furnilla*] *diuortium fecit*: *Titus* 4.2) with the group to which Corbulo himself had been aligned.

**unoque...inito:** Vespasian's first three victories in 67 were at Japha (20 June: *BJ* 3.306), Garizim (25 June: *BJ* 3.315) and Jotapata (27 June: *BJ* 3.339).

**tam constanter:** In his account of the Jewish campaign, Josephus tends to portray a somewhat different Vespasian from Suetonius' and to stress the bravery of his hero – Titus, So when Titus, Traianus and Vettulenus Cerialis urged Vespasian (towards the end of 67) to attack Jerusalem at once, he replied that they 'were anxious to make a theatrical, though hazardous, display of their gallantry;..."If any one thinks that the glory of victory will lose its zest without a fight, let him learn that success obtained by sitting still is more fruitful than won by uncertainty of arms"' (*BJ* 4.366-72). On the other hand, '(Titus') friends...all earnestly entreated him to retire before those Jews who courted death...and not act the part of a common soldier;...he on whom all depended ought not to face so imminent a risk' (*BJ* 5.87-8). Again, 'Titus was himself in arms and prepared to descend (from the Antonia) with his troops, but was restrained by his friends...(who) remarked that he would achieve more by sitting still in the Antonia...than by going down and fighting in the forefront' (*BJ* 6.132-3).

**in oppugnatione...sagittas:** The *castellum* was Jotapata in Galilee, where the defenders were led by Josephus; for the siege, see Adam-Bayewitz, 1997: 131-65.

In Josephus' version of this incident, 'one of the defenders of the ramparts hit Vespasian with an arrow in the sole of the foot. The wound was a slight one' (*BJ* 3.236).

Suetonius has nothing to say about Vespasian's activities in Judaea after June 67; but the next twelve months were not uneventful, with another eleven cities captured and the capital, Jerusalem, being the only significant city yet to be besieged. By the end of June 68, however, news of Nero's death had reached Vespasian in Caesarea (Jones, 1984: 42). A period of inactivity followed, in fact until June 69 according to Josephus (*BJ* 4.502), though it is more likely that hostilities recommenced in March 69, with Vespasian's command being confirmed by the new emperor Galba, possibly by December 68. That was when Titus set out for Rome – on reaching Corinth, he heard of Galba's assassination and decided to return to Judaea. See Jones, 1984: 44-7.

### 5.1

**post Neronem...iam pridem...conceptam:** Presumably, Suetonius means that Vespasian had long cherished the hope of becoming emperor and was now determined to bring it to fruition. Some (see Jones, 1984: 63 n.10) have therefore dated Vespasian's imperial aspirations to the occasion of Josephus' famous prediction (*BJ* 3.399-403) and of Titus' visit to Mucianus in Syria (*BJ* 4.32) – i.e. October 67. Possibly this is the force of Suetonius' *(spem) iam pridem conceptam*; however the timing is unrealistic. If Mucianus did not reach Syria until late in the summer of 67 (Nicols, 1978: 113-15), there would not have been time for the quarrel (*simultate* [*Vesp.* 6.4]; *odiis* [*Hist.* 2.5]) between him and Vespasian to begin and for reconciliation to occur by October of the same year. Tacitus dates the latter to the period after Nero's death (*exitu...Neronis positis odiis in medium consuluere*: *Hist.* 2.5) but before Jan. 69 (*proximus annus* [i.e. 69] *ciuili bello intentus*: *Hist.* 5.10).

**ostenta:** Of the eleven omens listed here, all apart from two (the branches of the oak tree and the three eagles at Bedriacum) are found in other authors: Dio has seven of them, Tacitus three and Plutarch and Orosius one each. The prophecy of *BJ* 3.399-403 appears in Suetonius (5.6 below), Dio and Orosius – but not in Tacitus who refers to the prophecies on three occasions (*Hist.* 1.10, 2.1 and 2.78) and dismisses them – *occulta fati et ostentis ac responsis destinatum Vespasiano liberisque eius imperium post fortunam credidimus* (*Hist.* 1.10). In fact, they were intended to advance the dynasty's claim to the throne, particularly amongst the members of the eastern legions, given the family's obscure origins, i.e. *ob humilitatem generis* (4.5) and Vespasian's lack of *auctoritas* and *maiestas* (7.2). For a discussion of the *ostenta* listed here and the cures attributed to Vespasian in 7.1 below, see Frassinetti, 1979: 115-27.

**5.2**

**quercus...Marti sacra:** Usually, the oak was regarded as sacred to Jupiter, as in Ovid's *sacra Ioui quercus* (*Met.* 7.623).

**tres Vespasiae partus:** Vespasia's three children by Flavius Sabinus were an unnamed daughter (*puella...non perannauit*), Flavius Sabinus (1.3) and Vespasian.

**patrem Sabinum:** See 1.3.

**haruspicio:** The *haruspex* ('entrail-observer') claimed to reveal the future by the appearance of the victim's entrails; see *OCD* 667-8.

**5.3**

**aedilem:** Vespasian was aedile in 38; see 2.3 above, s.u. *aedilitatis*.

**curam uerrendis uiis:** According to Cicero, *sunto aediles curatores urbis, annonae, ludorumque sollemnium* (*Leg.* 3.3.7). During the empire, the aediles were still responsible for the *cura urbis* and a few other minor tasks; see *OCD* 15-16.

**luto...oppleri:** Dio repeats the story and provides an explanation of its significance: '(Gaius) caught sight of a lot of mud in an alley, and ordered it to be thrown upon the toga of Flavius Vespasian, who was then aedile and had charge of keeping the alleys clean. This action was not regarded as of any special significance at the time, but later...it seemed to have signified that Gaius had entrusted the city to him outright for its improvement.' (59.12.3). The interpretation provided by Suetonius (*in tutelam...ac in gremium*) and Dio is a fine example of how the Flavian historians consulted by Suetonius and Dio dealt with certain aspects of Vespasian's career under the Julio-Claudians. Usually, loss of status or reputation before 68 (see, for example, 4.4 above, s.u. *praesens obdormisceret*) could be emphasised or exaggerated in order to disguise activities that would have earned from Tacitus labels such as *adulatio* or *libido adsentandi* (*Hist.* 1.1). However, having one's toga filled with what perhaps is euphemistically described as *lutum* could (so it would seem) only be interpreted as the low point in an ambitious senator's career and therefore best omitted; but, on the contrary, with an over-generous interpretation, it becomes an omen of future greatness.

**non defuerunt qui interpretarentur:** A favourite phrase of Suetonius, occurring also in *Galba* 8.2, *Titus* 5.3 and *Dom.* 23.2.

**praetextae:** The *toga praetexta*, a white toga with a purple border, could only be worn by curule magistrates. Vespasian, as plebeian aedile, was not entitled to wear one. Perhaps substitute *togae* for *praetextae*.

## 5.4

**canis extrarius...subiecit:** Dio has the same story – 'When he was eating, a dog dropped a human hand under the table' (66.1.2). Mooney (1930: 398) points out that the appearance of a strange dog was regarded as an omen and cites Terence's *quot res postilla monstra euenerunt mihi!/intro iit in aedes ater alienus canis/ anguis in inpluuium decidit de tegulis* (*Phorm.* 705).

**e triuio:** Rubbish, including human bodies (*quod purgamentum nocte calcasti in triuio aut cadauer?*: Petr., *Satyr.* 134) were often left at the cross-roads: hence the presence of the dog.

**manum humanam:** A sign of imperial power; for the legal implications of *manus*, see *OCD* 920.

**cenante...irrupit:** Dio's version is similar – 'As he was eating dinner on his country estate,...an ox approached him, knelt down and placed his head beneath his feet (Dio 66.1.2).

**ceruicem summisit:** The most obvious sign of Vespasian's future position.

**in agro auito:** The estate of Vespasian's grandmother Tertulla at Cosa; in Tacitus' version the tree is located *in agris eius* (*Hist.* 2.78: see the next item).

**arbor...resurrexit:** The story also occurs in Dio 66.1.3 and in Tacitus: *recursabant animo uetera omina: cupressus arbor in agris eius conspicua altitudine repente prociderat ac postera die eodem uestigio resurgens procera et latior uirebat. grande id prosperumque consensu haruspicum et summa claritudo iuueni admodum Vespasiano promissa* (*Hist.* 2.78). However, according to Tacitus, Vespasian was then *admodum iuuenis*, a phrase applied to 'the early pre-quaestorian years of a young man's life' (Syme, 1958: 671). Suetonius, on the other hand, who apparently arranged his omens chronologically (since the *quercus* in 5.2 is assigned to Augustus' reign, those in 5.3 to Gaius' and the later ones in 5.5 and 5.6 to Nero's), would have him in his late twenties at the time of the rise and fall of the cypress tree and so up to ten years older than Tacitus states (see Morgan, 1996: 43-4). If so, it was this omen, and not (or perhaps as well as) his mother's sarcastic comment in 2.2 above, that persuaded Vespasian to pursue a senatorial rather than an equestrian career. Note that the tree's destruction in 96, reported by Suetonius alone (*Dom.* 15.2), foretold the end of the Flavian dynasty.

**sine ulla ui tempestatis euulsa:** Tacitus' version (*repente prociderat: Hist.* 2.78) is similar, Dio's not so – it was 'uprooted and overthrown by a violent wind' (66.1.1).

5.5
**in Achaia...dens...exemptus...sequenti die:** Dio has a similar account – 'from a dream he learned that, when Nero Caesar should lose a tooth, he himself should be emperor. This prophecy about the tooth became a reality on the following day' (66.1.3). Suetonius adds that it occurred during the *peregrinatio Achaica* (4.4 above). So Vespasian and the other *comites* were respectfully waiting in the atrium of Nero's Greek residence throughout the 'operation'. It must, then, have taken place when Vespasian was in favour, i.e. at some point late in 66, either in the brief period after the retinue arrived in Achaea (following their departure from Rome late in September of that year) and before Vespasian's disgrace, or else after his return to favour and before his departure for Judaea early in 67. Once again, one must question the seriousness – or, indeed the existence – of the *faux pas* attributed to Vespasian during the *peregrinatio*; see 4.4 above, s.u. *latenti... extrema metuenti*.

5.6
**Carmeli dei oraculum:** Carmel (*Carmelus*) was the name of the mountain and the god: *est Iudaeam inter Syriamque Carmelus: ita uocant montem deumque. nec simulacrum deo aut templum (sic tradidere maiores): ara tantum et reuerentia* (*Hist.* 2.78). It is a mountain range 26 km long in the north-west of Israel, with the city of Haifa on its northeastern slope. Late in May 69, *illic sacrificanti Vespasiano, cum spes occultas uersaret animo, Basilides sacerdos* [on whom see 7.1 below, s.u. *Basilides libertus*] *inspectis identidem extis 'quicquid est, Vespasiane, quod paras, seu domum extruere seu prolatare agros siue ampliare seruitia, datur tibi magna sedes, ingentes termini, multum hominum'* (*Hist.* 2.78). Orosius, however, identifies the 'Messianic' oracle of *BJ* 6.312 ('An ambiguous oracle, found in their [Jewish] sacred scriptures, to the effect that one from their country would become ruler of the world') with the *Carmeli dei oraculum*, i.e. *Iudaei...quibusdam in Carmelo monte seducti sortibus quae portenderent exortos a Iudaea duces rerum potituros fore* (7.9.2).

There followed a series of meetings with Mucianus and their senior officers – and Vespasian was 'persuaded' to accept nomination. All this was intended to convince the soldiers of the eastern legions, with their imperfect knowledge of Roman customs and traditions (see Forni, 1953: 54-5, 1974: 383 and Keppie,

1997: 98) that Vespasian's success was predetermined, a conviction to be strengthened by the miracles ascribed to him at the time of his visit to the temple of Serapis at Alexandria (see 7.1 below for the details) – *has ambages et statim exceperat fama et tunc aperiebat; nec quicquam magis in ore uulgi* (*Hist.* 2.78).

Note that Suetonius, who apparently arranged the omens in chronological order (see 5.4 above, s.u. *arbor...resurrexit*), has placed the visit to Mt Carmel before Josephus' prophecy (of ca July 67). So, as with the omen of the cypress tree (5.4), Suetonius is in error; see Morgan, 1996: 50.

**sortes:** *Sortes* were small pieces of wood marked with various words; they were mixed together, one was drawn out at random and the omen interpreted; see Lindsay, 1995: 171. Here, though, the word is used in a broader sense of any kind of oracular utterance (*OLD* 1795, s.u. 3).

**unus ex nobilibus captiuis Iosephus:** This is the historian (Flavius) Josephus (*PIR*² F 293; Cohen, 1979; Rajak, 1983; Goodman, 1995), a Jewish priest with Hasmonaean connections – hence *nobilis*. Born in 37 or 38, he led the Jewish forces in Galilee against Vespasian but surrendered on the fall of Jotapata in 67. He assigns his prophecy to this period, immediately after his capture. That is the usually accepted time (see, for example, Schwartz, 1990: 4-5) and not just before 1 July 69 as stated by Schalit, 1975: 297-300. When interviewed by Vespasian, he addressed him as follows: 'You will be Caesar, Vespasian, you will be emperor, you and your son here' (*BJ* 3.401). Thanks to Titus, so Josephus claims, his life was spared; he was with Titus during the siege of Jerusalem and was later given Roman citizenship and an annual allowance. He remained in Rome for the rest of his life; for the details, see Cohen, 1979: 232-42 and Rajak, 1983: 223-9.

Josephus' motives in claiming to have made this prophecy have been questioned, but it would appear that it was intended to justify his personal conduct: not all agree, though – see Mason, 1991: 269-70. In the context of the similar prediction ascribed to Rabban Johanan ben Zakkai (on which see the discussion by Rajak, 1983: 188-9 and Price, 1992: 264-70), Rajak believes that the latter (and Josephus) would have explained their attitude as follows: 'if God had singled Vespasian out for greatness, it was surely right for a pious man to strike an agreement with him' (1983: 189). Vespasian encouraged the story for other reasons, not least *ob humilitatem generis ac nominis* (4.5).

**in uincula...iam imperatore:** Dio reports the same prophecy, but with minor differences (see Rajak, 1983: 191 with n.12), i.e. 'You may imprison me now, but a year from now, when you have become emperor, you will release me' (66.1.4). Presumably, Suetonius had no knowledge of the *BJ*, given the discrepancies in this section, i.e. the fate of Florus, the loss of the eagle, the composition of Vespasian's legionary and auxiliary forces, and the details of Vespasian's wound at Jotapata.

## 5.7

**Neronem...monitum per quietem:** Dio reports the same dream: 'Nero himself in his dreams once thought he had brought the chariot of Jupiter to Vespasian's house' (Dio 66.1.3).

**tensam...deduceret:** The *tensa* was the sacred chariot bearing the statues of the gods in a solemn procession that opened the *Ludi Circenses*. Leading senators provided an escort (*deducere*), a duty that apparently fell to the emperor – and, according to Nero's dream, would soon pass from him to Vespasian.

**e sacrario in domum Vespasiani:** The aediles were responsible for these sacred chariots which carried the statues of the gods to the Circus at the opening of the Ludi Circenses and which were stored in a building on the Capitol known as the *aedes tensarum* (see *Str* 2.500, n.2).

**comitia secundi consulatus ineunte Galba:** This phrase is not without its difficulties: apart from the precise meaning of the Latin, there is the contradictory version of Plutarch and Tacitus to the effect that the omen occurred after Galba's death.

Galba held his first consulship in 33 and his second in 69. During the empire, consular elections (or what passed for elections) were held twice a year, in March and October, and Galba reached Rome in the first days of October 68 (according to Chilver, 1979: 57). If Suetonius' text is sound (for some of the proposed emendations, see Mooney, 1930: 402), the phrase *comitia ineunte* must refer to the occasion when the people were assembled in the Campus Martius to hear the *renuntiatio* and the statue of Caesar on the island on the Tiber would be visible from there. The difficulty with this solution is that both Tacitus and Plutarch assigned the omen to the period after Galba's death: see the next item.

**statua&lt;m&gt;...conuersa&lt;m&gt;:** It predicted the transfer of imperial power from the West to the East. Suetonius assigns the portent to the last months of 68, whereas Tacitus prefers the following year, after Galba's death, when Vitellius was marching against Otho (*Hist.* 1.86), as does Plutarch who dates it to the time 'when Vespasian was at last openly trying to seize the supreme power' (*Otho* 4.5).

**acie Betriacensi:** Bedriacum (or Betriacum: both forms are found in the ancient sources) lies midway between Verona and Cremona, probably near the modern village of Tornata. The reference is to the first of two battles fought in this region during 69, i.e. between the armies of Otho and Vitellius with the second some months later between Vitellius' and Vespasian's forces. For the site plan of each battle, see Wellesley, 1975: 75 (first) and 146 (second).

**duas aquilas:** Otho and Vitellius with Vespasian being the *tertiam*. A simpler version of the story appears in Tacitus (*die, quo Bedriaci certabatur, auem inuisitata specie apud Regium Lepidum celebri luco consedisse incolae memorant...: Hist.* 2.50), Dio 63.10.3 and the Elder Pliny (*uenerunt in Italiam Bedriacensibus bellis ciuilibus trans Padum et nouae aues...: NH* 10.135). Plutarch describes another contest between two eagles before Philippi that foretold the outcome of the battle (*Brutus* 48.2) 2.

6.1

**promptissimis...suis:** Tacitus (*Hist.* 2.76-7) and Josephus have a similar theme: 'He was now (May/June 69) urged by Mucianus and the other generals to act as emperor and the rest of the army clamoured to be led against all opponents' (*BJ* 4.605).

**ignotorum...fauore:** The reference is to the Danubian vexillations mentioned in 6.2 and in no other ancient source. According to both Tacitus (*Hist.* 2.85) and Josephus (*BJ* 4.619), the Moesian legions (in Moesia) acted only after hearing of Vespasian's proclamation in Egypt.

6.2

**Moesiaci exercitus bina e tribus legionibus milia:** Suetonius' account is at considerable variance with that of Tacitus in *Hist.* 2.46 and 2.85. According to Suetonius (whose father Laetus was serving as tribune in the Pannonian XIII Gemina at this time), the rioting troops were in vexillations (i.e. detachments of the three legions garrisoned in Moesia, the III Gallica, VII Claudia and VIII Augusta). They rioted after Otho's death and they were the first, by some months, to declare for Vespasian, whereas Tacitus implies that complete legions were involved, that the rioting occurred whilst Otho was still alive and that the Moesian army declared for Vespasian only after those in the east. Chilver (1970/1: 105), Wellesley (1975: 114) and Nicols (1978: 75) accept (with reservations) Suetonius' account of the III Gallica's early support for Vespasian (e.g. 'the most trustworthy account...is probably...: Chilver, *loc. cit.*), but, for a full discussion of the two versions, see Chilver, 1979: 210-11 and 246; and, for a more sceptical reaction, compare Garzetti, 1974: 628, cited below, s.u. *consilium...imperatoris.*

**postquam...[Othonem] uim uitae suae attulisse:** Tacitus just as clearly assigns the incident to Otho's lifetime (*Hist.* 2.46).

**Aquileiam:** Aquileia was in Venetia, a few kilometres from the head of the Adriatic. See *OCD* 133 and the map in Wellesley, 1975: xvi.

**consilium inierunt eligendi...imperatoris:** Garzetti dismisses this account as 'obviously something invented later to give the army of the Danube priority in acclaiming the new Princeps' (1974: 628).

**Hispaniensi exercitu:** The VI Victrix; for the details, see Wellesley, 1975: 5.

**praetoriano:** Otho had seized power thanks to the *animum fidemque erga se praetorianorum* (*Otho* 8.1), the latter being described by Tacitus as *proprius Othonis miles* (*Hist.* 2.46). See *Hist.* 1.23-7 and Wellesley, 1975: 20-7.

**Germaniciano:** Vitellius had been proclaimed emperor by the armies of Upper and Lower Germany on 3 January; see *Otho* 8.1, *Vitell.* 8.1 and Wellesley, 1975: 15-17. According to Aurelius Victor, *milites praedicti* [from Moesia and Pannonia], *postquam Othonem praetoriis, Vitellium Germanicianis legionibus factum comperere, aemuli, ut inter se solent, ne dissimiles uiderentur, Vespasianum perpulere* (*De Caes.* 8.3); so too Orosius – *de Hispania siquidem ilico Galba surrexerat; quo mox oppresso, Otho Romae, Vitellius in Germania, Vespasianus in Syria imperia simul atque arma rapuerunt* (7.8.3).

6.3
**propositis...legatorum consularium:** The candidates would have been Pompeius Silvanus (in Dalmatia), Aponius Saturninus (Moesia), Tampius Flavianus (Pannonia), Licinius Mucianus (Syria), and, in theory, Vettius Bolanus (Britain) and Cluvius Rufus (Spain); see Eck, 1982: 284-6.

**quidam e legione tertia...in Moesiam:** In recent times (54 to 66), the Syrian III Gallica had served under Corbulo, gaining considerable success (*Ann.* 15.26; *Hist.* 3.24). Ordered to Moesia in 68, it helped defeat the Rhoxolani (early 69), with its commander Aurelius Fulvus (grandfather of the emperor Antoninus Pius) being awarded the *ornamenta consularia* (*Hist.* 1.79). After declaring first for Otho, the legion played a decisive role in Vespasian's elevation, for it was the first in Moesia to declare for him: *tertia legio exemplum ceteris Moesiae legionibus praebuit* (*Hist.* 2.85) and also *tertiam legionem, quod e Syria in Moesiam transisset, suam numerabat [Vespasianus]* (*Hist.* 2.74).

**nomenque eius uexillis omnibus...inscripserunt:** *Vexilla* were flags hanging from a crossbar attached to a staff; according to Dio, they 'resembled sails, with purple letters upon them to distinguish the army and its commander-in-chief' (40.10.3). At Aquileia, *vexilla* bearing the name of Vitellius were torn down: *laceratis uexillis nomen Vitellii praeferentibus* (*Hist.* 2.85) and *primores castrorum nomen atque imagines Vitellii amoliuntur* (*Hist.* 3.31); so *miles praescriptum Vespasiani nomen proiectas Vitellii effigies aspexit* (*Hist.* 3.13).

**numeris:** A *numerus* was a term applied to a body of soldiers and could be used of a legion, a cohort or even an *ala*; here it means vexillations.

**diuulgato facto:** Suetonius version of events is given greater credibility by the details he provides in this section and by the link with the July proclamation.

**Tiberius Alexander:** Prefect of Egypt in 69, Tiberius Julius Alexander (*PIR*² J 139; Pflaum, 1960: 46-9; and the bibliography in Jones, 1984: 69 n.57) was the first military governor to declare for Vespasian (1 July), and, though Vitellius survived until December 69, Vespasian officially dated his reign from Alexander's proclamation in Egypt. An apostate Jew, son of the alabarch in Alexandria and nephew of Philo, he became procurator of Judaea (ca 46-48), *minister bello datus* (*Ann.* 15.28) to Corbulo in Armenia and, subsequently, prefect of Egypt. Alexander, Agrippa II (his former brother-in-law) and Berenice (Agrippa's sister and Titus' mistress) formed part of the 'oriental group' that supported the Flavians in 69 – *Alexander consilia [Vespasiani] sociauerat* (*Hist.* 2.74). The relationship had probably been forged in the early decades of the century when Vespasian's father had sought and found influential patrons at court: according to Josephus, Tiberius Julius' father was 'an old friend of Claudius and looked after the interests of Claudius' mother Antonia' (*AJ* 19.276). Alexander later served as Titus' chief of staff during the siege of Jerusalem (*MW* 329), but was probably not praetorian prefect (cf. Jones, 1984: 85). Ti. Julius Alexander Iulianus (*PIR*² J 142), *cos.* 117 (Birley, 1998: 380) may be one of his descendants.

**praefectus Aegypti:** Egypt was the only major province under the control of an equestrian governor. As Tacitus explained: *Aegyptum copiasque, quibus coerceretur, iam inde a diuo Augusto equites Romani obtinent loco regum: ita uisum expedire, prouinciam aditu difficilem, annonae fecundam, superstitione ac lasciuia discordem ac mobilem, insciam legum, ignaram magistratuum, domi retinere* (*Hist.* 1.11). For a list of the prefects of Egypt, see Brunt, 1975a: 124-47 and Bastianini, 1988: 503-17.

**primus...legiones adegit:** Tacitus *(festinante Tiberio Alexandro, qui kalendis Iuliis sacramento eius legiones adegit: Hist.* 2.79) agrees with Suetonius' statement that Vespasian was first proclaimed Emperor in Egypt on 1 July 69 and not in Judaea as Josephus states *(BJ* 4.592-620). However, as Millar points out (1993: 73), it is significant that he was first hailed in person *(apud ipsum: Hist.* 2.79 and *Vesp.* 6.3) by his troops at Caesarea in Judaea – consequently, very early in his reign, it was granted the title *Colonia Prima Flavia Augusta Caesarea,* but note the reservations of Dabrowa (1993: 21) who argues that the title was purely honorary.

Alexander's legions were the III Cyrenaica and the XXII Deiotariana. One of his officers almost certainly involved in the proclamation was the young Ti. Julius Celsus Polemaeanus (see 9.2 below, s.u. *honestissimo...adlecto)* who reached the consulship in 92. His sepulchral inscription describes him as *cos., procos. Asiae, trib. legionis III Cyrenaicae, adlecto inter aedilicios ab diuo Vespasiano, pr(aetori) p(opuli) R(omani)...(ILS* 8971 = *MW* 316). It would seem that his adlection occurred 'in the field' (and not during the censorship of Vespasian and Titus in 73/74: hence the omission of a reference to Titus in the inscription). No doubt this was his reward for his well-timed support of Vespasian on 1 July 69.

**principatus dies in posterum obseruatus est:** Confirmation of Suetonius' statement is provided by Tacitus *(isque primus principatus dies in posterum celebratus: Hist.* 2.79) and by numerous coins and inscriptions (see Hammond, 1959: 72-3) which consistently date Vespasian's *tribunicia potestas* from 1 July 69. For this whole question, see Brunt, 1977: 95-116 and 12 below, s.u. *ne tribuniam... potestatem.* So both Tacitus and Suetonius mean to emphasise that, for Vespasian, the *primus principatus dies* was when he was acclaimed by the army, with the obvious 'constitutional' implications that emperors were appointed by the army and not by the senate: see the discussion in Chilver, 1979: 240.

**Iudaicus deinde exercitus:** Josephus reverses the order *(BJ* 4.592-620) in an attempt to disguise what had happened, an emperor proclaimed in Egypt with 'oriental' support (including the *Kleopatra in kleinen,* Berenice) that recalled events of a century before. The Judaean legions involved were the V Macedonica, X Fretensis and XV Apollinaris.

**V Idus Iul.:** 11 July, whereas Tacitus has 3 July *(quinto nonas Iulias: Hist.* 2.79). Braithwaite (1927) 26 prefers Suetonius' version on the grounds that it would give time for the news of the proclamation at Alexandria to have reached Caesarea, an argument rejected by Chilver (1979: 240) who believes that even the dates of the proclamation were arranged in advance. If Chilver is correct, one wonders why there should be any gap at all – as the pre-planning was so precise and detailed, there can be no doubt that the proclamation was to be made at Alexandria and Caesarea on the same day.

**apud ipsum iurauit:** cf. *apud ipsum iurasset* (*Hist.* 2.79) – see 6.3 above, s.u. *primus...* *adegit*. This suggests that Suetonius and Tacitus were using the same source.

6.4
**exemplar epistulae uerae siue falsae:** One is almost tempted to see here the 'hand' of the Flavian expert in such matters, i.e. *e pluribus comperi* (says Suetonius) *(Titum) imitari chirographa quaecumque uidisset ac saepe profiteri maximum falsarium esse potuisse* (*Titus* 3.2). That the letter was false is suggested by Suetonius' report that Otho wrote a number of letters just before he committed suicide, but *quicquid deinde epistularum erat, ne cui periculo aut noxae apud uictorem forent, concremauit* (*Otho* 10.2).

**extrema obtestatione:** i.e. '(urging him) as a last, solemn charge' rather than 'with the utmost earnestness'; see Mooney, 1930: 406.

**rumor...Germanicas transferre...ad securiorem...militiam:** Tacitus names Mucianus as the person responsible for spreading the report: *adseuerabat Mucianus statuisse Vitellium ut Germanicas legiones in Syriam ad militiam opulentam quietamque transferret* (*Hist.* 2.80).

**ex praesidibus prouinciarum:** *Praeses* was a general term for a senatorial proconsul or an imperial *legatus*, as Macer explains in the *Digest*: *praesidis nomen generale est, eoque et proconsules et legati Caesaris et omnes prouincias regentes, licet senatores sint, praesides appellantur* (1.18.1); and, by the middle of the second century, it had become the regular term for a provincial governor. At times, Suetonius distinguishes governors of imperial provinces *legati consulares* (6.3 above) from their senatorial counterparts (*proconsules*: e.g. *Galba* 7.1), but also makes use of the term *praeses*, e.g. at *Aug.* 23.1; *Tib.* 32.2; *Otho* 7.1 and *Dom.* 6.2.

**Licinius Mucianus:** Gaius Licinius Mucianus (*PIR*[2] L 216) was suffect consul on three occasions: ca 64, 70 and 72. On his early career, see *OCD* 859. Appointed to Syria late in Nero's reign, he came into dispute with Vespasian, his neighbour in Judaea (see below, s.u. *deposita simultate*). With this settled, he encouraged Vespasian's imperial ambitions and was instrumental in persuading the Syrian legions to support the Flavians, a far from easy task – the problems posed for

Vespasian and Mucianus by the soldiers of the much-lamented Corbulo are discussed in 4.6, s.u. *correcta...disciplina*. According to Dio, Mucianus' plan was that, 'while Vespasian should have the name of emperor, he himself as a result of the other's good nature might enjoy an equal share of power' (65.8.4). For his subsequent activities, see 7.1, s.u. *ducibus...praemissis* and 13, s.u. *Licinium Mucianum*.

**e regibus Vologaesus Parthus:** Vologaesus I (for the various forms of his name, see *PIR*[1] V 629) was king of Parthia for almost thirty years (51-79). For his relationship with Rome during Nero's reign, see Jones, 1996: 24. In July or August 69 (*Hist.* 2.81), Vespasian sent envoys to him, and it was only after hearing of the defeat and death of Vitellius, some six months later, that he received an offer of 40,000 cavalry (*Hist.* 4.51: see below). Unwilling to be seen as a dependant of the Parthian king, Vespasian thanked him: *gratiae Vologaeso actae mandatumque ut legatos ad senatum mitteret et pacem esse sciret* (*Hist.* 4.51). Vologaesus followed that advice and the *societas* with Rome was renewed (*Nero* 57.2): he sent Titus a 'golden crown in recognition of his victory over the Jews' (*BJ* 7.105) and later asked Vespasian (unsuccessfully) for help against the Alani (*Dom.* 2.2). The relationship seems to have deteriorated, though, if we accept the statement of Aurelius Victor: *bello rex Parthorum Vologaesus in pacem coactus* (*De Caes.* 9.10) – but compare his epitomator's claim that Vologaesus *metu solo in pacem coactus est* (9.12). For a discussion of Rome's relations with Parthia under Vespasian, see Dabrowa (1981) 187-204.

**ille deposita simultate:** Presumably, Vespasian would have reached Ptolemais early in 67, some months before Mucianus whose arrival (to take up his Syrian command) could, perhaps, be assigned to late July or early August. Their relationship rapidly deteriorated. While the precise cause of the dispute is uncertain, it could well have had its origin in the fact that Vespasian had set up his base camp in Syria (at Ptolemais) and maintained it there; see 4.4, s.u. *prouincia cum exercitu oblata*. Some of their *amici* tried to reconcile Vespasian and Mucianus, but it was Titus who acted as mediator, perhaps as early as August or September 67, when he was absent from the siege of Gamala, 'having been sent off to Syria to Mucianus'(*BJ* 4.32). After providing a character sketch of Vespasian and Mucianus, Tacitus states *ceterum hic Syriae, ille Iudaeae praepositus, uicinis prouinciarum administrationibus inuidia discordes, exitu demum Neronis positis odiis in medium consuluere, primum per amicos, dein praecipua concordiae fides Titus praua certamina communi utilitate aboleuerat, natura atque arte compositus adliciendis etiam Muciani moribus* (*Hist.* 2.5).

**Syriacum promisit exercitum:** Syria originally had four legions (III Gallica, IV Scythica, VI Ferrata and XII Fulminata) but the III Gallica was transferred to Moesia (6.3 above, s.u. *quidam...in Moesiam*). Mucianus, in urging Vespasian to seize power, said *tibi e Iudaea et Syria et Aegypto nouem legiones integrae* (*Hist.* 2.76), i.e. 3 in Judaea (V Macedonica, X Fretensis and XV Apollinaris), 4 in Syria and 2 in Egypt (III Cyrenaica and XXII Deiotariana).

**hic quadraginta milia sagittariorum:** Tacitus (*Hist.* 4.51) refers to them as *equites* (i.e. *quadraginta milia Parthorum equitum*) because these were mounted archers.

7.1

**suscepto igitur ciuili bello:** Suetonius is imprecise. As far as Vespasian was concerned, the civil war had already begun on 1 July 69, with the events described in 6.3 above, and not with the subsequent activities of 6.4 or even 7.1.

**ducibus copiisque...praemissis:** The *duces* were Mucianus and Antonius Primus. The former set out for Italy *cum expedita manu, socium magis imperii quam ministrum agens...legio sexta et tredecim uexillariorum milia ingenti agmine sequebantur* (*Hist.* 2.83): so too Dio 65.9.2. However, without waiting for him to arrive, Antonius Primus, with the Dalmatian, Pannonian and Moesian armies, moved against Vitellius and defeated him; for a concise summary of Primus' activities, see Murison, 1992: 166. The Tacitean passage is discussed by Morgan, 1994: 167-8, 174-5.

**Alexandriam transiit:** Similarly Dio 65.9.2 and Orosius 7.9.3 (*per Alexandriam profectus est Romam*). Whilst Mucianus marched against the Vitellians, Titus remained in Judaea and Vespasian crossed to Alexandria (*Titum instare Iudaeae, Vespasianum obtinere claustra Aegypti placuit*: *Hist.* 2.82) where he arrived no later than November 69 (Henrichs, 1968: 55 n.15). For a detailed discussion of Vespasian's activities there, including a comparison of Suetonius' version with that of Tacitus, *Hist.* 4.81-4, see Scott, 1975: 9-13; Henrichs, 1968: 54-65 (Vespasian in the Temple of Serapis) and 65-72 (Vespasian the thaumaturge): the most recent discussion is that of Levick, 1999: 68-9 and 227-8. The visit was important for a number of reasons. Apart from Alexandria's strategic position (see next item), Vespasian needed to be seen as remote from the pillaging and slaughter (cf. 6.2 above, i.e. *ibi* [at Aquileia] *per occasionem ac licentiam omni rapinarum genere grassati*) inevitable in a civil war so that blame could be assigned elsewhere. Furthermore, his representatives, prominent amongst whom was Tiberius Julius Alexander, needed time to strengthen his support amongst the members of the nine eastern legions (see 6.4 above, s.u. *Syriacum promisit exercitum*) who had to be assured that Vespasian's ultimate success was pre-determined.

Henrichs (1968: 55) argues that, in their accounts of what happened (or what was alleged to have happened) in Alexandria, both Suetonius and Tacitus seem to have relied on a common source (see below, s.u. *solus, de firmitate* and *hortantibus amicis*) that was derived from an account of Alexander the Great's visit some four hundred years before to the oasis of Siwah to consult the oracle of Ammon; if so, Vespasian's agents would have been far from hesitant in stressing links of this sort. But, despite the reliance on a common source, the accounts of Suetonius and Tacitus differ in certain vital details: Tacitus assigns Vespasian's visit to the Serapeum after, and as a result of his miraculous cures (so *Hist.* 4.82 begins *altior inde* [the cures] *cupido adeundi sacram sedem* – cited below, s.u. *de firmitate*) and, unlike Suetonius, assigns both events to the period in 70 when Vespasian, now assured of supreme power, was only waiting for the *statos aestiuis flatibus dies et certa maris* (*Hist.* 4.81) to leave Alexandria for Rome.

**ut claustra Aegypti obtineret:** Suetonius probably means Alexandria and Pelusium as in *B. Alex.* 26.2 (*tota Aegyptos maritimo accessu Pharo, pedestri Pelusio, uelut claustris munita existimatur*), despite Braithwaite, 1927: 38. The same phrase occurs in Tacitus (*Vespasianum obtinere claustra Aegypti placuit*: *Hist.* 2.82) who explains the strategic significance of Egypt: *Augustus inter alia dominationis arcana...seposuit Aegyptum ne fame urgeret Italiam, quisquis eam prouinciam claustraque terrae ac maris quamuis leui praesidio aduersum ingentis exercitus insedisset* (*Ann.* 2.59). Vespasian outlined Egypt's role in his plans to overcome Vitellius: *quando Aegyptus, claustra annonae, uectigalia opulentissimarum prouinciarum obtinerentur, posse Vitellii exercitum egestate stipendii frumentique ad deditionem subigi* (*Hist.* 3.8).

**de firmitate imperii auspicium:** So, too, in Tacitus: *altior inde Vespasiano cupido adeundi sacram sedem ut super rebus imperii consuleret* (*Hist.* 4.82) and, for Alexander the Great, see Plutarch, *Alex.* 27.6.

**aedem Serapidis:** the Serapeum at Alexandria, described by Ammianus Marcellinus as *atriis...columnatis amplissimis et spirantibus signorum figmentis et reliqua operum multitudine ita est exornatum ut post Capitolium...nihil orbis terrarum ambitiosius cernat* (22.16.12). For the *origo dei*, see *Hist.* 4.83-84 and, for the Temple's location, Henrichs, 1968: 55 n.13. On Serapis in general, see Stambaugh, 1972; Engelmann, 1975; Takacs, 1995 and *OCD* 1355-6.

**summotis omnibus solus:** So, too, in Tacitus: *arceri templo cunctos iubet* (*Hist.* 4.81) and, for Alexander, see Strabo 17.1.43.

**uerbenas coronasque et panificia uisus est:** *Verbena* is 'a leafy branch or twig from any of various aromatic trees or shrubs used in religious ceremonies' (*OLD* 2033; a *corona* is 'a wreath of flowers' (*OLD* 447) and *paneficia* are 'baked loaves or cakes' (OLD 1290). In a number of documents from Ptolemaic times, these items appear as symbols of kingship; for the texts, see Henrichs, 1968: 61 n.30.

**Basilides libertus:** The reading has been questioned with *liberius, uberius* and *Libye ortus* being preferred to *libertus*; see Mooney, 1930: 409-10. This Basilides has been identified (e.g. by Scott, 1975: 11-13) with the Egyptian noble (*e primoribus Aegyptiorum*: *Hist.* 4.82) of the same name consulted by Vespasian at Mt Carmel (see 5.6, s.u. *Carmeli dei oraculum*: named by Tacitus at *Hist.* 2.78 but not by Suetonius); there is also another Basilides, the procurator in Egypt in 49 – see *PIR*[2] B 60 and 61. Basilides' name was in itself an omen – Tacitus, but not Suetonius, stressed the point: *diuinam speciem et uim responsi ex nomine Basilidis interpretatus est* (*Hist.* 4.82).

**statim:** So, too, in Tacitus: *usum statim conuersa ad manus* (*Hist.* 4.81). Suetonius' use of *statim* renders his version even more suspect (see below), since swiftness is a standard feature in the terminology of ancient thaumaturgical literature; see Henrichs, 1968: 55.

**aduenere litterae:** Tacitus' account differs from that of Suetonius and Josephus. The latter states that he accompanied Vespasian to Alexandria (*Vita* 415; *Ap.* 1.48), and that, once there, Vespasian heard of both the victory at Cremona and the death of Vitellius (*BJ* 4.656); Suetonius agrees. There was, however, an interval of some eight weeks between the two events. So Tacitus' version is obviously correct: Vespasian probably heard of Cremona in the middle of November (Wellesley, 1972: 144) before reaching Alexandria, whereas news of Vitellius' death (December 20) came later (*Hist.* 3.48: cf. 4.51). See Nicols, 1978: 84-5.

**Cremonam:** After this, the second battle of Bedriacum (October 24/25), Antonius Primus' forces sacked Cremona (Bedriacum lies midway between Verona and Cremona); for the two battles fought there in 69, see 5.7 above, s.u. *acie Betriacensi*.

**fusas...interemptum:** For the details, see the account of Wellesley, 1975: 128-50 (Cremona) and 188-203 (Vitellius).

7.2

**auctoritas...accessit:** Much the same point is made by Tacitus: *caelestis favor et quaedam in Vespasiano inclinatio numinum* (*Hist.* 4.81). Portents indicating support from the gods helped to supply the *auctoritas* and *maiestas* he lacked, for they enabled his agents to convince the credulous, ordinary soldiers that his success was in fact predetermined. Note how the various portents were deliberately designed to appeal to the prejudices, or beliefs, of each particular group of likely supporters, for example in Italy (5.2-5.5: *in suburbano Flauiorum quercus antiqua...*; and 5.7: *ex urbe praesagia...*), in Greece (7.3: *Tegeae in Arcadia...*) and in the East (5.6: *Apud Iudaeam Carmeli dei oraculum...*; and 7.1-2: *cum... aedem Serapidis...intrasset...*).

Vespasian's wonder-working abilities have been discussed by a number of scholars including Gagé (1952: 292), Herrmann (1953: 312-15), Derchain and Hubaux (1953: 38-52), Derchain (1953: 261-79), Gagé (1976: 145-66) and Montevecchi (1981: 483-95). See also the bibliography in Garzetti, 1974: 631-2 and in Benediktson, 1993: 325-7.

**inopinato...principi:** That was indeed Nero's (correct) assessment: he saw Vespasian as one *cui...tuto tanta res committeretur* (4.5 above). Yet Titus' marriage to Marcia Furnilla (probably niece of Barea Soranus; see Jones, 1992: 10-11) and Vespasian's *amicitia* with people like Barea Soranus and Thrasea Paetus (*Hist.* 4.7) – before the Pisonian conspiracy – were well known. Both relationships must been severed at precisely the right time for Nero to have entrusted Vespasian with the Judaean command and to have, unprecedentedly, given him *carte blanche* in the selection of his three legionary commander. See 4.6 above, s.u. *inter legatos...assumpto*.

**e plebe quidam:** Tacitus' version of the incident begins with the same phrase: *e plebe Alexandrina quidam* (*Hist.* 4.81).

**debili crure:** The same story appears in both Tacitus (*Hist.* 4.81) and Dio: 'Vespasian himself healed two persons, one having a withered hand (*manum aeger* in Tacitus), the other being blind, who had come to him because of a vision seen in dreams; he cured the one by stepping on his hand and the other by spitting upon his eyes. Yet, though Heaven was thus magnifying him...' (66.8.2).

**per quietem:** The same detail occurs in both Dio (66.8.2 above) and Tacitus (*monitu Serapidis dei*: *Hist.* 4.81).

**restituturum...inspuisset:** For the use of saliva in such cases, see *NH* 28.7 and the gospel of *John* 9.6-7 (from the Vulgate): *Iesus...expuit in terram, et fecit lutum ex sputo et liniuit lutum super oculos eius* [i.e. *caeci*] *et dixit ei 'Vade, laua in natatoria Siloe...' Abiit ergo, et lauit, et uenit uidens*; similarly *Mark* 8.23.

**calce contingere:** The presumed magical power of Serapis' feet is indicated by the votive offerings to the god consisting of a marble foot together with part of the ankle as a base for the god's head; there are also gems (and coins) inscribed with Serapis-headed feet. So, for the Alexandrians, Vespasian was indeed Serapis (Henrichs, 1968: 68-70) and, on what seems to be a contemporary papyrus fragment, he was addressed as 'Serapis, Son of Ammon, Saviour and Benefactor' (*P. Fouad* 8 = *MW* 41: the document is translated in 19.2, s.u. *Alexandrini*). Pyrrhus of Epirus, too, (so it seems) could heal diseases of the spleen: 'while the patient lay flat upon his back, Pyrrhus would press gently with his right foot against the spleen [and the big toe of this foot had divine power because] after the rest of his body had been consumed, it was found to be untouched and unharmed by the fire' (Plutarch, *Pyrrhus* 3.4-5); later, it was venerated as a relic (*NH* 7.20).

### 7.3

**ne experiri quidem auderet:** Tacitus (*Hist.* 4.81) discusses Vespasian's reluctance in some detail.

**hortantibus amicis:** Tacitus has the same detail (taken, no doubt, from a common source): *uocibus adulantium in spem induci* (*Hist.* 4.81); see Henrichs, 1968: 65 n.12.

**Tegeae in Arc[h]adia:** Tegea (in south east Arcadia) was one of the oldest towns in the Peloponnesus with an important cult centre of Athena Alea outside it; see Pausanias 8.45 and *OCD* 1478-9.

### 8.1

**in urbem reuersus:** The Arval Brethren offered sacrifice *in Capitolio ob diem [quo urbem ingressus est imperator C]aesar Vespasianus Aug.* (*MW* 4) – unfortunately, without any (surviving) reference to the date; but there are other indications. According to Dio (66.8.1), Vespasian was still in Alexandria at the time of the extremely high Nile flood (and the Nile reaches its maximum around 20 July) but he had left for Rome before learning of the fall of Jerusalem in early September (Dio 66.9.2a). Moreover, Josephus (*BJ* 7.39) has Titus celebrating Vespasian's birthday (Nov. 17) in Berytus and, soon after (*BJ* 7.63), receiving news of Vespasian's arrival in Italy. So it could be suggested that Vespasian, travelling via Asia Minor and Greece, probably reached Rome early in October 70.

Dio describes the journey as follows: 'Vespasian...sailed as far as Lycia, and from there he proceeded partly by land and partly by sea to Brundisium' (66.9.2a); Josephus states that 'he crossed from Alexandria to Rhodes (and) from there sailed on triremes, touching at all towns on his route; he passed over from Ionia to Greece and thence from Corcyra to the Iapygian promontory (*BJ* 7.21-2).

**acto...triumpho:** On Titus' return to Rome in the middle of June 71 (his tribunician power is dated from 1 July of that year), the senate voted to honour the Flavian victory and decreed triumphs for both Vespasian and Titus, the first time that a father and son had triumphed together. But they preferred a common ceremony (*BJ* 7.121) that was described in detail by Josephus, i.e. *BJ* 7.123-31 (preliminaries), 132-47 (procession), 148-52 (spoils) and 153-7 (execution of Simon, the Jewish leader). Suetonius refers to it on two other occasions (*Dom.* 2.1 and *Titus* 6.1), as does Pliny (*NH Praef.* 3). Orosius describes it as *magnificum...pulchrum et ignotum antea cunctis mortalibus inter trecentos uiginti triumphos* (7.9.8); it is also commemmorated on the coinage (e.g. *BMC* 2.397). The Roman triumph is examined in detail by Versnel (1970); see also Hammond, 1959: 35-8, 52-6; Maxfield, 1981: 101-9 and Scullard, 1981: 213-17.

**consulatus octo ueteri addidit:** His only suffect consulship (*ueteri*) was his first, with Claudius in 51; the other eight were ordinary. His second was held in 70 with Titus as colleague (both *in absentia*), the third in 71 with Nerva and then six more (in 72, 74, 75, 76, 77 and 79), all with Titus. For the evidence, see Gallivan, 1981: 186-9. The Flavians' fondness for the ordinary consulship, derided by Pliny (*miseros ambitionis qui ita consules semper ut semper principes erant*: *Pan.* 58.4), was intended to supply the *auctoritas et...maiestas (quae) nouo principi deerat* (7.2).

**suscepit et censuram:** Vespasian and Titus assumed the censorship (*census quem intra quadriennium imperatores Caesares Vespasiani pater filiusque censores egerunt*: *NH* 7.162) between March and 1 July 73 (*ILS* 260: see below), presumably in April as was the practice in the Republic; and the *lustrum* of 74 marked the censorship's end, according to Censorinus: *lustrum ab imperatore Vespasiano V et [T.] Caesare III cos. factum est* (*De Die Natali* 18.14). Buttrey (1980: 15, 23) has rejected the widely-accepted theory (e.g. by Weynand, *RE* 6.2655, Hammond, 1959: 85, 120 n.177 and others) that the designated censorship appeared on inscriptions as early as 71. The earliest reliable epigraphic evidence (*ILS* 260) points to 73, for it refers to Titus as *censor, cos. II des. III* (so after March 73), *trib. pot. II* (before 1 July 73) as does *CIL* 2.5217 where Vespasian appears as *censor, cos. IIII des. V, trib. pot. IIII* (again March - 1 July 73). As far as Vespasian was concerned, there were sound reasons (not the least of them financial) for assuming the office. To take but one example: granting the *ius Latii* to all Spain (*NH* 3.30: see Sherwin-White, 1973: 252, 361-2) meant that the local magistrates now had to pay the inheritance tax. Apart from revising membership of the senate and the equestrian order (see 9.2 below), exercising a general supervision over the community's morals and conducting the census, the censors saw to the leasing of revenue-producing state property (e.g. mines) and to letting out contracts for new buildings and for restoring those that were old or damaged (8.5, 9.1 below). Moreover, the census traditionally concluded with a religious ceremony of purification or *lustratio*, performed in the Campus Martius by one of the censors, entirely appropriate after the recent civil war. See Brunt, 1971: 536-7; *OCD* 307-8 (censor), 308 (census) and 893 (lustration); for the censor's powers, see Dio 53.17.7 and *Str* 2.334 and, for imperial censorships, Millar, 1977: 293-4.

**per totum...et ornare:** Suetonius' neat summary of Vespasian's policy recalls the phrase *imperium...firmauit* in 1.1.

8.2

**milites...processerant:** Suetonius fails to mention anywhere in the *Life* the most pressing and immediate reason for army reform, i.e. the rebellion on the Rhine (in the latter part of 69 and early in 70: *Hist.* 4 *passim*) and the surrender to (or collusion with) the Batavian Julius Civilis and the pro-Vitellian legions.

**ignominiae:** The 'humiliating' defeat of the Vitellians at Cremona; see Wellesley, 1975: 128-50.

**regna:** Commagene and Lesser Armenia, for example (see 8.4 below), were not acting *tumultuosius* – though that may well have been Vespasian's excuse to justify annexing them. On client kings and kingdoms, see Braund, 1984: *passim*.

**prouinciae...inter se agebant:** His policy towards the *prouinciae* and the *ciuitates liberae* was, in the main, based on the need to increase taxation revenue (but see 16.1) and to reorganise and strengthen the eastern frontier; internal dissensions may have provided the official excuse for intervention – if one was felt necessary: see the changes in status noted below, in 8.3.

**ciuitatesque liberae:** Free cities were communities which, by a special agreement with Rome, had local autonomy and, sometimes, immunity from taxation.

**Vitellianorum...exauctorauit plurimos:** Suetonius' statement needs considerable emendation. Three of the four Vitellian legions present at the second battle of Cremona (I Italica, XXI Rapax and XXII Primigenia) were not disbanded; the other (the V Alaudae) may have suffered that fate or else it was transferred to Moesia, to be wiped out either there in 86 or in Pannonia in 92. Those disbanded (I Germanica, IV Macedonica, XVI Gallica and, probably, XV Primigenia) had only vexillations fighting for Vitellius at the second battle of Cremona but the legions themselves were punished for either colluding with or surrendering to Civilis and were replaced by the II Adiutrix, IV Flavia Felix and XVI Flavia Firma. Another serious problem was the sixteen praetorian cohorts that Vitellius had raised from the German legions and the pro-Vespasianic praetorians he had dismissed. Before Vespasian reached Rome, Mucianus had begun to reduce the former: *quibus aetas et iusta stipendia, dimissi cum honore, alii ob culpam carptim ac singuli* (*Hist.* 4.46). Ultimately, they were replaced by nine cohorts, the traditional number. See Durry, 1968: 243-5, 376-7.

**adeo nihil:** By the time of Claudius, it was customary for an incoming emperor to give his troops a special sum of money or donative (*donatiuum*) with the intention or hope of ensuring their support; see Jones, 1996: 26. The amounts paid by each ruler varied considerably: Augustus gave the praetorians 1,000 sesterces each (but in his will), Claudius and Nero made an annual grant of 15,000 per man, Galba refused to pay any and Mucianus offered them 100 sesterces each (Dio 65.22.2). Tacitus' summary is important, i.e. *donatiuum militi neque Mucianus...nisi modice ostenderat, ne Vespasianus quidem plus ciuili bello obtulit quam alii in pace, egregie firmus aduersus militarem largitionem eoque exercitu meliore* (*Hist.* 2.82). The *donatiuum* is discussed by Watson, 1969: 108-11.

**legitima praemia sero:** Those veterans granted *honesta missio* (above, 1.2) were entitled to certain 'bounties' (*praemia*): so the soldiers of Caesar's tenth legion demanded *missionem et praemia* (*Iul.* 70). According to Dio, the praetorians received 20,000 sesterces in Augustus' reign and the legionaries 12,000 (55.23.1), the latter being reduced to 6,000 by Gaius (*Cal.* 44.1). *Legitima* is explained by Tacitus' *ne Vespasianus...in pace* (*Hist.* 2.82, cited in the previous item). By *sero*, Suetonius presumably means a payment by Vespasian after his arrival to supplement the one hundred sesterces previously paid by Mucianus (Dio 65.22.2).

8.3

**occasionem corrigendi disciplinam:** That Vespasian was a noted disciplinarian is apparent from Tacitus' estimate of his character: *Vespasianus acer militiae anteire agmen, locum castris capere, noctu diuque consilio ac, si res posceret,* *manu hostibus obniti, cibo fortuito, ueste habituque uix a gregario milite discrepans* (*Hist.* 2.5).

**praefectura:** The command of an *ala*, an auxiliary cavalry squadron. The significance of such a posting is explained by Suetonius: *liberis senatorum...militiam auspicantibus non tribunatum modo legionum, sed et praefecturas alarum dedit [Augustus]; ac ne qui expers castrorum esset, binos plerumque laticlauios praeposuit singulis alis* (*Aug.* 38.2).

***maluissem alium oboluisses*:** Braithwaite's comment (1927: 44) is worth quoting: 'I suppose the point of Vespasian's remark was that he would rather have a boorish, manly *praefectus* than a cultured effeminate one (to smell of garlic being the mark of the yokel).' For a discussion of the anecdote, see Millar, 1977: 285.

**alium:** The Italian for 'garlic' is *aglio* and the French *ail*.

**litteras:** *litterae* in the sense of 'commission' as here or 'official ordinances' as in Cicero's *cedo mihi eiusdem praetoris litteras et rerum decretarum et frumenti imperati* (*Verr.* 2.5.22).

**classiarios:** The *classiarii* at Ostia (25 km from Rome at mouth of the Tiber: *OCD* 1081-2) and Puteoli (12 km north of Naples: *OCD* 1280-1) belonged to the naval base of Misenum (*OCD* 989) on the bay of Naples. The other major base was at Ravenna (*OCD* 1294). The first extant diploma of Vespasian's principate (dated 26 February 70) was issued to a member of the latter fleet; see Roxan, 1996: 248-54 for the details. The cohorts that Claudius stationed at Ostia and Puteoli to deal with fires may have been *classiarii*: *Puteolis et Ostiae singulas cohortes ad arcendos incendiorum casus collocauit* (*Claud.* 25.2).

**calciarii:** Understand *argenti*, i.e. 'shoe-money': so *calciator* = 'a shoemaker' (*OLD* 256).

**cursitare:** It would seem that the *classiarii* were being used as couriers; see Mooney, 1930: 415.

8.4

**Achaiam...equite Romano:** When were these changes made? Whilst Suetonius' list is repeated precisely by Eutropius (7.19.4), Orosius (7.9.10) and Jerome (*Chron.* p. 188: Helm), only the latter goes further and allocates the same date to all the changes, i.e. the Year of Abraham 2090 (1 Oct. 73/30 Sept. 74), a date accepted by Garzetti, 1974: 641. Suetonius nowhere assigns a specific time to any of the changes and other evidence goes against Jerome – Achaea lost its *libertas* in 70; the Elder Pliny, whose *NH* was dedicated to Titus in 77, describes Samos and Byzantium as free cities (*liberae condicionis*: see below). The changes in Trachia Cilicia and Commagene occurred in 72 and the Cappadocia-Galatia complex was not created before 75.

To complicate matters further, Suetonius does not even mention the annexation of Emesa (probably not long after 72, according to Kennedy, 1996: 731; Schwartz, however, argues [1990: 116 n.31] for the period between 72 and 78) or of Palmyra (around the same time: Millar, 1993: 83-4) or of Lesser Armenia (in the middle of 71: Kokkinos, 1992: 312) – even though the latter entailed the removal of Aristobulus, Rome's consistent ally in recent years (Schieber, 1976: 64-5). He could also have noted that Judaea was now an imperial praetorian province, with Sex. Vettulenus Cerialis as its first governor (Eck, 1982: 287) and Sex. Lucilius Bassus as his successor (Dabrowa, 1993: 28-9); both were simultaneously legates of the X Fretensis, the legion that had seen three legates in the tumult of 69/70 (M. Ulpius Traianus, A. Larcius Lepidus Sulpicianus and Terentius Rufus: Dabrowa, 1993: 52). On the other hand, Suetonius' inclusion of Lycia has been challenged (see below) as has his exclusion of Cos (Magie, 1950: 1428-9 at n.10). Finally, there is Festus' statement – unsupported by any other evidence – that Vespasian formed a province called *Insulae* (i.e. *sub Vespasiano principe Insularum prouincia facta est: Breu.* 10). Whilst this should be rejected, Vespasian may, according to Magie (1950: 1428 n. 9), have created a post analogous to the *prouincia Hellesponti* of *ILS* 1374 (an office held by the procurator C. Minicius Italus – see now *PIR²* M 614) to deal with the financial administration of the Aegean islands.

Why were such extensive changes made so early in the reign? The reasons were financial (a need to increase sources of taxation) and strategic (a need to strengthen the eastern frontier) – but the official excuse was the need to settle internal dissensions (see above, 8.2 s.u. *prouinciae...inter se agebant*) and below, s.u. *adsiduos barbarorum incursus*.

**Achaiam:** Assigned to the senate by Augustus (Dio 53.12.40), Achaea was made an imperial province by Tiberius (*Ann.* 1.76), but returned to the senate by Claudius (*Claud.* 25.3). Then Nero *prouinciam uniuersam libertate donauit* (*Nero* 24.2; see the discussion by Gallivan, 1973: 230-4; also Bradley, 1978: 66-71 and 1978a: 145-7). When Vespasian arrived in 70 (see 8.1 above, s.u. *reuersus*), he deprived it of its liberty (Philostratus, *V. Apoll.* 5.41) since 'the Hellenes had forgotten the meaning of freedom' (Pausanias 7.17.2) and it became a senatorial province, governed by a proconsul of praetorian rank. Braithwaite (1927: 44-5) argues *ex silentio* (and unconvincingly) that Jerome's date (73/74) for Achaea's new status ought to be preferred on the grounds that Josephus fails to mention the change in his reference to Vespasian's visit in 70 (*BJ* 7.21).

**Lyciam:** As the Lycians lost their liberty under Claudius *ob exitiabiles inter se discordias* (*Claud.* 25.3), it must have been restored at some point by Nero. Suetonius' testimony that Lycia had lost it again under Vespasian has been firmly rejected by Eck (1970: 113 and 1982: 285-6, n.16), who argues that the loss occurred towards the end of Nero's reign and that all Vespasian did was to disallow some internal privileges, later (ca 74) joining it to Pamphylia. His argument has been rejected by Bosworth, 1976: 65 n.18 and C.P. Jones, 1973: 690-1, but accepted (with hesitation) by Syme, 1995: 275; see also Levick, 1999: 146. Paltiel, however, attempts to reconcile Suetonius' statement with Eck's evidence by suggesting that Galba freed Lycia but that his act was not recognised by his successors (1991: 251). On Lycia, see Magie, 1950: 529-33; 1427 n.9 and Jones, 1971: 95-109. Lycia-Pamphylia became an imperial province of praetorian rank, with Vespasian's first governor being M. Hirrius Fronto Neratius Pansa (Strobel, 1985: 173-80) rather than L. Luscius Ocrea (Eck, 1982: 295 with n.54).

**Rhodum:** Rhodes' freedom, *adempta saepe aut firmata* (*Ann.* 12.58), had been lost in 44 ('because the Rhodians...had impaled some Romans': Dio 60.24.4) and restored in 53 (*ob paenitentiam ueterum delictorum*: *Claud.* 25.3). Presumably, Rhodes lost it again at the time of Vespasian's visit (see *BJ* 7.21) in 70 and was included in the province of Asia. See Magie, 1950: 1427-8 n.9; Jones, 1971: 76-7; Bosworth, 1973: 60-1 and *OCD* 1315-16.

**Byzantium:** Its freedom, like that of Rhodes, was frequently lost and restored. A *ciuitas libera* in Cicero's time (*Prou. Cons.* 4.7), it was controlled by the senate in 53, as is clear from Tacitus' account in *Ann.* 12.62-3. Since the Elder Pliny described it as an *oppidum liberae condicionis* (*NH* 4.46), it presumably did not lose its *libertas* until late in Vespasian's reign. Either then or not long afterwards, it was incorporated into the senatorial province of Pontus-Bithynia (Pliny, *Ep.* 10.43.1). See *OCD* 266.

**Samum:** Part of the province of Asia since 129 BC, Samos was granted its freedom by Augustus (Dio 54.9.7.) and was described as a free city by the Elder Pliny (*NH* 5.135). Presumably, it was late in Vespasian's reign that it was, once again, incorporated into the province fo Asia. See *OCD* 1351.

**Trachiam Ciliciam:** Turnebus first proposed the celebrated emendation *Trachiam* for the *Thraciam* of the MSS (see the discussion by Magie, 1950: 1439-40), but the MSS of the epitome of the *De Caesaribus* have *Ciliciaque ac Trachia*, whilst, in those of Orosius, we find *Tracia Cilicia, Trachia Cilicia* and *Thracia Cilicia*. *Thracia* is obviously wrong (but see Suceveanu, 1991: 255-76 who argues that *Thracia = ripa Thraciae*, i.e. Dobrudja) as Thrace had been a procuratorial province from the time of Claudius and remained so until Trajan's reign. As for Cilicia Trachia (also known as Cilicia Maritima or Cilicia Aspera), Gaius had, on his accession, given it to Antiochus IV (and he is, presumably, the 'king' referred to here by Suetonius) together with Commagene (Dio 59.8.2); previously, it had been ruled by Cleopatra (a gift from Antony) and then by Amyntas (king of Galatia). Vespasian now detached Cilicia Campestris from Syria and added it to Trachia to form the new province. The change in status is probably to be assigned to the period between 1 July and 1 October 72 (Gwatkin, 1930: 60), i.e. at the same time as Commagene's. The history and geography of the area is discussed by Magie (1950: 266-77), Jones (1971: 191-214), Mitford (Terence, 1980: 1230-261) and Syme (1995: 218, 230). The first governor of the 'new' province of Cilicia seems to have been (P. Nonius) Asprenas Caesius Cassianus; see Eck, 1982: 291-2 with n.38.

**et Commagenen dicionis regiae usque ad id tempus:** Situated to the south of Cappadocia, the north of Syria, the east of Cilicia and the west of the Parthian empire, Commagene together with its capital Samosata was of considerable strategic significance. Moreover, in view of its position on the right bank of the Euphrates, Samosata (modern Samsât) guarded an important crossing of the river on one of the main caravan routes from East to West and so was of tremendous commercial importance as well.

However, Suetonius is wrong: it was Cilicia Trachia but not Commagene that was 'ruled by kings up to that time'. In 18, after the death of Antiochus III, *Commagenis Q. Seruaeus praeponitur, tum primum ad ius praetoris translatis* (*Ann.* 2.56); under Gaius, Commagene was restored to Antiochus IV and then taken back again (Dio 59.8.2). On his accession, Claudius returned it to Antiochus (Dio 60.8.1), but, between 1 July and 1 October 72 (Gwatkin, 1930: 60; Kokkinos, 1998: 312), it was absorbed into Syria, as were Emesa (Kennedy, 1996: 731) and Palmyra (Millar, 1993: 83-4). Antiochus IV, described by Tacitus as *uetustis opibus ingens et seruientium regum ditissimus* (*Hist.* 2.81: similarly, *BJ* 5.461), had been consistently loyal to Rome, having provided forces for Corbulo's war (*Ann.* 13.7), for the Jewish war (*Hist.* 5.1) and for Vespasian in the civil war (*Hist.* 2.81).

Despite this, on the pretext (but see Dabrowa, 1981: 197-9) that Antiochus had been in league with the Parthians, the governor of Syria, Caesennius Paetus was authorised to invade the country (*BJ* 7.219-43); hence the *bellum Commagenicum* (*MW* 49). The only (short-lived) resistance came from two of Antiochus' sons, Epiphanes and Callinicus. They took refuge in Parthia but a Roman officer, Gaius Velius Rufus, *missus in Parthiam Epiphanen et Callinicum regis Antiochi filios ad Imp[eratorem] Vespasianum cum ampla manu tributariorum reduxit* (*MW* 372). All were treated generously by Vespasian. It is, of course, just possible, as Braithwaite (1927: 46-7) has noted, that Antiochus and Vespasian had met three or four decades previously as members of Antonia's court (see 4.1 above, s.u. *Auli Plauti*), for Antiochus seems to have been there, according to Dio (59.24.1), serving Gaius as 'tyrant-trainer'! – Dio refers to Agrippa I and Antiochus as *tyrannodidaskaloi*. After the *bellum Commagenicum* was over, Antiochus' family was settled in Rome; when Antiochus' daughter (Jotape: for the family tree, see Kokkinos, 1998: 251) married Alexander IV (later, at an advanced age, consul under Trajan before 103) in Rome, Vespasian's wedding present was a kingdom (*AJ* 18.140); the entire family 'took up abode in Rome and were treated with honour' (*BJ* 7.243) and Epiphanes' son (C. Julius Antiochus Epiphanes Philopappus) became consul in 109. The latter ('lover of his grandfather') was the 'King Philopappus' of Plutarch; see Birley, 1998: 62-4. Commagene now became part of Syria, its capital being renamed Flavia Samosata.

**in prouinciarum formam redegit:** This is technical language, implying the imposition of a governor: *Str* 3.1166.

**Cappadociae:** With the death of Archelaus in 17, Cappadocia had become a procuratorial province (Dio 57.17.3-7) and remained so until Vespasian's reign. For an overview of its history and geography, see Jones (1971: 174-90), Sullivan (1980: 1147-68) and Mitford (Timothy, 1980: 1169-228). Until recently, scholars believed that, between 71 and 72, it became the centre of the new Cappadocia-Galatia complex, a consular province with two legions which covered almost the entire central plateau of Asia Minor with an area of some 112,000 square miles (Magie, 1950: 574). The first legion moved eastwards was the XII Fulminata, sent by Vespasian to Melitene (in Cappadocia) immediately after the end of the siege of Jerusalem in September 70 (*BJ* 7.18) and it has been generally assumed that the second legion was the XVI Flavia Felix that had been raised 'by Vespasian in Syria' (Dio 55.24.2-3). Dabrowa (1980: 382) argued that the latter was probably moved to Satala between 71 and 72, a date supported by Mitford (Timothy), 1980: 1186 and by Sherk who claimed Trajan's father as the new province's first consular legate (1980: 996-7, as had been suggested by Syme, 1958: 31 n.1 and accepted by Eck, 1970: 3 n.7). But it is now clear that, as late as 75, the XVI Flavia was still in Syria (van Berchem, 1983: 186 and 1985: 85-7; Sherk, 1988: 129; and Dabrowa, 1996: 289), based perhaps first at Samosata and later at Satala (French, 1994: 29-46). So the XII Fulminata was sent to Melitene as a reinforcement for that frontier (Keppie, 1986: 421) – or 'as a punishment' (Schieber, 1976: 215 n.30) – rather than as a first step in the creation of Cappadocia-Galatia.

The component parts of this new huge complex were Cappadocia, Galatia, Pontus, Pisidia, Paphlagonia, Lycaonia and Armenia Minor (*MW* 105, 423 and 464), with Pompeius Collega as its first attested governor (see below, s.u. *consularemque...Romano*). The province previously named Galatia had consisted of Galatia, Pamphylia, Paphlagonia and Pisidia (*MW* 303): Pamphylia was now joined with Lycia.

**propter adsiduos barbarorum incursus:** Scholars from Mommsen (1909: 62) to Sherk (1980: 997) have assumed that Suetonius' *barbari* were the Alani; but they were not 'the bogeymen of the eastern frontier' (Bosworth, 1976: 67) as early as the first century, and they never posed a serious frontier problem for the Flavians; see Jones, 1996: 24. Suetonius was probably referring to the Heniochi, Colchians and other tribes of the Pontic coast listed by Josephus (*BJ* 2.367). In the summer of 69, one group massacred a cohort stationed at Trapezus, forcing Vespasian to send several vexillations from Judaea to deal with the problem (*Hist.* 3.47-8). The same Pontic coast *barbari* had caused concern before: Caesennius Paetus had been obliged to maintain the *quintam legionem...in Ponto habebat* (*Ann.* 15.9) and it seems that the fleet stationed there (40 ships) was directed against these same *barbari* (*BJ* 2.367). What Vespasian needed before annexing a client kingdom was a plausible excuse and the Pontic *barbari* provided it. On all this, see Bosworth, 1976: 67-72. For a discussion of Rome's relationship with Parthia during Vespasian's reign, see Dabrowa, 1981: 187-204; and for an overview of Roman policy in Transcaucasia from Pompey to Domitian, Dabrowa, 1988: 67-76.

**legiones addidit:** i.e. the new province was to have more than one legion and thus a governor (*legatus*) of consular rank. At the time of Vespasian's acclamation in July 69, however, *inermes legati regebant, nondum additis Cappadociae legionibus* (*Hist.* 2.81). For the first few years, presumably, the commander of the XII Fulminata at Melitene could act as governor, as his counterpart in the X Fretensis did in Judaea. Consular status came after the incorporation of Lesser Armenia and the transfer of the XVI Flavia Firma from Antioch to Satala. For a description of Melitene and Satala, see Mitford (Timothy), 1980: 1186-7 and 1220-4 [maps]).

**consularemque rectorem...Romano:** On the possibility that the first *rector pro equite Romano* was of praetorian rank, see the previous item. The earliest known consular governor of the enlarged province was Cn. Pompeius Collega (*PIR*² P 600), attested in 76 (*MW* 86: 1 Jan. to 31 June).

8.5

**deformis urbs:** In this section and the next, Suetonius provides *exempla* from within Rome of Vespasian's attempts to deal with the second part of the task mentioned in 8.1, i.e. *rem publicam stabilire primo, deinde et ornare.* There is a brief reference to Vespasian's work in the *Epit. de Caes.* (*Romam deformem incendiis ueteribus ac ruinis permissa, si domini deessent, uolentibus aedificandi copia, Capitolium, aedem Pacis, Claudii monumenta reparauit multaque noua instituit:* 9.8) and in Dio ('He also repaired the sacred precincts and the public works which had suffered injury and rebuilt such as had already fallen into ruin': 66.10.1a). Inscriptions attest to his restoration, at his own expense, of Rome's streets (*Imp. Caesari Vespasiano Aug., pont. max., tr. p. III, imp. IIX, p.p., cos. III des. IIII, s.c., quod uias urbis neglegentia superior. tempor. corruptas inpensa sua restituit: MW* 412) and aqueducts (*imp. Caesar Vespasianus August., pontif. max., trib. pot. II imp. VI cos. III desig. IIII, p.p. aquas Curtiam et Caeruleam perductas a diuo Claudio et postea intermissas dilapsasque per annos nouem sua impensa urbi restituit: MW* 408 a: see Platner-Ashby, 1929: 413, 417).

In discussing the implications of Vespasian's action in being the first to move the debris in the area of the old temple (*primus admouit ac suo collo quaedam extulit*), both Casson (1978: 43-50) and Brunt (1971: 376-88, 1980: 81-100) attempt to link the restoration of the Capitol with the rebuilding of Rome. There is no support whatever for this in Suetonius (or, for that matter in Dio 66,10.2, quoted below, s.u. *ruderibus purgandis...extulit*) – these are completely separate activities that are credited to Vespasian; for a detailed discussion, see Wardle, 1996: 208 ff. who correctly points out that 'juxtaposition in Suetonius is no guide to position in his sources' (1996: 208). See also Keaveney, 1987: 213-16 and 18 below, s.u. *sineret se plebiculam pascere.*

**ueteribus incendiis:** The fire of June 64 (*Nero* 38.1-3) and the burning of the Capitol in December 69 (*Vit.* 15.3).

**uacuas areas:** The word *area* is defined in the *Digest: locus...sine aedificio in urbe area, rure ager appellatur* (1.16.211).

**ipse restitutionem Capitolii adgressus:** Well before Vespasian reached Rome, the senate had voted (*Hist.* 4.4) for the restoration of the Capitoline temple that had been destroyed by the army of Vitellius in December 69 (*Vit.* 15.3; Dio 65.17.3). Both Suetonius (here) and Dio describe what happened on Vespasian's return: he 'immediately began to construct the temple on the Capitoline. He was himself the first to carry out a load of soil, thereby evidently bidding all the other leading citizens to do likewise, in order that the rest of the populace might have no excuse for shirking this service' (66.10.2).

However, Tacitus' chapter on the restoration of the temple has caused some confusion. According to him, control of the rebuilding was assigned by (the still-absent) Vespasian to L. Julius Vestinus and the initial ceremony (on 21 June 70) was described by Tacitus: *curam restituendi Capitolii in Lucium Vestinum confert, equestris ordinis uirum, sed auctoritate famaque inter proceres. ab eo contracti haruspices monuere ut reliquiae prioris delubri in paludes aueherentur, templum isdem uestigiis sisteretur: nolle deos mutari ueterem formam. XI kalendas Iulias serena luce...uittas, quis ligatus lapis innexique funes erant, contigit [Heluidius Priscus]; simul ceteri magistratus et sacerdotes et senatus et eques et magna pars populi, studio laetitiaque conixi, saxum ingens traxere...* (*Hist.* 4.53). A number of scholars have found this passage far from easy to interpret, e.g. 'The difficulty is that Vespasian did not arrive in Italy and Rome till the late summer of 70, and Tacitus (who was probably an eyewitness) in describing the ceremonies at the dedication of the site and the laying of the foundation-stone of the new temple on June 21 does not mention the emperor as taking part but says that he commissioned Vestinus to supervise the work' (Mooney, 1930: 418).

However, the ceremony reported by Tacitus had nothing whatsoever to do with 'laying the foundation-stone' of the restored temple as is usually assumed. On the contrary, as Townend (1987: 243-8) has shown, what Tacitus was describing was the moving of the cult-stone of the god Terminus whose presence guaranteed the permanence of Roman power; for the details of the festivities at the *Terminalia*, see Scullard, 1981: 79-80. In brief, our sources mention two quite separate activities – the moving of the cult-stone and actual preparations for the rebuilding of the temple.

Vespasian regarded the *restitutio Capitolii* and the worship of Jupiter as vital, not least in providing the new dynasty with some sort of legitimacy. Now whilst the temple of Jupiter on the Capitol was Rome's most significant religious building throughout the Republic, it lost status under the immediate successors of Augustus; and even though Galba, Otho and Vitellius made use of Capitoline Jupiter on their coinage, it was Vespasian who employed every means of demonstrating his connection with Jupiter. The restored temple in particular was intended to show that he now had divine approval of all his actions; on this, see especially Wardle, 1996: 221-2.

In 80, the temple was again destroyed (Dio 66.24.2), but almost immediately partly restored. On the temple itself, see Platner-Ashby, 1929: 5-8, 297-303 and Steinby, 1996: 144-53.

**ruderibus purgandis...extulit:** Suetonius and Dio (66.10.2) both mention preliminaries to the rebuilding, started after Vespasian reached Rome in the early part of October (see 8.1 above, s.u. *in urbem reuersus*).

**aerearum tabularum...restituenda suscepit:** All official arrangements between Rome and foreigners were engraved on bronze tablets and attached to the walls of public buildings and temples, especially those close to the temple of Jupiter. So, in Cicero, *toto Capitolio tabulae figebantur, neque solum singulis uenibant immunitates, sed etiam populis uniuersis; ciuitas non iam singillatim, sed prouinciis totis dabatur...unum egregium de rege Deiotaro, populi Romani amicissimo, decretum in Capitolio fixum (Phil.* 2.36-7). Recorded also were the original notifications of the awards of *ciuitas* made to former soldiers in the form of the so-called military diplomas, e.g. *MW* 397 indicates that a certain *Dule Datui f., natione Bessus,* became a citizen on 7 March 70 and gives the precise location in Rome of the bronze original: *descriptum et recognitum ex tabula ahenea, quae fixa est Romae in Capitolio ad aram gentis Iuliae latere dextro ante signum Liberi patris tabula I, pag. I. loco XXV.*

Bauman (1982: 115-16) raises the interesting question as to whether all the material Suetonius mentions was readily available. If not (as seems likely), then the work would have involved restatement and interpretation that would have resulted in a revision of Rome's international relations – a revision that was inevitable in view of the major changes on the eastern frontier (*Achaiam...in prouinciarum formam redegit*: 8.4).

A similar theme occurs in Tacitus. According to him, before Vespasian reached Rome in 70, the senate had appointed a commission *qui aera legum uetustate delapsa noscerent figerentque (Hist.* 4.40). This could perhaps be another version of what Suetonius says (see Mooney, 1930: 419), but, as Bauman points out (1982: 116 n.165), that solution presents difficulties, i.e. *aera legum* is more general than the items listed by Suetonius, *uestustate delapsa* is vastly different from *quae simul conflagauerant* and Suetonius has no reference to a commission.

**undique inuestigatis exemplaribus:** Domitian acted in similar fashion when restoring the libraries destroyed by fire: *exemplaribus undique petitis (Dom.* 20).

**instrumentum:** It is used here in the sense of 'official record' as in *Calig.* 8.5: *sequenda est...publici instrumenti auctoritas.*

**senatus consulta:** A *senatusconsultum* was, during the Republic, the advice or recommendation of the senate to the magistrates and it was binding (subject to veto). In the empire, it was implemented by a clause in the praetor's edict and, after Hadrian, it usually had the force of law; see *OCD* 1733. The most interesting example of a *SC* is the recently-discovered *SC de Cn. Pisone patre*, published with a detailed commentary by Eck, 1996 (discussed by Meyer, 1998: 315-24 and Potter, 1998: 437-57); note also the *SC Claudianum* and the *SC Macedonianum* in 11 below.

**plebi[s] scita:** A *plebiscitum* was a resolution of the plebeian tribal assembly that, by the *Lex Hortensia* of 287 BC, gained the force of law; see *OCD* 1389.

**priuilegio:** According to the *OLD*, a *priuilegium* was 'a law passed against (in Cicero's time) and in favour of (later) a specific individual or individuals' (1461).

9.1
**noua opera:** Apart from the *opera* he mentions in this section, Suetonius elsewhere notes Vespasian's restoration of the temple of Jupiter (8.5) and of the *scaena* of Marcellus' theatre (19). There was also his extension of the *pomerium* (Platner-Ashby, 1929: 395 and Blake, 1959: 96), his restoration of the temple of Honos and Virtus (*Cornelius Primus et Attius Priscus...Honoris Virtutis aedes Imperatori Vespasiano Augusto restituenti pinxerunt: NH* 35.120 and see Platner-Ashby, 1929: 258-9), the erection of the *Horrea Vespasiani* (Jones, 1992: 85) and of the *sacellum* to Jupiter Conservator (built by Domitian in the seventies). A number of triumphal arches were also erected in his reign ('triumphal arches were voted to them': Dio 65.7.2). Kleiner (1989: 85-91 and 1990: 127-36) discusses three of them.

In addition, there is considerable epigraphic evidence of his building activity in Rome, e.g. *MW* 151 (where Vespasian is described as *conseruator caerimoniarum publicarum et restitutor aedium sacrarum*), *MW* 430 (where he *locum uiniae publicae occupatum a priuatis per collegium pontificum restituit*) and *MW* 431 (which refers to the *collegium subrutor(um)* whose members, according to Mommsen in *CIL* 6.940, had to dig out the ruins of buildings destroyed by fire or from some other cause); see also *MW* 79, 413, 425, 426 and 443 together with the discussion by Castagnoli, 1981: 261-74. For evidence of his building activities in Italy, see *MW* 432 (from Rocca Giovine in Sabini, where Vespasian, as *censor, aedem Victoriae uetustate dilapsam sua impensa restituit*) and *MW* 433 (from Herculaneum, where Vespasian *templum Matris deum terrae motu conlapsum restituit*); see also *MW* 339, 414, 415, 444, 469. For his work in the provinces, see *MW* 418 (from Baetica, where he *uiam Aug. ab Iano ad Oceanum refecit pontes fecit ueteres restituit*) and *MW* 86, 337, 416, 419, 421, 424, 434, 435, 446, 448 and 449. Mitchell discusses inscriptions from Cadyanda (*IGRR* 3.507 = *MW* 437) and Patara in Lycia (*IGRR* 3.659) where Vespasian 'appears to have been diverting funds normally destined for imperial revenues to local building projects' (1987: 347).

**templum Pacis:** It also appears in Aurelius Victor's list: *Romae Capitolium, quod conflagrauisse supra memorauimus, aedes Pacis, Claudii monumenta, amphitheatri tanta uis, multaque alia ac forum coepta seu patrata (De Caes. 9.7).* Work on the temple (later referred to as the *Forum Pacis* or *Vespasiani*) started soon after the triumph of 71 (*BJ* 7.158 and see 8.1 above, s.u. *acto...triumpho*) to celebrate the return of peace and the closing of the gates of the temple of Janus (Orosius 7.9.9) and the building was quickly completed, with the dedication taking place in 75 (Dio 66.15.1; Martial 1.2.5). Statius, however, ascribes this temple's completion to Domitian (*qui...Pacem propria domo reponit: Silvae* 4.3.17), but the topographers tend to reject his evidence, e.g. Platner-Ashby, 1929: 386. Some fifteen to twenty years later, however, it seems that Domitian altered it radically: clearing all traffic from the Argiletum, he meant to join it to the other *fora* by means of the *Forum Transitorium*, thereby greatly enhancing the general overall effect; see Anderson, 1983: 110.

According to the Elder Pliny, it was *inter magnifica et pulcherrima operum quae umquam uidit orbis* (*NH* 36.102) and he adds that *ex omnibus, quae rettuli, clarissima* [works of art] *quaeque in urbe iam sunt dicata a Vespasiano principe in templo Pacis aliisque eius operibus; uiolenta Neronis in urbem conuecta et in sellariis domus aureae disposita* (*NH* 34.84). He mentions its famous statue of Venus − *ignoratur artifex eius quoque Veneris quam Vespasianus imperator in operibus Pacis suae dicauit antiquorum dignam fama* (*NH* 36.27); and, at *NH* 35.74, 109 and 122, he gives examples of the paintings and sculptures that were placed within it. Josephus provides more details: '(The temple) was very speedily completed and in a style surpassing all human conception. For, besides having prodigious resources of wealth on which to draw, Vespasian also embellished it with ancient masterpieces of painting and sculpture; indeed, into that shrine were accumulated and stored all objects for the sight of which men had once wandered over the whole world, eager to see them severally while they lay in various countries. Here, too, he laid up the vessels of gold from the temple of the Jews' (*BJ* 7.158-61). Whilst no inscriptions from the *templum Pacis* itself are known, there are several epigraphic references to the *Pax Vespasiani*, e.g. *Paci aeternae domus imp. Vespasiani Caesaris Aug. liberorumque eius sacrum* (*ILS* 6049 = *MW* 513). See Platner-Ashby, 1929: 386-8; Blake, 1959: 89-90 and Nash I, 1961/2: 439-45.

**foro:** *Forum Romanum*, to the south of the temple. The enclosed space in which the temple stood was later called the *Forum Pacis* or *Forum Vespasiani* and the link between it and the *Forum Augustum* was converted by Domitian into the *Forum Transitorium* (or *Forum Neruae*: see *Dom.* 5). See Anderson, 1984: *passim.*

**Diui Claudi (templum):** This temple was situated on the Caelian, with its colonnade occupying part of the site of Nero's Golden House – *Claudia diffusas ubi porticus explicat umbras,/ultima pars aulae deficientis erat* (Martial, *Spect.* 2.9-10). It had been more or less destroyed by Nero to enable him to build a huge nymphaeum as part of the Golden House. Both Pliny and Suetonius refer to Nero's neglect of the honours due to Claudius: *dicauit caelo...Claudium Nero sed ut irrideret (Pan.* 11.1) and *funeratus est sollemni principum pompa et in numerum deorum relatus; quem honorem a Nerone destitutum abolitumque recepit mox per Vespasianum (Claud.* 45). The epigraphic evidence contradicts part of that statement, for Claudius always appears as *diuus* on Neronian inscriptions (though not on the so-called *Lex de Imperio Vespasiani*); see Charlesworth, 1937: 57-60. Vespasian's action in completing the temple was consistent with his efforts to distance the new dynasty from Nero's policies, as also appears in the final sentence of Plautius Silvanus' sepulchral inscription, consisting of the *uerba ex oratione eius* [i.e. *Vespasiani*] – *Moesiae ita praefuit ut non debuerit in me differri honor triumphalium eius ornamentorum (ILS* 986 = *MW* 261). Moreover, according to Fishwick (1987: 297), he may also, at this time, have completed and dedicated the temple of Divus Claudius in Britain. For the temple itself, see Platner-Ashby, 1929: 120-1; Blake, 1959: 90-1; Richardson, 1992: 87-8; Steinby, 1993: 277-8 together with the illustrations in Barrett, 1996: 148-51.

**in Caelio monte:** Situated south of the Esquiline, it was the most south-easterly of the seven hills of Rome. Its chief buildings, apart from Claudius' temple, were Nero's food-market and the barracks for various military units including the *uigiles,* the *equites singulares* and the *frumentarii.* See Platner-Ashby, 1929: 88-9; Richardson, 1992: 61-3 and Steinby, 1993: 208-11.

**Agrippina:** Claudius' wife: 2.3 above, s.u. *coniuratorum* and *insepulti.*

**a Nerone prope funditus destructum:** Nero needed to make room for his Golden House and for work on the Claudian Aqueduct: so, according to Frontinus, *hi (arcus) directi per Caelium montem iuxta templum diui Claudii terminantur (Aq.*1.20) and *postquam Nero imperator (Aquam) Claudiam...usque ad templum diui Claudii perduxit ut inde distribueretur...(Aq.* 2.76. See Platner-Ashby, 1929: 120.

**amphitheatrum urbe media:** The reference is to the monumental Flavian Amphitheatre (*omnis Caesareo cedit labor Amphitheatro;/unum pro cunctis fama loquetur opus*: Martial, *Spect.* 1.7-8) that was not known as the Colosseum until the middle ages. Built on the site previously occupied by the lake of Nero's Golden House (*hic ubi conspicui uenerabilis Amphitheatri/erigitur moles, stagna Neronis erant*: ibid., 2.5-6), it was begun by Vespasian, enlarged and dedicated by Titus in 80, with games lasting 100 days (*Titus* 7.3; Dio 66.25.1-5 and *BMC* 2.190-1, 270) and completed by Domitian who added the fourth level and was probably responsible for the Amphitheatre's subterranean rooms and equipment (Anderson, 1983: 95). The building held some 45,000 spectators, with standing-room for another 5,000. See Platner-Ashby, 1929: 6-11; Blake, 1959: 91-6; Richardson, 1992: 7-10; Steinby, 1993: 30-5 and Auguet, 1994: 34-42.

**ut destinasse compererat Augustum:** This is the only reference to Augustus' intention to build an amphitheatre in the centre of Rome, but both Suetonius (*Aug.* 29.5) and Dio (51.23.1) do mention a stone amphitheatre built 'in the Campus Martius' by Statilius Taurus in 29 BC, on which see Steinby, 1993: 36-7 and compare *RG* 22.3: *uenationes bestiarum Africanarum meo nomine aut filiorum meorum et nepotum in circo aut in foro aut in amphitheatris populo dedi sexiens et uiciens.*

9.2

**amplissimos ordines:** The senatorial and equestrian orders; sometimes, Suetonius refers to the senatorial order alone as *amplissimus* (e.g. 2.3 above), but Cicero had already used it of both, e.g. he describes Autronius as *inimicus amplissimis ordinibus* (*Pro Sulla* 15).

**exhaustos caede uaria...purgauit suppleuitque recenso...equite:** Aurelius Victor's version is interesting in that he supplies a detail not mentioned by Suetonius: *censu more ueterum exercito senatu motus probrosior quisque, ac lectis undique optimis uiris mille gentes compositae, cum ducentas aegerrime repperisset exstinctis saeuitia tyrannorum plerisque* (*De Caes.* 9.9) – with the additional information (*mille gentes...plerisque*) repeated verbatim by his so-called epitomator (9.11).

**purgauit:** Mommsen (*Str* 3.883-5) discusses the expulsion of senators from the senate both by the emperor and by a vote of the senate itself. In *Dom.* 8.3, Suetonius provides examples of different types of 'removal' by Domitian: (i) *quaestorium uirum, quod gesticulandi saltandique studio teneretur, mouit senatu* and (ii) *quosdam ex utroque ordine lege Scantinia condemnauit.*

**suppleuit:** For an analysis of the composition of Vespasian's senate, see Devreker, 1980a: 257-68 and especially the table on p. 265.

**recenso senatu et equite:** The precedent was established by Augustus whose 'review of the knights' is mentioned by Dio (55.31.2); Gaius and Claudius are similarly attested as having held a *recognitio equitum*: *equites Romanos seuere curioseque nec sine moderatione [Gaius] recognouit* (*Calig.* 16.2) and *recognitione equitum iuuenem probri plenum...sine ignominia [Claudius] dimisit* (*Claud.* 16.1) held periodically by the censors; for further details, see Mooney, 1930: 422.

**summotis indignissimis:** One of these was M. Palfurius Sura (*pulsum olim senatu*: *Dom.* 13.1 – see *PIR²* P 63), who, according to the Scholiast on Juvenal (4.53), *a Vespasiano senatu motus transiuit ad stoicam sectam...[Domitiano] interfecto, senatu accusante damnatus est, cum fuisset inter delatores potentes apud Domitianum...sicut Marius Maximus scribit*; he may be 'Seras', a Domitianic informer executed by Nerva (Dio 68.1.2). Domitian also *quaestorium uirum, quod gesticulandi saltandique studio teneretur, mouit senatu* (*Dom.* 8.3).

**honestissimo:** The word *honestissimus* was regularly applied to one of the wealthy and influential members of the municipal aristocracy; see Devreker, 1980a: 258.

**honestissimo...allecto:** Tacitus also refers to the adlections of this period: *multos praefecturis et procurationibus, plerosque senatorii ordinis honore percoluit, egregios uiros et mox summa adeptos; quibusdam fortuna pro uirtutibus fuit* (*Hist* 2.82). Adlection to the senate could and did occur at times other than during an imperial censorship (see *OCD* 12) and a number of Vespasian's supporters were so honoured during the civil war as a reward for the stance adopted at that time. There were, it seems, two types of *adlectio*, (a) enabling a member of the equestrian order to enter the senate by means of a grant of the *latus clauus* and (b) promoting senators to a higher senatorial rank. Devreker (1980: 70-87) lists twenty-eight in category (a), six in (b) and believes that seven of the twenty-eight (an asterisk appears before their names in the list below) were promoted before 73/74 thanks to their stance in the civil war. Of the twenty-eight in category (a), Devreker names four equestrians who were granted the *latus clauus*, i.e. (?) C. Clodius Nummus, Raecius Gallus, T. Rutilius Varus and C. Settidius Firmus; then sixteen former equestrians who are attested as *adlecti in senatum*, i.e. M. Annius Messalla, C. Caristanius Fronto, *Ti. Julius Celsus Polemaeanus, *(L.) Plotius Grypus, C. Salvius Liberalis Nonius Bassus, the *Ignotus* of *CIL* 2.4130, Annius Verus, L. Antonius Saturninus, L. Baebius Avitus, M. Cornelius Nigrinus

Curiatius Maternus, *C. Fulvius Lupus Servilianus, *C. Antius A. Julius Quad-
ratus, *...tilius Lo[ng ?]us, *Sex. Lucilius Bassus, Q. Aurelius Pactumeius
Clemens, Q. Aurelius Pactumeius Fronto; and finally he suggests that another
eight were probably or possibly adlected to senatorial rank, i.e. L. Javolenus
Priscus, Julius Secundus, M. Sempronius Fuscus, C. Cornelius Gallicanus,
Pomponius, Q. Pomponius Rufus, *L. Pupius Praesens and the *Ignotus* of the
Elder Pliny, *NH* 20.215.

In category (b), i.e. senators promoted to a higher senatorial rank: Devreker
includes L. Antistius Rusticus, L. Flavius Silva Nonius Bassus, C. Julius...Cor-
nutus Tertullus, M. Annius Messalla, C. Caristanius Fronto and C. Salvius
Liberalis Nonius Bassus.

Of the twenty-eight *adlecti*, three were of unknown origin, six were Italians,
nineteen provincials (and thirteen of these came from the western provinces)
whereas the senate as a whole was 63.2% Italian against 33.6% provincial
(Devreker, 1980: 86). However, the presence of six Italians amongst Vespasian's
*adlecti* is consistent with the general picture, i.e. 24.1% of the new senators were
Italian, whilst the fact that nineteen out of the twenty-eight seem to have been
provincials suggests supports Suetonius' *honestissimo quoque Italicorum ac
prouincialium allecto.*

Finally, it is worth noting that adlection to the senate in 73/74 or in the
preceding years did not automatically mean that subsequent favours could be
expected, as the belated consulships of C. Antius A. Julius Quadratus (in 94), Ti.
Julius Celsus Polemaeanus (92) and C. Caristanius Fronto (90) indicate.

A number of senators were also adlected into the patriciate (for a list, see Eck,
1970: 108-9) including Cn. Julius Agricola, M. Ulpius Traianus (father of the
future emperor) and the Aurelii Fulvi (father and grandfather of Antoninus Pius).
The adlections of 73/74 have been discussed by Eck, 1970: 103-5; Chastagnol,
1975: 375-94; Houston, 1977: 35-63; Millar, 1977: 293-6; Devreker, 1980: 70-87
and Talbert, 1984: 133-4.

**Italicorum ac prouincialium:** Similarly, Tacitus refers to *noui homines e
municipiis et coloniis atque etiam prouinciis in senatum crebro adsumpti* (*Ann.*
3.55). We have a fair amount of information about Vespasian's senatorial
appointments, three of the more interesting being the provincials M. Cornelius
Nigrinus Curiatius Maternus (who was to govern three vital consular provinces
in the eighties and nineties, i.e. Moesia, Lower Moesia and Syria), Ti. Julius
Celsus Polemaeanus (who became proconsul of Asia under Trajan) and C. Antius
A. Julius Quadratus (who governed Syria and was proconsul of Asia also under
Trajan). Of the *Italici*, the best known is the conqueror of Masada, L. Flavius
Silva Nonius Bassus from Urbs Salvia in Picenum (on him, see McDermott,

1973: 335-51), who was one of the very few non-Flavians to receive an ordinary consulship in the period 70-81; for his close relative (see Salomies, 1992: 80, 132-3) C. Salvius Liberalis Nonius Bassus, see 13 below, s.u. *Saluium Liberalem*. Vespasian's policy towards the appointment of eastern and other provincial senators is examined by Devreker, 1980a: 257-68 and 1982: 492-516; and the parallel with Augustus on the recruitment of senators from the towns of Italy is discussed by Wallace-Hadrill, 1995: 116-17.

**non tam libertate...quam dignitate differre:** This was the theoretical distinction between the orders, i.e. one of rank rather than privilege. Note that Vespasian's equestrian father married into a senatorial family (1.3 above) and that, when Suetonius describes the families of Titus' wives, the first (Arrecina Tertulla) is *patre equite Romano sed praefecto quondam praetorianarum cohortium* whereas the second (the senatorial Marcia Furnilla) is simply *splendidi generis* (*Titus* 4.2).

**ciuile:** The behaviour to be expected of a citizen; see 12 below, s.u. *ciuilis*.

10
**litium series...tumultuque temporum:** The theme of repairing the losses caused by the civil war is continued. The interruption of jurisdiction in 68/69 had resulted in a vast build-up of cases, and the violation of property rights at that time had exacerbated the situation. Special commissioners were chosen by lot to restore property illegally seized and they were empowered to act *extra ordinem* so as to speed up the process.

**sorte elegit...restituerentur:** Tacitus' version is different; according to him, this took place under the aegis of the senate and before Vespasian returned to Rome: *tum sorte ducti per quos redderentur bello rapta* (*Hist.* 4.40). Those *per quos rapta bello restituerentur* would be *reciperatores* ('regainers' or 'recoverers'; see 3 above, s.u. *reciperatorio iudicio*) who were usually chosen by the praetor by lot and used instead of a single judge in certain cases; see *Dom.* 8.1 and Dio 67.13.1 for some examples.

**iudicia centumuiralia:** In the early Republic, the *centumuiri* were nominated by the praetor, three from each of the thirty-five tribes, i.e. after 241 BC, when the number of tribes was increased to thirty-five. Before that time, the court presumably consisted of one hundred members who were nominated on an unknown basis. During the empire, the panel was increased from 105 to 180 (four courts or *consilia* of forty-five members each) and they dealt with civil cases, problems of status (e.g. *Dom.* 8.1), inheritance, right of way etc. They were controlled by the *X uiri stlitibus iudicandis* and sat in the *Basilica Julia*. This was where the younger Pliny delivered most of his speeches. The procedure in these courts tended to be 'lengthy and leisurely' (Braithwaite, 1927: 53), for they provided an opportunity for the ambitious to display their forensic eloquence; hence the need to expedite the hearing of urgent cases. See Pliny, *Ep.* 1.20 and 6.2; Sherwin-White, 1966: 791 and *OCD* 309-10.

**uix suffectura...aetas:** This was not the only time that the legal system had to deal with a back-log of cases. Martial (7.65) refers to a trial lasting twenty years, Juvenal to *mille ferenda taedia, mille morae* (16.43) and Suetonius lists measures passed by Augustus, Claudius and Galba (*Aug.* 32.2; *Claud.* 23.1 and *Galba* 14.3) to reduce delays in the courts. It was a problem that Justinian too had to face – *properandum nobis uisum est ne lites fiant paene immortales et uitae hominum modum excedant* (*Cod. Iust.* 3.1.13).

**extra ordinem diiudicarent:** The commissioners were given special powers to give preference to the most urgent cases; hence Nero's edict with regard to trials involving *publicani*: *Romae praetor, per prouincias qui pro praetore aut consule essent iura aduersus publicanos extra ordinem redderent* (*Ann.* 13.51). Possibly, they were also given the right to sit on special occasions, such as on days exempt from legal business: at the time of Caelius' trial, a visitor to Rome would have been surprised *quod diebus festis ludisque publicis, omnibus forensibus negotiis intermissis unum hoc iudicium exerceatur* (Cicero, *Cael.* 1.1).

11

**libido atque luxuria...inualuerat:** Vespasian, according to Aurelius Victor (*De Caes.* 9.5) *legibus aequissimus...uitiorum plura aboleuerat*. But Suetonius' account of his legislative programme, compared with that of Domitian's is remarkably thin; see Bauman, 1982: 113-16.

The words *libido...inualuerat* introduce two senatorial decrees proposed (so Suetonius states) by Vespasian and subsequently carried by the senate. They represent most of what he has to say about Vespasian's legislative programme, but even the accuracy of this has been impugned. Both decrees, so it is argued (see Bauman, 1982: 114 for the details), were really the work of Claudius and Suetonius wrongly attributed them to Vespasian. Yet it is hard to believe that Suetonius could have confused the authors of two such different decrees and then list them as Vespasian's sole legislative achievements when other material was available; see Bauman, 1982: 114 and n.160. Again, Suetonius' language (*nullo coercente inualuerat*) implies that [Claudius'] legislation against *libido atque luxuria* had existed but had fallen into disuse in recent years, so that what now happened was a restatement of that legislation.

Thus, whilst the wording of the two Claudian proposals is very close to what Suetonius says here, that is no reason to deny Vespasian's role. Bauman adds that 'there is room for the suggestion that these two decrees were restated by Vespasian at the same time as he revived Claudius' deification after its cancellation by Nero, in which case the flourishing condition of *libido atque luxuria* was due to the laws against them having not so much fallen into disuse as ceased to exist: the *SC Claudianum* concerning *ancilla haberetur* will have recovered its original appellation with the revival of its author's deification' (1982: 114-15).

**auctor senatui fuit decernendi:** Vespasian's attitude towards the senate is outlined by Dio: 'He regularly attended meetings of the senate, whose members he consulted on all matters...Whatever items he was prevented by old age from reading and whatever communications he sent to the senate when unable to be present, he usually caused to be read by his sons, thus showing honour to the House even in this detail' (66.10.5-6); on this, see Talbert, 1984: 179 and 278. But emperors did more than just attend the senate. Augustus had been given 'the privilege of bringing before the senate at each meeting any one matter at whatever time he liked, even if he were not consul at the time' (Dio 53.32.6) and other emperors had the right of making up to five such *relationes* (*Str* 2.898). The *Lex de imperio Vespasiani* confirms Vespasian's rights in this regard: *utique ei senatum habere relationem facere remittere senatus consulta per relationem discessionemque facere liceat*; for the full text, see *MW* 1, Crawford (1996: 549-53) and, for a discussion of its significance, Brunt (1977: 95-116). In addition, an emperor did not have to present his *relatio* in person – it could be in the form of an *epistula* or an *oratio*; and thus it was presumably towards the end of the reign that Titus *orationes [Vespasiani] in senatu recitaret etiam quaestoris uice* (*Titus* 6.1).

**ut...ancilla haberetur:** 'a free woman who cohabited with another's slave would be deemed to be an *ancilla*' (so Bauman, 1982: 114). The *senatus consultum Claudianum*, re-enacted by Vespasian, had been carried by the senate in 52, on the proposal of Claudius. According to Tacitus, *inter quae refert ad patres de poena feminarum quae seruis coniungerentur; statuiturque ut ignaro domino ad id prolapsae in seruitute, sin consensisset pro libertis haberentur* (*Ann.* 12.53). For further discussion, see Mooney, 1930: 425-6.

**neue filiorum familiarum faeneratoribus exigendi crediti ius umquam esset, hoc est ne post patrum quidem mortem:** Loans made to minors would not be repayable even on the father's death. Suetonius' summary resembles closely the wording of the *SC Macedonianum*, named after the usurer involved, a certain Macedo. Compare Suetonius' version and the underlined section of the *senatus consultum*: *uerba senatus consulti Macedoniani haec sunt:* '*cum inter ceteras sceleris causas Macedo, quas illi natura administrabat, etiam aes alienum adhibuisset, et saepe materiam peccandi malis moribus praestaret, qui pecuniam, ne quid amplius diceretur, incertis nominibus crederet: <u>placere ne cui qui filio familias mutuam pecuniam dedisset etiam post mortem parentis eius cuius in potestate fuisset, actio petitioque daretur</u>: ut scirent qui pessimo exemplo faenerarent, nullius posse filii familias bonum nomen exspectata patris morte fieri*' (*Digest, De Senatusconsulto Macedoniano* 14.6). Tacitus complicates matters by referring to a similar Claudian *lex*: *lege lata saeuitiam creditorum coercuit ne in mortem parentum pecunias filiis familiarum faenori darent* (*Ann.* 11.13). For Macedo, see Daube (1947: 261-311, together with the discussion of Talbert, 1984: 443-4) and, for the *SC*, Mooney (1930: 426), May (1936: 230-3) and especially Bauman (1982: 113-16).

## 12

**ciuilis:** *Ciuilitas* was the quality expected of citizens – they should treat each other with respect, insult no one and accept insults from no one. Suetonius used this quality, or the lack of it, in his assessment of most emperors, e.g. of Augustus (*ciuilitatis eius multa et magna documenta sunt*: *Aug.* 51.1), Claudius (*quamquam iactator ciuilitatis...: Claud.* 35.1 – see below, s.u. *consuetudinem scrutandi salutantes...omiserat*) and Domitian (*minime ciuilis animi: Dom.* 12.3). According to Dio, Vespasian behaved 'not as an emperor, but as a private citizen' (66.10.1); in fact, 'he was looked upon as emperor only by reason of his oversight of the public business, whereas in all other respects he was democratic and lived on a footing of equality with his subjects.... He indulged in jests like a man of the people and enjoyed jokes at his own expense' (66.11.1). Eutropius' judgement was similar: *Romae se in imperio moderatissime gessit* (7.19). See the discussion by Wallace-Hadrill, 1982: 32-48 and 1995: 164-6.

**clemens:** But see 15 below, s.u. *inlacrimauit etiam et ingemuit*, for the fate of Julius Sabinus and his family. That Vespasian was highly regarded by Suetonius is very evident and especially so from the fact that only three of his twelve *Caesares* (Julius Caesar, Augustus and Vespasian) are assigned this quality (i.e. *clementiam...admirabilem exhibuit: Iul.* 75.1 and *clementiae...multa et magna documenta sunt*: *Aug.* 51.1) and others are criticised for their lack of it, e.g. *neque in clementiae neque in abstinentiae tenore permansit [Domitianus]* (*Dom.* 10.1); similarly, *Tib.* 53,2, *Nero* 10.1, *Vit.* 14.2 and *Dom.* 11.2.

**mediocritatem pristinam:** *Mediocritas* in this context is defined as 'moderateness of means' (*OLD* 1089). Braithwaite summarises his attitude as 'that of the affable and benevolent autocrat, too good-natured to be haughty, and conscious, moreover, that regal display would contrast ludicrously with his former plebeian position' (1927: 54). Even though, for most of the Julio-Claudian period, the Flavians were a wealthy, well-connected equestrian family, the term *mediocritas* could be applied to them – but only in comparison with the riches and status of certain senatorial families.

**conantis...referre:** This sort of flattery was not without parallels, e.g. the Julians claimed descent from Venus (*Iul.* 6.1), Galba from Jupiter and Pasiphae, wife of Minos (*Galb.* 2) – and Claudius' freedman Pallas was said to be *regibus Arcadiae ortus* (*Ann.* 12.53).

**conditores Reatinos:** Varro discusses the legends on the foundation of Reate (*Ling.* 5.53).

**comitem Herculis:** Hercules passed through Italy on his way back from Spain with the oxen of Geryon but there is no reference anywhere to a companion or to any monument on the Via Salaria.

**Salaria uia:** The 'salt road' ran northeast from Rome (there were salt-pits near Ostia) to Reate in the Sabine country and, later, as far as the Adriatic via Asculum in Picenum and Amiternum. It started at the Colline Gate, formerly called the *Porta Salaria*.

**triumphi die:** The joint triumph with Titus for their victory over the Jews; see 8.1 above, s.u. *acto...triumpho.*

*senex*: He was over 60 (born 9).

**ne tribuniciam quidem potestatem <...>:** Something like *statim nec* needs to be supplied: *STATIM* may have fallen out after *POTE-STATEM* – for other suggestions, see Levick, 1999: 226-27. Suetonius' statement has been described as 'mysterious' and 'doubtful'; see Braithwaite (1927: 54), Mooney (1930: 428) and Buttrey (1980: 13). According to Rolfe in the Loeb edn (305), 'the meaning ...is not clear'.

    Mommsen (*Str* 2.875) and others assume that Suetonius is referring to an unusually lengthy interval between the *Senatus Consultum* (of 22 December 69) that decreed *cuncta principibus solita* (*Hist.* 4.3) to Vespasian and the *comitia tribuniciae potestatis* which passed the law. In theory, the procedure was for *tribunicia potestas* to be promulgated by a decree of the senate, and, following an interval that included three market days (*trinum nundinum*), to be conferred officially by a *rogatio* put before the people in the Comitia. So *tribunicia potestas* was assumed some time after the *dies imperii*, i.e. fifty-three days in the case of Nero (see Bradley, 1978: 65), of Otho forty-five, of Domitian seventeen and of Vitellius twelve. But, with Vespasian, this explanation is far from satisfactory.

Despite the *SC* of 22 December 69, coins and inscriptions date his *trib. pot.* from 1 July 69 – however, the confusion is only apparent. Vespasian's inscriptions of 69 (i.e. those that can definitely be assigned to that year) never list the so-called 'Republican' titles of *TRIB. POT., COS., P.M.* or *P.P.* (and such omissions are unusual, particularly on milestones – see Isaac, 1984: 143) and refer to him simply as *IMP. CAES. VESP. AVG.* However, by 26 Feb. 70, the date of our earliest Vespasianic military diploma (Roxan, 1996: 248-56), the titles *TRIB. POT., COS. II* are also present. As Isaac has noted, 'the milestone of 69 [which omits Vespasian's "Republican" titles] makes it perfectly clear what Suetonius meant and that he was right: Vespasian did not immediately lay claim to titles which were to be endowed by the senate in December (and they) are omitted on the milestone of 69 in recognition of the fact that Vespasian was formally a usurper at the time' (1984: 144 and n.5). It was only later (but before 26 Feb. 70) that he 'back-dated' (Brunt, 1977: 107) it to 1 July 69.

**patris patriae appellationem:** Cicero was so named by Catulus for 'saving the state' at the time of the Catilinarian conspiracy (63 BC) – *Roma patrem patriae Ciceronem libera dixit* (Juv. 8.244), as was Augustus in 2 BC on his sixtieth birthday. His successors (apart from Tiberius who refused to accept the title) did not receive it until some time after their accession – as long as they lived long enough (so not Galba, Otho or Vitellius). The purpose of this (Republican) title is stated by Dio: 'The term "father" perhaps gives them a certain authority over us all, the authority which fathers once had over their children; yet it did not signify this at first, but betokened honour, and served as an admonition both to them that they should love their subjects as they would their children, and to their subjects, that they should revere them as they would their fathers' (53.18.3).

**nisi sero recepit:** According to Buttrey, '*nisi sero* seems exaggerated' (1980: 14). But Vespasian did not assume the title of *PP* until after his return to Rome late in 70 (it does not appear in the new diploma, Vespasian's earliest, of 26 Feb. 70: see above) and, as Isaac notes, 'this may well have seemed surprisingly long to an author who lived through the reign of Domitian' (1984: 144 n.5) and who is describing Vespasian's *ciuilitas*.

**consuetudinem scrutandi salutantes...omiserat:** The use of *scrutatores* to search all callers is attested for various emperors, e.g. Claudius (*salutatoribus scrutatores semper apposuit, et quidem omnibus et acerbissimos: Claud.* 35.1) and Gaius ('Gaius caused all who came near him, men and women alike, to be searched, for fear they might have a dagger, and at banquets he was sure to have some soldiers present. The latter practice, thus established by him, continues to this day; but the indiscriminate searching of everybody came to an end under Vespasian': Dio 60.3.3). Many other kings and tyrants had all visitors searched. Exceptions were rare; according to Plutarch, Dionysius 'gave Plato a special token of his trust, which no one else had, of coming into his presence without being searched' (*Dion.* 19.1). Plutarch also tells the story of Dionysius II, when he was living in Corinth, no longer tyrant of Syracuse – a visitor 'shook out his robe on coming into his presence, as if into the presence of a tyrant, Dionysius turned the jest upon him by bidding him to do so when he went out from his presence, that he might not take anything in the house away with him' (*Timol.* 15.3).

Vespasian's practice is consistent with his reputation for being *ciuilis* (see above) and in complete contrast to that of Claudius who, *quamquam iactator ciuilitatis, neque conuiuia inire ausus est nisi ut speculatores cum lanceis circumstarent militesque uice ministrorum fungerentur (Claud.* 35.1). Not surprisingly, under Claudius, access to the emperor was limited. The Elder Pliny refers to the importance of the *imaginem principis ex auro in anulo* and adds *quae omnia salutaris exortus Vespasiani imperatoris aboleuit aequaliter publicando principem (NH* 33.41).

However, as Domitian said, *condicionem principum miserrimam...quibus de coniuratione comperta non crederetur nisi occisis (Dom.* 21).

## 13

**amicorum libertatem...lenissime tulit:** Other sources agree. Dio refers to Vespasian's tolerant attitude, stating that 'he indulged in jests like a man of the people and enjoyed jokes at his own expense; and whenever any anonymous bulletins, such as are regularly addressed to the emperors, were posted, if they contained scurrilous references to himself, he would simply post a reply in kind, without showing the least resentment' (66.11.1). Tacitus calls him *patientisimus ueri (Dial.* 8.3) and, according to the *Epit. de Caes., ferebat patienter amicorum motus, contumeliis eorum, ut erat facetissimus, iocularibus respondens* (9.3). Suetonius now proceeds to give an example from each of his three categories: *amici* (Mucianus), *causidici* (Liberalis) and *philosophi* (Demetrius).

**causidicorum:** Eutropius states that Vespasian *conuicia a causidicis et philosophis in se dicta leniter tulit* (7.20).

**figuras:** Quintilian examines *figurae* (innuendos or indirect attacks – called *obliqua dicta* in the *Epit. de Caes.* 9.4: *quid mirum in amicis, cum etiam causidicorum obliqua dicta et philosophorum contumaciam contemneret?*) at some length (9.2.65-84), claiming that *quamlibet enim apertum, quod modo et aliter intelligi possit, in illos tyrannos bene dixeris, quia periculum tantum, non etiam offensa uitatur. quod si ambiguitate sententiae possit eludi, nemo non illi furto fauet* (9.2.67) and he also provides an example, i.e. *duxi uxorem, quae patri placuit.* In discussing this *figura*, Bauman links it with the fate of Hermogenes of Tarsus, executed by Domitian *propter quasdam in historia figuras* (*Dom.* 10.1) and offers the attractive suggestion that *patri* is Quintilian's 'discreet emendation of a *fratri* in Hermogenes' history' (1974: 162), the allusion being to Titus' alleged affair with Domitia (Dio 66.26.4). Another *figura* occurs in the *HA*, viz. *damnabantur autem plerique, cur iocati essent, alii, cur tacuissent, alii cur pleraque figurata dixissent, ut 'ecce imperator uere nominis sui, uere Pertinax, uere Seuerus'* (*Seu.* 14.13). See also the discussion by Ahl, 1984: 174-208 and especially 193.

**philosophorum contumaciam:** Vespasian was ultimately forced to exile a number of them; see below, s.u. *Demetrium Cynicum.*

**Licinium Mucianum:** On his early career and his role in the events of 69, see 6.4, s.u. *Licinius Mucianus* and 7.1, s.u. *deposita simultate.* Until Vespasian reached Rome, he was in control and not the least of his services to the new emperor was his elimination of Calpurnius Galerianus (*Hist.* 4.11), of L. Piso (4.48-50) and of Vitellius' brother and son (4.80; Dio 65.22.1): as Levick notes, Vespasian was able to 'keep his hands clean' (1999: 80). In essence, Mucianus was an efficient and successful organiser and this was apparent in the early months of 70. He effectively silenced the ambitious Antonius Primus and began to reduce the excessively large praetorian guard and dealt with the confusion prevalent in the senate; he had to deal with the behaviour of Domitian and with the moves against the alleged Neronian delators, starting with P. Egnatius Celer (*Hist.* 4.39 ff.; Evans, 1979: 198-202). Particularly revealing was the problem posed by Tettius Julianus and Mucianus' quick and diplomatic reaction to it. Praetor in 70, Julianus was demoted but quickly (by 3 January) reinstated. His enemies included the governor of Moesia, Aponius Saturninus whose support Mucianus needed in dealing with Antonius Primus, whereas Julianus had the support of his powerful relative and prominent Flavian freedman Tiberius Julius Aug. lib. This decided the matter, even though Julianus had, at the very least, been guilty of 'extended procrastination' (Evans, 1978: 123) in joining the Flavian cause; see the full discussion in Evans, 1978: 102-28 and Jones, 1984:

97-8. Mucianus' reward was a suffect consulship in 70 and another in 72 – but nothing more. That was not what he had expected; before Vespasian returned to Rome in 70, Mucianus had sent the senators a letter, regarded by them as *erga principem contumeliosum, quod in manu sua fuisse imperium donatumque Vespasiano iactabat* (*Hist.* 4.4). In the seventies, he was pushed aside and seems to have devoted himself to writing, no doubt out of bitterness and frustration.

His literary output was certainly considerable. He collated and edited versions of ancient speeches and documents, including those of Pompey, Crassus and other prominent Republican politicians; his *libri actorum* comprised eleven books and his *epistulae* three (*Dial.* 37). The Elder Pliny cited him by name on thirty-two occasions, using him for information about Asia (*NH* 7.36), Lycia (12.9), Syria (5.128), the Greek islands (2.231) and as an eye-witness for a number of exotic animals (7.36). He had died (*NH* 32.62) by the time Pliny composed the *Naturalis Historia*, but if, as seems reasonable, he spent the years after his third consulship (72) in virtual retirement, these last few years of his life may well have been very productive.

There is little – if any – ancient evidence for the alleged rivalry between him and Titus; see Crook, 1951: 162-75 and the response of Rogers, 1980: 86-95 and Jones, 1984: 87-100. The role assigned to him in the early seventies was consistent with his abilities and with his activities in the previous decade; the part he had played in securing Vespasian's accession was appropriately rewarded. He may well have been resentful and bitter yet he would not have been so foolish as to intrigue against Titus. Had he done so, he would not have been the butt of one of Vespasian's jokes – he would have shared the fate of Helvidius Priscus.

**notae impudicitiae:** i.e. his homosexuality, hinted at in Tacitus' famous character sketch – *luxuria industria, comitate adrogantia, malis bonisque artibus mixtus: nimiae uoluptates, cum uacaret; quotiens expedierat, magnae uirtutes: palam laudares, secreta male audiebant* (*Hist.* 1.10). The accusation, presumably, is that he was a passive homosexual. Recently, it has been argued that, according to the *lex Scantinia*, 'a Roman male, if he engaged in homosexual relations, so long as he did not violate a *puer*, incurred punishment only if he took a passive role' (Cantarella, 1994: 113). That it was the passive partner in a homosexual relationship who was liable to criticism is apparent from Cicero's attack on Antony for prostituting himself: *primo uulgare scortum, certa flagitii merces, nec ea parua: sed cito Curio interuenit, qui te (Antonium) a meretricio quaestu abduxit et, tamquam stolam dedisset, in matrimonio stabili et certo collocauit* (*Phil.* 2.44). Again, there was the defence offered by Suillius Caesoninus. During the trials that followed the execution of Messalina in 48, *Suillio Caesonino et Plautio Laterano mors remittitur, huic ob patrui egregium meritum: Caesoninus uitiis* *protectus est tamquam in illo foedissimo coetu passus muliebria* (*Ann.* 11.36). No doubt this is what Vespasian meant with the *clausula, ego tamen uir sum.*

**uir sum:** See previous item and compare the version in the *Epit. de Caes.*: *namque Licinium Mucianum, quo adiutore ad imperium peruenerat, fiducia meritorum insolentem lepide flectebat, adhibito aliquo utrique familiari, id unum dicens*: **nosti me uirum esse** (9.3).

**Saluium Liberalem:** An equestrian from Urbs Salvia in Picenum, Salvius Liberalis (C. Salvius Liberalis Nonius Bassus: *PIR*[1] S 105, McDermott, 1973: 335-51; Mcdermott-Orentzel, 1979: 45-58 and A.R. Birley, 1981: 211-2, 404-7; for his career inscription, see *ILS* 1011 = *MW* 311) was adlected *inter tribunicios* by Vespasian and Titus in 73/4 and immediately promoted to praetorian rank (see 9.2 above, s.u. *honestissimo...allecto*); appointed legate of the V Macedonica in Moesia, he then became *legatus iuridicus* in Britain. On Domitian's accession, he was in Rome (*CIL* 6.2060), serving as a one of the Arval Brothers, and was subsequently appointed to the proconsulship of Macedonia, probably for 83/4 (Eck, 1982: 307-8) and to a suffect consulship. Banished ca 87 (so it seems), he returned on Domitian's death and *sorte [proconsul fac]tus prouinciae Asiae se excusauit* (*MW* 311). He was known for his outspokenness and as a *uehemens et disertus* (*Ep.* 3.9.36) advocate for senators accused of extortion during their terms as proconsul (i.e. Marius Priscus in Africa and Caecilius Classicus in Baetica). Elsewhere, Pliny describes him as *uir subtilis dispositus acer disertus* (*Ep.* 2.11.17). On the possibility of determining his precise relationship with the conqueror of Masada (L. Flavius Silva Nonius Bassus), see Salomies, 1992: 80, 132-3.

**quid...habet:** Liberalis' *figura* implies that Vespasian, noted for his *auaritia*, might have had Hipparchus condemned so that his 100 million (i.e. *milies centena milia sestertium*) sesterces would revert to the emperor.

**Hipparchus:** He was presumably the Hipparchus (*PIR*[2] C 889, i.e. Ti. Claudius Hipparchus) whose property was confiscated after he had been condemned for treason (Philostratus, *V. Soph.* 2.1.2). On his son Ti. Claudius Atticus Herodes (*cos.* ca 132) and grandson (*cos. ord.* 143), see Birley, 1998: 63.

**Demetrium Cynicum:** This famous Cynic managed to earn Seneca's praise (*uirum exactae...sapientiae firmaeque in iis quae proposuit constantiae, eloquentiae uero eius quae res fortissimas deceat...huic non dubito quin prouidentia et talem uitam et talem dicendi facultatem dederit ne aut exemplum saeculo nostro aut conuicium deesset*: *Ben.* 7.8.2-3), to reject a benefaction from Gaius (ibid. 11), to attack Nero ('You threatened me with death; nature threatens you': Epictetus, *Dissert.* 1.25, 22), in 66 to discuss the *natura animi et dissociatio spiritus* (*Ann.* 16.34) with Thrasea Paetus during his last hours and, in 70, to defend the *delator* Egnatius Celer when attacked by Musonius Rufus (*Hist.* 4.40 – Tacitus was not impressed, *quod [Demetrius] manifestum reum ambitiosius quam honestius defendisset*). But, according to Dio, it was Mucianus who had him and other philosophers expelled from Rome: 'Inasmuch as many others, too, including Demetrius the Cynic, actuated by the Stoic principles, were taking advantage of the name of philosophy to teach publicly many doctrines inappropriate to the times, and in this way were subtly corrupting some of their hearers, Mucianus, prompted rather by anger than by any passion for philosophy, inveighed at length against them and persuaded Vespasian to expel all such persons from the city... And Vespasian immediately expelled from Rome all the philosophers except Musonius; Demetrius and Hostilianus he even deported to the islands' (66.13.1). Philostratus also mentions Demetrius, claiming that he was exiled by Tigellinus (*VA* 4.42), taught Titus (at Antioch) how to rule (*VA* 6.31) and lived at Puteoli during Domitian's reign (*VA* 7.10).

**oblatrantem:** Dio's version is a little different: 'Demetrius and Hostilianus he even deported to the islands...Demetrius would not yield even then (i.e. even though 'Hostilianus immediately withdrew'), and Vespasian commanded that this message should be given to him "You are doing everything to force me to kill you, but I do not slay a barking dog"' (66.13.2-3).

**satis...appellare:** Canis was often used of Cynic philosophers. So Martial has *esse putas Cynicum deceptus imagine ficta./non est hic Cynicus, Cosme: quid ergo? canis* (4.53.7-8). Mooney cites Ausinius' version of the inscription on Diogenes' tomb (bearing the emblem of a dog): *Dic, canis, hic cuius tumulus? Canis. At canis hic quis?/Diogenes. Obiit? Non obiit, sed abit.*

14

**offensarum...minime memor:** Eutropius states that Vespasian *offensarum et inimicitiarum immemor fuit* (7.20) and, in the *Epit. de Caes.*, *huius inter cetera bona illud singulare fuit inimicitias obliuisci* (9.2). Vespasian was hardly *inimicitiarum immemor* when he authorised the execution of Julius Sabinus and his family for Sabinus' actions some nine years previously; see 15 below, s.u. *inlacrimauit...ingemuit.*

**Vitelli...splendidisime maritauit:** The only daughter of Vitellius mentioned in our sources is that by his second wife Galeria Fundana (*Vitell.* 6; *PIR*² G 33;

Raepsaet-Charlier, 1987: 344-6). She had been betrothed (rather than married; see Raepsaet-Charlier, 1987: 640) to D. Valerius Asiaticus, governor of Gallia Belgica in 69 and partisan of Vitellius (*accessere partibus [Vitellii] Valerius Asiaticus, Belgicae prouinciae legatus*: *Hist.* 1.59).

However, he made peace with the new régime and was designated consul for 70 but died before taking up office. Vespasian then arranged for her to marry another senator – that is how *splendidissime* is interpreted in the *Epit. de Caes.* 9.2 (*splendidissimo coniungeret uiro*). Although Mucianus executed Vitellius' young son Germanicus (*Hist.* 4.80), Vespasian treated other Vitellian relatives very generously, perhaps in view of that family's assistance some decades previously (see 4.1 above, s.u. *Auli Plauti*) – L. Tampius Flavianus (Tacitus mentions his *adfinitas cum Vitellio* in *Hist.* 3.4) received a second consulship in 74 and C. Calpetanus Rantius Quirinalis Valerius Festus (for his *adfinitas Vitellii*, see *Hist.* 4.49) was awarded a suffect consulship as early as 71. Note, too, that Silius Italicus' *Vitellii amicitia* (Pliny, Ep. 3.7.3) did not prevent him from holding the proconsulship of Asia in 77/78 (Eck, 1982: 299).

**interdicta aula:** See the discussion by Gascou, 1984: 323-6 and, for the details of Vespasian's lapse during Nero's *peregrinatio Achaica*, see 4.4 above and Wallace-Hadrill, 1996: 283-4.

**quidam:** Dio gives his name as Phoebus (*PIR*[2] P 391 [Ti. Claudius?]): 'During Nero's reign, Vespasian while in the theatre in Greece had frowned when he saw the emperor behaving himself in unseeming fashion, whereupon Phoebus had angrily bidden him go away. And when Vespasian asked "Go where?" Phoebus had replied, "To the Deuce". So when Phoebus now apologised for this remark, Vespasian did him no harm, and gave him no answer other than this same retort: "To the deuce with you"' (66.11.2). Dio assigns the anecdote to the *peregrinatio Achaica*, yet, in Suetonius' account of Vespasian's lapse during that tour (*grauissimam contraxit offensam*: 4.4 above), there is not a hint of Phoebus' role; once again, the accuracy of 4.4 is open to question.

**ex officio admissionis:** Entry to an emperor's *salutationes* was controlled by a special department, the *officium admissionis*. The imperial freedman in charge, the *ab officiis et admissione* admitted callers according to their rank: *prima admissio, secunda admissio*: Seneca refers to *amici...qui in primas et secundas admissiones digerentur* (*Ben.* 6.33.4) and, in the *HA*, Severus Alexander was gracious to *amicos non solum primi aut secundi loci sed etiam inferiores* (*Alex. Seu.* 20.1), even though Trajan is supposed to have abolished the *contumeliarum gradus* (*Pan.* 47.5).

*abire Morbouiam*: The word is not found elsewhere but is presumably formed from *morbus* and *uia*. See *OLD* 1133.

**ut suspicione aliqua uel metu ad perniciem cuiusquam compelleretur tantum afuit:** Suetonius has conveniently not cited the execution of Julius Sabinus and his family; see 15 below, s.u. *inlacrimauit...ingemuit*.

**Mettium Pompusianum:** Apart from a consulship during the seventies, nothing is known of Mettius' career (*PIR²* M 570: despite Mooney [1930: 435] and Braithwaite [1927: 57], he is not to be identified with L. Pompusius Mettius [...]nus, *praefectus aerarii Saturni* [*PIR²* P 783]). Dio provides further information: 'Among the many who perished at this time [i.e. under Domitian] was Mettius Pompusianus, whom Vespasian had failed to harm after learning from some report that he would one day be sovereign, but on the contrary had shown him honour, declaring: "He will surely remember me and will surely honour me in return." But Domitian first exiled him to Corsica and now put him to death' (67.12.2-4). Suetonius provides the details: *[interemit Domitianus] Mettium Pompusianum, quod habere imperatoriam genesim uulgo ferebatur et quod depictum orbem terrae in membrana[s] contionesque regum ac ducum ex Tito Liuio circumferret quodque seruis nomina Magonis et Hannibalis indidisset* (*Dom.* 10.3). See Arnaud, 1983: 677-99 and Gascou, 1984: 326-8.

It would seem that he was one of the Mettii from Arles who felt the full force of imperial disfavour during Domitian's reign. Three generations of the family are known (*PIR²* M 566-71). M. Mettius Modestus (*PIR²* M 566), equestrian procurator of Syria under Claudius, seems to have left two sons, viz. Mettius Modestus (M 565 and ?567: suffect consul in 82) and M. Mettius Rufus (M 572: prefect of Egypt, attested there in September 89 and in 91/92). Furthermore, the prefect's two sons held senatorial offices after 96 with the return from exile of their father and uncle. During the nineties, the Mettii must have fallen into disfavour – the consular Modestus was exiled (*Ep.* 1.5.5, 13) and, in a number of papyri, the prefect's name was erased. Perhaps he and his brother had come to grief through involvement in the fall of Mettius Pompusianus.

**genesim...imperatoriam:** The astrologer had predicted that Mettius would one day be emperor. During the early empire, astrology was widely practised and its predictions were often accepted as accurate and scientific – so eminent senators consulting an astrologer for an emperor's *genesis* were assumed by emperors such as Domitian to have been planning to murder him. By Ulpian's time, consulting an astrologer even about an emperor's health was punishable by death (*De Officio Proconsulis* 7; Liebeschuetz, 1979: 124 n.8). But Vespasian preferred to accept the prediction that his sons would succeed him – see 25 below.

**spondens:** The same anecdote occurs in the *Epit. de Caes.* 9.14 and in Dio (67.12.3). The irony of Vespasian's reply – for he 'knew' that Mettius' horoscope had not been cast correctly (25 below) – is stressed by the former, with *alludens (tali) cauillo* being substituted for Suetonius' *spondens: monentibus amicis ut caueret a Mettio Pompusiano, de quo sermo percrebuerat regnaturum fore, consulem fecit, alludens tali cauillo: 'quandoque memor erit tanti beneficii'.*

**beneficii:** The consulship, seen as the first step in Mettius' rise to supreme power.

## 15

**non temere quis punitus insons:** For Vespasian's leniency, see Aurelius Victor, *De Caes.* 9.2 (*namque primum satellites tyrannidis, nisi qui forte atrocius longe processerant, flectere potius maluit quam excruciatos delere*) and Eutropius 7.19.2 (*placidissimae lenitatis, ut qui maiestatis quoque contra se reos non facile puniret ultra exilii poenam*).

**absente eo:** For the executions carried out by Mucianus before Vespasian's arrival in 70, see 13, s.u. *Licinium Mucianum.*

**decepto:** The reference may well be to Titus' activities as praetorian prefect (*praefecturam praetori suscepit...egitque aliquanto inciuilius et uiolentius, siquidem suspectissimum quemque sibi summissis qui per theatra et castra quasi consensu ad poenam deposcerent, haud cunctanter oppressit: Titus* 6.1), activities that Vespasian chose – officially – to ignore. No wonder Titus was regarded as an *alius Nero* (*Titus* 7.1; similarly 6.2) whilst Vespasian was portrayed as publicly lamenting even *iusta supplicia* (*inlacrimauit etiam et ingemuit*; see below).

**Heluidio Prisco...altercationibus insolentissimis:** Not long after Nero's accession, Gaius Helvidius Priscus (*PIR²* H 59) married Fannia, the daughter of Thrasea Paetus. In his *encomium* of Helvidius (*Hist.* 4.5), Tacitus aptly describes him as *recti peruicax*. Suetonius is less enthusiastic and Dio positively hostile: Helvidius, he claims, attacked *basileia*, praised *demokratia* and incited the mob to revolution (66.12.2), charges that must be treated with caution, for Dio is merely repeating the standard attacks on philosophy. On his father-in-law's suicide in 66, Helvidius suffered *relegatio* (*Ann.* 16.33), was recalled by Galba (*Hist.* 4.6) and became praetor in 70.

Determined 'to find traces of the autocrat in what Vespasian did, he was disappointed when there was none to find' (Braithwaite, 1927: 58; see also Epictetus,

*Dissert.* 1.19-21, cited below s.u. *altercationibus*) and treated the emperor with disdain, addressing him as 'Vespasian' and even reducing him to tears (Dio 66.12.1). In Dio's account, '(Helvidius Priscus) would not cease reviling Vespasian. Therefore the tribunes once arrested him and gave him in charge of their assistants, a procedure at which Vespasian was overcome by emotion and went out of the chamber in tears, saying merely: "My successor shall be my son or no one at all"' (66.12.1). So, if we believe Dio's version of the incident (compare Suetonius' account in 25 below, s.u. *aut filios...aut neminem*), Helvidius could well have voiced his opposition to Vespasian's dynastic policy (accepted by Birley, 1978: 143 ['no doubt'] but rejected by Pigon, 1992: 240 ['impossible to prove']); on the other hand, his objection might have been not to the principle of dynastic succession but to the character of the successor, i.e. he had attacked the promotion of someone with Titus' reputation, the *alius Nero* of *Titus* 7.

What brought about his downfall was, in all probability, his persistence in asserting the senate's traditional rights (what Dio called *demokratia* – see Brunt, 1975: 29 n.38). He was *recti peruicax*, sorely tried the emperor's patience ('Helvidius...would not let him alone in private or in public': Dio 66.12.2) and was again exiled. Subsequently, Vespasian had him executed. Birley has pointed out that, in the exchange between Helvidius and Vespasian reported by Epictetus (*Diss.* 1.2.19-21, cited below, s.u. *altercationibus*), the implication is that the emperor could well deprive Helvidius of his senatorial rank (1978: 152), which gives force to Syme's suggestion that he was executed in 74 (1958: 212). His career is discussed by Sherwin-White (1966: 424-5), Gascou (1984: 328-32), Chilver/Townend (1985) 6-8, Malitz (1985: 231-46), Syme (*RP* 7.574-7), Pigon (1992: 235-46) and Levick (1999: 87-9).

**priuato nomine:** i.e. as '*Vespasiane*', omitting all the usual titles. Compare Seneca, *De Const.* 18.4 – *Gaius Caligula iratus fuit Herennio Macro, quod illum Gaium salutauerat, nec impune cessit primipilari quod Caligulam dixerat*. Pigon argues that the picture of Helvidius presented by Suetonius is impaired by his 'highly favourable' attitude towards Vespasian (1992: 243).

**in praetura:** As praetor in 70, Helvidius had officiated at the ceremony held at the Capitoline temple on 21 June 70 to celebrate the moving of the cult-stone of the god Terminus; see *Hist.* 4.3 (cited in 8.5 above, s.u. *ipse restitutionem Capitolii adgressus*), Townend (1987: 243-8) and Wardle (1996: 221-2). During his praetorship, Helvidius opposed all measures that in any way involved the emperor, e.g. the selection by lot of an embassy to congratulate Vespasian (he wanted it chosen by the magistrates under oath), the curtailment of public expenditure by the emperor (he wanted it left to the senate etc. (*Hist.* 4.6-9 and *passim*).

**edictis:** The reference is, presumably, to the edict's preamble where the emperor's name and titles should appear or just possibly to the *subscriptio* which should contain an expression of goodwill along the lines of Pliny's first letter to Trajan: *fortem te et hilarem, Imperator optime, et priuatim et publice opto* (*Ep.* 10.1).

**altercationibus:** An exchange between opposing lawyers; Epictetus provides an example of such an 'exchange': 'When Vespasian sent a message to him (Helvidius) not to come into the senate, he replied, "It is in your power not to let me be a senator, but, as long as I am one, I must come to the meetings". "All right" replied Vespasian, "but when you come, keep quiet". "Don't ask me my opinion and I'll keep quiet". "But I must ask your opinion". "And I must say what appears just". "But, if you speak, I'll put you to death". "Did I ever say to you that I was immortal? You do yours, I'll do mine. It's yours to kill, mine to die without trembling. It's yours to send into exile, mine to leave without grieving"' (*Dissert.* 1.19-21).

**in ordinem redactus:** This military expression could be applied to a magistrate who had been treated as though he were a private citizen, e.g. Livy 3.35.6; Pliny, *Ep* 1.23.1; and *Claud.* 38.1: of the emperor himself.

**relegatum:** This was his second banishment, the first occurring in 66 (see above). Pliny describes them both as *exsilium* (*bis maritum secuta [Fannia] in exsilium est, tertio ipsa propter maritum relegata*: *Ep.* 7.19.4) but, despite the reference to *relegata* for what happened to Fannia in Domitian's reign, he must have been using *exsilium* loosely, for what he suffered under Nero was certainly *relegatio* to Apollonia in Macedonia. *Relegatio*, the milder penalty, involved residence for a specified time (or indefinitely) outside (or within) a specified place or region, but did not necessarily include the loss of all civil and personal rights: *Digest* 48.19.4.

**neque caede...laetatus:** The *neque* is difficult; it ought to be *non*. Mooney compares *Tib.* 62.1, where Suetonius has *neque tormentis neque supplicio cuiusquam pepercit* and, arguing that this might have been another instance of Suetonius' coupling synonymous words, suggests the reading <que nece> neque caede cuiusquam (1930: 438).

**inlacrimauit etiam et ingemuit:** Vespasian's deliberate ploy, a public display of emotion, is not particularly convincing – and it seems to have been a family trait; compare *Titus* 9.3 (*lacrimis orans*) and 10.1 (*ubertim fleuerat*). But Suetonius' comment is at least consistent with his other efforts, again not always

90

convincing, to portray Vespasian in the best possible light. So his readiness here to present the 'lenient' Vespasian has led him to be selective in his choice of *exempla* and to avoid reference to any damaging evidence such as the fate of Julius Sabinus who 'had once styled himself Caesar and, after taking up arms, had been defeated and...brought to Rome. With him perished also his wife Peponila... She threw her children at Vespasian's feet and delivered a most pitiful plea in their behalf: "These little ones, Caesar, I bore and reared...that we might be a greater number to supplicate you." Yet, though she caused both him and the rest to weep, no mercy was shown to the family' (Dio 66.16.1).

## 16.1

**sola est, in qua merito culpetur, pecuniae cupiditas:** References to Vespasian's *auaritia* appear in a number of sources, with the later writers Aurelius Victor, Eutropius and Ausonius being less disapproving than Suetonius and Tacitus: compare Suetonius' *merito culpetur* with Aurelius Victor's reference to those accusing Vespasian of *auaritia* (*uti quidam praue putant*) and his assessment of Vespasian's financial practices (*prudentiam magis quam auaritiam*). Apart from Tacitus' famous *prorsus, si auaritia abesset, antiquis ducibus par* (*Hist.* 2.5), we have Pliny's *numquam principibus defuerunt, qui fronte tristi et graui supercilio utilitatibus fisci contumaciter adessent. et erant principes ipsi sua sponte auidi et rapaces et qui magistris non egerent* (*Pan.* 41.3), which seems to classify Vespasian as *auidus et rapax*, if only because the other possible candidate, Domitian, had already been mentioned, surely to be included in the preceding section amongst those who *cum omnia raperent et rapta retinerent* (*Pan.* 41.2).

On the other hand, there is Aurelius Victor's judgement: *infirmus tamen, uti quidam praue putant, aduersum pecuniam, cum satis constet aerarii inopia ac labe urbium nouas eum neque aliquamdiu postea habitas uectigalium pensiones exquisiuisse* (*De Caes.* 9.6); and he adds that Vespasian's public works *tot tantaque breui confecta...prudentiam magis quam auaritiam probauere* (9.9). Eutropius, too, is less censorious than earlier writers: *pecuniae tantum auidior fuit ita tamen ut eam nulli iniuste auferret; quam cum omni diligentiae prouisione colligeret, tamen studiosissime largiebatur, praecipue indigentibus; nec facile ante eum cuiusquam principis uel maior est libertas comperta uel iustior* (7.19.2). Ausonius is also more generous in his assessment: *quaerendi adtentus, moderato commodus usu,/auget nec reprimit Vespasianus opes: De XII Caes., Tetrasticha* 41-2).

Again, Dio suggests that Mucianus set the pattern for Vespasian: 'Now Mucianus was gathering countless sums into the public treasury with the greatest eagerness from every possible quarter, thereby relieving Vespasian of the censure which such a proceeding entailed. He was forever declaring that money was the sinews of sovereignty' (66.2.5); and he provides *exempla* of Vespasian's generosity at times when there was minimal political advantage: 'The property of his opponents who had fallen in the various conflicts he left to their children or to other kinsmen of theirs; furthermore, he destroyed the notes that were long overdue belonging to the public treasury' (66.10.2a). Similarly, at 17 below, Suetonius lists his grants to those who could not afford the senatorial census or to cities suffering from fires and earthquakes.

However, to accuse Vespasian of *pecuniae cupiditas* is to miss the central point. He was far more interested in financial matters – and far more capable and expert – than were his Julio-Claudian predecessors. Unlike them, he had inherited an interest in finance; his grandfather was a *coactor* and his father a wealthy banker (see above 1.2-1.3). So, for example, he reduced the size of provincial embassies (for the financial implications, i.e. savings, see 24 below, s.u. *legationes*); when (in 77) the people of Sabora were having difficulties in collecting local taxes, Vespasian would not allow them to raise new ones unless they had the permission of the proconsul (*MW* 461). And, let it be admitted, even when Vespasian met Berenice, what impressed him was not her obvious physical attractions but rather her money: *nec minore animo regina Berenice partis iuuabat, florens aetate formaque et seni quoque Vespasiano magnificentia munerum grata* (*Hist*. 2.81).

One example of his efficient management of the economy (no doubt translated as *pecuniae cupiditas* by unkind observers) appears in his policy towards the *subseciua*. When a colony was being founded, the *agrimensores* divided the territory into rectangular areas (*centuriae*) and any irregular sections left over were known as *subseciua*. They were still technically *ager publicus*, even though occupied by owners of the nearby plots. Domitian's policy was to confirm such squatters in their occupancy, as was recorded in an *epistula* of July 82 (*MW* 462), by Hyginus (*per totam Italiam subseciua possidentibus donauit, edictoque hoc notum uniuersis fecit: De Generibus Controuersiarum* 133) and by Frontinus (*uno edicto totius Italiae metum liberauit: Corpus Agrimensorum Romanorum* 1.1 = Thulin, 1913: 54). Whereas this was in line with a provision of the Twelve Tables (6.3) by which uninterrupted possession of land for two years conferred ownership of it, Vespasian was less generous – according to Frontinus (as reported by Agennius Urbicus), Vespasian collected *non enim exiguum pecuniae fisco...uenditis subseciuis* (*Corpus Agrimensorum Romanorum* 1.1 = Thulin, 1913: 41); for a translation of the entire passage from the *Corpus*, see Millar (1977: 444). In Arausio (Orange), for instance, he had new maps drawn up with *centuriae* and *subseciua* clearly indicated, followed by the sale of the latter and the enrichment of the imperial treasury; on all this, see Dilke (1971: 40-1). The relevant text of one of Vespasian's decisions in Arausio (*MW* 447 [a], [b] and [c]: illustrated by Levick, 1999: Plates xii and xiii) has been restored (with slight differences from

*MW*) and translated by Dilke as follows: *Imperator Caesar Vespasianus Augustus, pontifex maximus, tribunicia potestate VIII, imperator XVIII, pater patriae, consul VIII, censor, ad restituenda publica quae diuus Augustus militibus legionis II Gallicae dederat, possessa a priuatis per aliquod annos, formam proponi iussit, adnotato in singulas centurias annuo uectigali, agente curam...Ummidio Basso proconsule prouinciae Narbonensis*, i.e. 'The emperor Vespasian, in the eighth year of his tribunician power (i.e. 77), so as to restore the state lands which the emperor Augustus had given to the soldiers of the second legion Gallica, but which for some years had been occupied by private individuals, ordered a survey map to be set up, with a record on each *centuria* of the annual rental...Ummidius Bassus, proconsul of the province of Gallia Narbonensis' (1971: 160, 168).

In brief, it is difficult to go beyond Aurelius Victor's assessment of Vespasian's financial policy as indicating *prudentiam magis quam auaritiam* (*De Caes.* 9.9). See also the discussion of his *auaritia* by Homo (1940: 453-65) and Wallace-Hadrill (1995: 14).

**non contentus...uectigalia reuocasse:** In Alexandria, according to Dio, Vespasian 'renewed many taxes that had fallen into disuse, increased many that were customary and introduced still other new ones' (66.8.3) and Dio adds that he also 'adopted this same course later in the rest of the subject territory, in Italy, and in Rome itself (66.8.4). There were various types of *uectigalia*: the *portoria* (see 1.2 above, s.u. *publicum...egit*), the *uicesima libertatis* (5% tax on the value of manumitted slaves), the *centesima rerum uenalium* (1% on auction sales), the *uicesima hereditatum* (5% on legacies to those not close relatives), the *quinta et uicesima uenalium mancipiorum* (4% on the sale of slaves to provide pay for the *uigiles*), rents from imperial properties and also local taxes on property.

**omissa sub Galba uectigalia:** Despite Galba's reputation for meanness (*praecesserat de eo fama...auaritiae*: *Galba* 12.1), we have two statements by Tacitus to the effect that he granted some reduction in tribute to Spain and Gaul, provinces that had supported his bid for the throne: *Galliae...obligatae recenti dono Romanae ciuitatis et in posterum tributi leuamento* (*Hist.* 1.8) and *remissam...a Galba quartem tributorum partem* (*Hist.* 1.51). Numismatic evidence points to the *quadragesima Galliarum* (see 1.2, s.u. *publicum quadragesimae* in Asia egit and De Laet, 1940: 122, 170-3), the two-and-a-half per cent customs duty levied on the frontier between Gaul and Spain. The coin in question, an As of 68-9 from Spain, bears the legend *[SER.] GALBA IMP. CAESAR AVG. P.M. [TR.P.]* on the Obverse and, on the Reverse, *QVADRAG[ENS.] REMISSAE] S.C.* (*BMC* 1 p. 345, no. 205 = *MW* 29). No doubt this was one of the 'many taxes renewed' (Dio 66.8.3) by Vespasian. On the other hand, we know that, in at least one instance, he allowed a reduction approved by previous emperors to stand: in a letter to the Vanacini (north Corsica), he stated that *beneficia tributa uobis ab diuo Augusto post septimum consulatum, quae in tempora Galbae retinuistis, confirmo* (*MW* 460: see the discussion by Millar, 1977: 435-6).

**noua et grauia addidisse:** Dio states that the Alexandrians soon came to detest Vespasian, for, 'instead of securing anything, they had additional contributions levied upon them. In the first place, he collected large sums from them in various ways, overlooking no source, however trivial or however reprehensible it might be, but drawing upon every source, sacred and profane alike, from which money could be secured. He also renewed many taxes that had fallen into disuse, increased many that were customary and introduced new ones (66.8.3); and, later, 'adopted the same course' throughout Italy and the provinces (66.8.4).

Neither Suetonius nor Dio, though, refer to the fact that these *uectigalia noua* were imposed for a limited time only – information reported by Aurelius Victor alone: *cum satis constet aerarii inopia ac labe urbium nouas eum neque aliquamdiu postea habitas uestigalium pensiones exquisiuisse* (*De Caes.* 9.6).

Little detail about the 'new' taxes survives. Suetonius mentions one, the *uectigal urinae* (23.3 below), presumably one of those categorised as 'trivial or reprehensible' by Dio. We know most about another, the *fiscus Iudaicus*. Traditionally, all free male Jews between the ages of twenty and fifty, wherever they lived, paid an annual contribution of half a shekel (two *denarii*) for the upkeep of the temple in Jerusalem, the *aurum Iudaicum* as Cicero called it (*Pro Flacco* 28). Vespasian, however, converted it into an annual tax of the same amount for the maintenance of the Capitoline temple (*BJ* 7.218; Dio 66.7.2); and he went further, applying the tax to women, slaves and children from the age of three (*CPJ* 2.421) and appointing procurators to collect it, e.g. T. Flavius Aug. lib. Euschemon, *qui fuit... procurator ad capitularia Iudaeorum* (*ILS* 1519 = *MW* 203). For Domitian's stricter enforcement of the tax, see Smallwood, 1976: 376-85; Thompson, 1982: 329-42; Williams, 1990: 196-211 and Sordi, 1994: 47-8.

Another *uectigal nouum* is probably the *fiscus Alexandrinus*. Johnson (in Frank 2, 1933-40: 46 and n.31) argues that its institution is probably to be explained by the conversion into cash of Julio-Claudian property. On Nero's death, there had been left legally vacant not only a considerable amount of crown property (that had increased considerably thanks to the confiscations of Tiberius, Gaius and Claudius) but also the personal estates of the various members of the Julio-Claudian family. Whilst Vespasian could not personally inherit all this, he could have it sold – note Dio's comment that 'the Alexandrians were angry... because he had sold the greater part of the palaces' (66.8.4). In addition, he could no doubt collect more in taxation from the new local owners than from their imperial predecessors; see Johnson in Frank 2, 1933-40: 45-7. Apart from the *fiscus Alexandrinus*, Vespasian may well have organised another *uectigal nouum* along the same lines by converting into cash the imperial properties in Asia, i.e. the *fiscus Asiaticus*: see Magie (1950) 568, 1425 n.5 and *RE* 6.2403. In addition, it may well be, as Heichelheim suggests (in Frank 4, 1933-40: 237), that the *fiscus Asiaticus* had some connection with the Syrian *tributum capitis* payable by all men from fourteen to sixty-five and all women from twelve to sixty-five (Ulpian in *Digest* 50.15.3).

In more general terms, the careful census of Vespasian's early years (see Bosworth, 1973: 62) must have resulted in a more thorough exaction of tribute. Thus, as the epigraphic evidence (see Garzetti, 1974: 635 and Le Glay, 1981: 175-84) indicates, Vespasian attempted to define and widen the taxation base in Thrace, Cyrenaica, Tunisia, Algeria, Canusium, Orange and Africa. One example is provided by Haywood in Frank 4, 1933-40: 38. He notes that Vespasian resurveyed the 146 BC boundaries in Roman Africa that separated the land of the original province which was subject to a *uectigal* from that of the Marian colonists which was not; some in the former area may well have claimed that their holdings were Marian and so avoided the tax, a situation easily remedied by a careful Vespasianic survey. Finally, it is also possible, as Loane argues (1944: 10-21), that Vespasian helped to balance his budget by engaging in the spice trade and that he converted part of the *domus aurea* into the *Horrea Piperatoria*. On the latter, see Platner-Ashby, 1929: 262-3 and Steinby, 1996: 45-6.

For a discussion of the various imperial taxes, see the articles by Burton in the *OCD*, i.e. 596-7 (*Finance, Roman*), 1551 (*tributum*) and 1583 (*vectigal*) as well as Johnson's examination of Vespasian's income from taxes (in Frank 2, 1933-40: 47-51).

**auxisse tributa prouinciis...duplicasse:** The provincial tribute could be paid as (i) a *decuma*: a tithe paid in kind; (ii) a *stipendium*: a fixed amount, either a land tax (*tributum soli*) or a poll tax (*tributum capitis*); or (iii), especially in Egypt, a combination of taxes in cash and kind (e.g. the *annona* or supply of corn). Whilst we have no data on which provinces were required to pay twice as much in tribute, it is clear that with the new régime came massive changes. Bosworth has argued that, in the first year after his accession to power, Vespasian 'ruthlessly reduced independent communities to provincial and tributary status, almost obsessively preoccupied with the problems of raising funds for the state treasuries' (1973: 61) and that, as 'censuses in Spain and Africa were the necessary basis for new and increased taxation,...it would be natural if they were carried out rapidly as an urgent priority (1973: 62).

Late in 70 came the end of Greek liberty when Achaea returned to imperial control with the appointment of a proconsul; we may reasonably assume that the income from taxing this peaceful province would have well and truly surpassed the expense involved in direct control. At the same time, there must have been a substantial increase in revenue resulting from his reorganisation in the east – the incorporation of Lesser Armenia, Commagene and Trachia Cilicia in the early seventies and, some years later, that of Rhodes, Byzantium and Samos (see 8.4 above). In addition, Festus claimed that *sub Vespasiano principe Insularum prouincia facta est* (*Breu.* 10), a somewhat dubious statement, but Vespasian may (according to Magie, 1950: 1428 n.9) have created a post analogous to the *prouincia Hellesponti* of *ILS* 1374 to deal with the financial administration of the Aegean islands.

On the other hand, there is also no evidence that Vespasian's grants of Latin rights to various communities in Spain were accompanied by a reduction in tribute, and the only financial concession he made to his own colony at Caesarea was exemption from the Syrian poll tax (see Bosworth, 1973: 55). For a discussion of the various taxes payable by the provinces at this time, see the authorities cited above, s.u. *noua et grauia addidisse.*

**negotiationes...uel priuato pudendas propalam exercuit:** Suetonius explains precisely the activities that were *pudendas*: *coemendo quaedam tantum ut pluris postea distraheret.* A Roman senator did not engage in trade. As for those who did, *sordidi etiam putandi qui mercantur a mercatoribus quod statim uendant; nihil enim proficiant, nisi admodum mentiantur, nec uero est quicquam turpius uanitate* (Cicero, *Off.* 1.42).

16.2

**ne candidatis quidem honores...uenditare cunctatus est:** According to Dio, it was Caenis (see 3 above) who acted as intermediary. She had 'the greatest influence and she amassed untold wealth,...for she received vast sums from many sources, sometimes selling governorships, sometimes procuratorships, generalships and priesthoods, and in some instances even imperial decisions' (66.14.3).

**creditur etiam:** An unpromising prelude, usually (as here) to a story that was almost certainly untrue.

**procuratorum:** A *procurator* was an imperial agent or employee, holding a post in the civil administration; the more important procurators were members of the equestrian order. At least six different types of procuratorial posts are attested; see Brunt, 1966: 461-87; *OCD* 1251-2 and Burton, 1993: 13-28.

Commentary

**exprimeret umentis:** cf. 4.3 above, i.e. *conuictus quoque dicitur ducenta sestertia expressisse iuueni...*

16.3

**quidam natura cupidissimum tradunt:** Aurelius Victor was clearly not one of the *quidam* who so regarded Vespasian, i.e. *infirmus tamen, uti quidam praue putant, aduersum pecuniam* (*De Caes.* 9.6).

**negata[m] sibi gratuita[m] libertate[m]:** A slave could purchase his freedom from the money he had saved (his *peculium*), cf. Seneca's *peculium suum, quod comparauerunt uentre fraudato, pro capite numerant: Ep.* 80.4), so long as his master agreed. So, with Pedanius Secundus: *Pedanium Secundum seruus ipsius interfecit, seu negata libertate cui pretium pepigerat...* (*Ann.* 14.42).

***uulpem pilum mutare, non mores*:** Perhaps *mores* refers to the rumour that, when Vespasian was still a *priuatus*, he had been found guilty (*conuictus dicitur*) of obtaining the *latus clauus* for a young man and demanding payment for his services (4.3 above).

**manubias et rapinas:** Gellius (*NA* 13.25) claims that the money obtained from the sale of booty (*praeda*) was called *manubiae*, but, according to Asconius on *Verr.* 2.1.154, *manubiae sunt praeda imperatoris pro portione de hostibus capta.* Suetonius, however, is obviously referring in unflattering (but general) terms to Vespasian's money-raising methods. Braithwaite, however, believes that he is far more precise and means 'one of Vespasian's most oppressive measures,...the appropriation of the *subseciua*...(which) proved so exceptionally unpopular' (1927: 61). There may be some support for that thesis in Frontinus' comment on Domitian's edict reversing his father's practice and granting virtual ownership to those squatting (illegally) on the *subseciua: uno edicto totius Italiae metum liberauit* (*Corpus Agrimensorum Romanorum* 1.1 = Thulin, 1913: 54). For a discussion of the *subseciua*, see 16.1 above, s.u. *sola est...cupiditas.*

**aerarii fiscique inopia:** From its basic meaning of 'basket', the term *fiscus* came to be used, not only for the emperor's personal funds as opposed to the public *aerarium* (see *OCD* 24-5), but also for the imperial financial administration in a broad sense. The precise nature of the *fiscus* has inspired extensive scholarly debate (for the details, see *OCD* 598-9), a difficulty that (according to Dio) did not worry Augustus: 'In reality, Caesar himself was destined to have absolute control of all matters for all time, because he was not only master of the funds (nominally, to be sure, he had separated the public funds from his own, but as a matter of fact, he always spent the former also as he saw fit), but also commanded the soldiers' (53.16.1).

**quadringenties milies opus esse ut res publica stare posset**: *quadringenties milies centena milia sestertium* (= 40,000,000,000 sesterces). Suetonius had already (16.1-2) discussed Vespasian's attempts to reduce his huge deficit, though some (e.g. Watkins, 1988/89: 119) query the figure, the largest sum of money mentioned in antiquity. Its causes were clear enough, i.e. the economic disaster of Nero's reign, the widespread destruction caused by the civil war together with the need to pension off unsatisfactory and surplus soldiers from the Praetorian Guard and the legions. It has been suggested that the purpose of Vespasian's statement may have been to justify his transfer to the *fiscus* of all the Julio-Claudian properties left vacant at Nero's death; see Johnson in Frank 2, 1933-40: 45 and 16.1 above, s.u. *noua et grauia addidisse*. Some idea of the problems Vespasian faced and the need for desperate measures emerges from Johnson's attempt (in Frank 2, 1933-40: 53-4) to draw up a Vespasianic 'balance sheet'. His 'very hypothetical' set of figures indicates that Vespasian's maximum annual income would have been in the vicinity of 1,200,000,000 to 1,500,000,000 sesterces, i.e. under four per cent of the deficit mentioned by Suetonius.

**quod et ueri similius uidetur:** Suetonius, whilst softening his earlier assessment (i.e. *merito culpetur* in 16.1), nonetheless adds *male partis optime usus est*. But even Ausonius is more generous: *quaerendi adtentus, moderato commodus usu,/auget nec reprimit Vespasianus opes* (*Caes.* 10).

## 17

**in omne hominum genus liberalissimus:** Eutropius also praises Vespasian's *liberalitas* (7.19.2: see 16.1 above, s.u. *sola est...cupiditas*) but towards *indigentes*, with no mention of the senatorial order.

**expleuit censum senatorium:** According to Dio, Augustus 'permitted all to stand for office who possessed property worth four hundred thousand sesterces and were eligible by the laws to hold office. This was the senatorial rating which he at first established; but later he raised it to one million sesterces' (54.17.3). Suetonius, however, believes that at first Augustus fixed the property qualification at eight hundred thousand sesterces but then raised it to twelve hundred thousand, at the same time making up the amount for those with insufficient property (*suppleuit non habentibus: Aug.* 41.1). See also the discussion in Talbert, 1984: 10-11. Dio's figure has been generally accepted, since Tacitus refers to grants of one million sesterces for this purpose by both Augustus (*Ann.* 2.37, to

Hortensius Hortalus) and Tiberius (*Ann.* 1.75, to Propertius Celer). For a discussion of imperial assistance in making up the senatorial census qualification, see Talbert, 1984: 52-3. Frontinus reports a 'not easily intelligible case' (Millar, 1977: 298 n.64) of Vespasian giving the *census* to a young man: *diuus Augustus Vespasianus, cum quendam adulescentem honeste natum, militiae inhabilem, angustiarum rei familiaris causa deductum ad longiorem ordinem rescisset, censu constituto honesta missione exauctorauit* (*Strat.* 4.6.4).

**consulares inopes quingenis sestertiis annuis sustentauit:** Nero made the same annual grants – according to Suetonius (*senatorum nobilissimo cuique, sed a re familiari destituto, annua salaria et quibusdam quingena constituit: Nero* 10.1) and Tacitus (*sed nobili familiae honor auctus est oblatis in singulos annos quingenis sestertiis quibus Messala paupertatem innoxiam sustentaret. Aurelio quoque Cottae et Haterio Antonio annuam pecuniam statuit princeps, quamuis per luxum auitas opes dissipassent: Ann.* 13.34).

**plurimas...restituit in melius:** Aurelius Victor similarly states that *per omnes terras, qua ius Romanum est, renouatae urbes cultu egregio uiaeque operibus maximis munitae* (*De Caes.* 9.8) but provides a detail not recorded elsewhere: *et cauati montes per Flaminiam prono transgressui* (9.8), with the so-called epitomator repeating this precisely but adding the comment *quae uulgariter Pertunsa petra uocitatur* (9.10). For examples of his work in restoring bridges and buildings, see the examples quoted in 9.1 above, s.u. *noua opera*.

**ciuitates terrae motu aut incendio afflictas:** At Herculaneum in 76, he restored the temple of Rhea, Mother of the Gods that had been destroyed by an earthquake during Nero's reign (*Ann.* 15.22): *Imp. Caesar Vespasianus Aug. pontif. max. trib. pot. vii imp. xvii p.p. cos. vii desig. viii templum Matris Deum terrae motu conlapsum restituit* (*ILS* 250 = *MW* 433). Earthquakes were not infrequent during the first century AD – see *RG* 6.4, *Ann.* 2.47 and *Tib.* 48.2; for grants by Claudius and Nero to cities damaged by fire, see *Ann.* 12.58 and 16.13.

**ingenia et artes uel maxime fouit:** In this, Vespasian was yet again following Augustus' example: *ingenia saeculi sui omnibus modis fouit [Augustus]: Aug.* 89.3). On the basis of the evidence provided by Suetonius, especially the grant from the *fiscus* to professors of rhetoric (18 below), Vespasian's patronage of the arts was genuine. Even before he became emperor, he had been on terms of friendship with Thrasea Paetus and Barea Soranus (*Hist* 4.7) and, in the seventies, the two leading orators of the day, Vibius Crispus and Eprius Marcellus were *principes in Caesaris amicitia* (*Dial.* 8.3). Another was the Elder Pliny who *ante lucem* *ibat ad Vespasianum imperatorem* (*Ep.* 3.5.9).

Moreover, he seems to have been determined that his sons' education should not be neglected; see the discussion of Bardon, 1981: 178-94. As Titus was educated at court, it is not surprising to learn that he was *Latine Graeceque uel in orando uel in fingendis poematibus promptus et facilis ad extemporalitatem usque; sed ne musicae quidem rudis, ut qui cantaret et psalleret iucunde scienterque* (*Titus* 3.2). One of the more obvious indications of Domitian's interests in the arts appears in the *Epit. de Caes.*: *bibliothecas incendio consumptas petitis undique, praesertim Alexandria, exemplis reparauit* (11.4); and, for a detailed assessment of his writings and sponsorship of literature, see Coleman, 1986: 3088-111. Bardon, however, believes that Vespasian had little genuine interest in the arts – '(Vespasien) resta toute sa vie une manière de bourgeois peu sensible aux lettres' (1981: 178).

## 18

**primus e fisco Latinis Graecisque rhetoribus annua centena constituit:** The grant is noteworthy for two reasons – it represents an important milestone in the history of Roman education and it also supports the suggestion that Vespasian was guilty not of *auaritia* but of careful financial management that included spending money when considered necessary.

One hundred and fifty years previously, teachers of Latin rhetoric were expelled from Rome; Suetonius reports verbatim the decree of Cn. Domitius Ahenobarbus and L. Licinius Crassus (censors in 92 BC) in reference to *Latini rhetores, homines qui nouum genus disciplinae instituerunt...haec noua, quae praeter consuetudinem ac morem maiorum fiunt, neque placent neque recta uidentur. quapropter et eis qui eos ludos habent, et eis qui eo uenire consuerunt, uidetur faciundum ut ostenderemus nostram sententiam, nobis non placere* (*Rhet.* 1.1). By the time of Augustus, however, attitudes had changed dramatically and it was possible for such teachers to gain great wealth and status: *nonnulli ex infima fortuna in ordinem senatorium atque ad summos honores processerint* (ibid.). Finally, under Vespasian, they achieved imperial recognition, with the first appointee being Quintilian (*PIR*² F 59; according to Eusebius, *Quintilianus ex Hispania Calagurritanus primus Romae publicum scholam et salarium e fisco accepit et claruit* [*Chron. Canon. A. Abr.* 2104, i.e. 1 Oct. 87 - 30 Sept. 88]). He taught for some twenty years and numbered the younger Pliny amongst his pupils. The education of Domitian's heirs, the sons of Flavius Clemens (on whom, see 1.3 above, s.u. *Sabinus*), had also been entrusted to Quintilian, probably ca 90, for which, so it seems, he received the rare award of *ornamenta consularia* (*Quintilianus consularia per Clementem ornamenta sortitus honestamenta nominis potius uidetur quam insignia potestatis habuisse*: Ausonius, *Grat. Act.* 10.7) that provoked bitter resentment on the part of some senators at least: *quos tibi, Fortuna, ludos facis? facis enim ex senatoribus professores, ex professoribus senatores (Ep.* 4.11.2); similarly, Juvenal, 7.197-8: *si Fortuna uolet, fies de rhetore consul;/si uolet haec eadem, fiet de consule rhetor.* On these passages, see McDermott-Orentzel, 1979: 24 and Coleman, 1986: 3108-9.

While this was a fine example of Vespasian's initiative, it was limited in so far as it applied only in Rome, as Dio attests: 'Vespasian afterwards established in Rome teachers of both Latin and Greek learning, who drew their pay from the public treasury' (Dio 66.12.1a). Other literary evidence supports Dio. Philostratus always refers to the chair of Greek rhetoric in the singular, e.g. 'the chair of Rome' (*VS* 2.8.580 and 2.33.627) or 'the highest chair' (*VS* 2.10.589).

From an edict found at Pergamum (*AE* 1936, 128 = *MW* 458), it appears that Vespasian also granted to teachers and doctors exemption from the payment of taxes and from the obligation of providing lodgings for officials or troops: 'The emperor Caesar Vespasian Augustus, pontifex maximus, with tribunician power for the sixth time, saluted as victorious commander for the fourteenth time, father of his country, consul for the fifth time, designated for the sixth time, censor declares... Because these men (grammarians and rhetoricians...physicians and medical practitioners) are thus regarded as (?) sacred and godlike, I order that no billeting be made against them and no taxes are to be exacted from them in any manner...and they are permitted [to assemble in their associations] in precincts, sanctuaries and temples wherever they choose' (trans. adapted from N. Lewis and M. Reinhold, 1966: 295). But this may not have been an innovation; for an instance of *immunitas* dating back to the triumviral period, see Marrou, 1956: 301. In the *Digest*, however, credit is given to Vespasian and Hadrian for granting exemption from providing accommodation to *magistris qui ciuilium munerum uacationem habent, item grammaticis et oratoribus et medicis et philosophis* (1.4.18.30).

Marrou argues that, although Vespasian had introduced a whole system of economic privilege by exempting these people from municipal levies, the net result was hostility on the part of the municipal authorities who objected to all these exemptions (1956: 301-2). See also Wallace-Hadrill's discussion of Vespasianic salaries and privileges (1995: 36).

**centena:** *centena sestertia,* 100,000 sesterces, a salary that, it would appear, remained unchanged at least until the beginning of the third century, as an inscription from Sicca Veneria in Africa mentions a *procurator centenarius primae cathedrae* (*ILS* 9020).

**praestantis poetas:** One who can be identified is Saleius Bassus (*PIR*[1] S 50):

*laudauimus nuper ut miram et eximiam Vespasiani liberalitatem, quod quingenta sestertia Basso donasset (Dial.* 9.5). According to Quintilian, *uehemens et poeticum ingenium Salei Bassi fuit, nec ipsum senectute maturuit (Inst. Or.* 10.90).

**Coae Veneris:** Graevius proposed this correction for the manuscripts' *coeuenerit* (or *coemerit* or *coemit*) on the basis of the Elder Pliny's reference to a statue of Venus that Vespasian set up in his Temple of Peace: *ignoratur artifex eius quoque Veneris quam Vespasianus imperator in operibus Pacis suae dicauit antiquorum dignam fama (NH* 36.27). So the statue would have come from Cos. But Suetonius may possibly have been referring to a picture, and, if so, the likeliest candidate is the famous 'Aphrodite Anadyomene' of Apelles that was originally in the temple of Aesculapius at Cos. The Elder Pliny recounts its history: *Venerem exeuntem e mari diuus Augustus dicauit in delubro patris Caesaris, quae anadyomene uocatur...cuius inferiorem partem corruptam qui reficeret non potuit reperiri...consenuit haec tabula carie, aliamque pro ea substituit Nero in principatu suo Dorothei manu (NH* 35.91). However, Pliny then proceeds to mention another, even better, Aphrodite that Apelles started at Cos but which remained unfinished when he died: *Apelles inchoauerat et aliam Venerem Coi, superaturus etiam illam suam priorem. inuidit mors peracta parte, nec qui succederet operi ad praescripta liniamenta inuentus est (NH* 35.92). Of the three possibilities, perhaps preference should be given to the restored statue rather than to the pictures – at least it would be consonant with the next item.

**Colossi refectorem:** The colossal (120 ft high: but the ancient accounts differ) bronze statue of Nero by Zenodorus was (according to the Elder Pliny) changed by Vespasian into a statue of the Sun (*dicatus Soli uenerationi est damnatis sceleribus illius principis*: *NH* 34.45) with the addition of a radiate crown, each of the seven rays being $23^{1}/_{2}$ Roman feet long (Howell, 1968: 295 with n.7; Richardson, 1992: 92-3). It had first been set up in the entrance court of the *domus aurea* (*hic ubi sidereus propius uidet astra colossus/et crescunt media pegmata celsa uia,/inuidiosa feri radiabant atria regis*: Martial, *Spect.* 1.2.1-3), and, according to Dio, it was moved by Vespasian: 'in the sixth consulship of Vespasian and the fourth of Titus (i.e. 75),...the "Colossus" was set up on the Sacred Way. This statue is said...to have borne the features of Nero, according to some, or those of Titus, according to others' (66.15.1). Later, Hadrian moved it to the north-west of the Flavian Amphitheatre: *transtulit (Hadrianus) et Colossum...ita ut operi etiam elephantos uiginti quattuor exhiberet. et cum hoc simulacrum post Neronis uultum deletum, cui antea dicatum fuerat, Soli consacrasset* (*HA, Hadrian* 19.12-13). Subsequently, Commodus is said to have 'actually cut off the head of the Colossus and substituted for it a likeness of his own head' (Dio 72.22.3: the same account appears in *HA, Comm.* 17.9 and Herodian 1.15.9). For a suggestion that it was not Nero who actually erected the Colossus (it does not appear on his coins), see Howell (1968: 292-9); he argues that it was set up by Vespasian ca 75, but only after it had been converted into a statue of the sun. Despite Platner-Ashby, 1929: 130, it is not to be identified with the *Palatinus Colossus* of Martial (8.60). On the Colossus, see Bradley, 1978: 175-6; Castagnoli, *Atti* 261-74 and Steinby, 1993: 295-8.

**congiario:** Originally, the *congiarium* was a quantity (one *congius* = about six pints) of wine or oil distributed as a gift by the magistrats to the people. Later, cash was distributed instead (from the emperor's private funds) and the *congiarium* became the civilian equivalent of the donative (*populo congiarium, militi donatiuum proposuit: Nero* 7.2); for a detailed discussion of the official *congiaria*, see *OCD* 376 and especially van Berchem (1939) 119-76. Here, though, the word is used in the more general sense of a gift, as in *Iul.* 27: *[Caesar] uel inuitatos uel sponte ad se commeantis uberrimo congiario prosequebatur.*

**mechanico:** He was an engineer or technician, and possibly a freedman like the *machinator* of *ILS* 7727; note that half of the architects attested epigraphically have been found to be slaves or freedmen (Brunt, 1980: 82 n.9). So it is hard to accept Casson's theory (1978: 44-51) that he was, in essence, discussing labour problems with the emperor and proffering economic advice.

**commento:** Casson's argument (1978: 43) that the *mechanicus* proposed what could be described as a 'work for the dole scheme' has been persuasively rejected by Brunt (1980: 82). The *commentum* was not, despite Casson, an economic plan; rather it must have been some sort of labour-saving mechanical device, one that Vespasian rejected (*remisit*) precisely because he had no intention of saving labour costs.

**grandes columnas...perducturum:** Compare the machine designed by a certain Paronius that was supposed to convey stone from a quarry (Vitruvius, *De Arch.* 10.2.13).

**in Capitolium:** See 8.5 above, s.u. *ipse restitutionem Capitolii adgressus.*

*sineret se plebeculam pascere:* For *plebeculam* in preference to Ihm's *plebiculam,* see Mooney, 1930: 446. Brunt has shown that the common people in Rome had to earn their living in casual employment and partly in the building trade (1980: 81-98 and also 1971: 376-8). Despite Casson (1978: 43-51), there is not even a hint in Suetonius that Vespasian was forced to resort to a gang of slaves. On the contrary, Vespasian was not trying to save money, his so-called *auaritia* notwithstanding; he wanted to maintain (*pascere*) his people (*plebeculam*). The anecdote should be taken at face value – Levick, on the other hand, treats it with scepticism (1999: 129 and 248 n.16). See also Keaveney, 1987: 213-16 and Wardle, 1996: 208-9.

## 19.1

In this section, Suetonius provides further *exempla* of Vespasian's generosity, balancing it in 19.2 with two indications of his *cupiditas*, both quite unconvincing, i.e. insults from the Alexandrians (something to be expected by any visiting Roman emperor) and, in effect, an anecdote on how to save the state ten million (less 100,000) sesterces.

**ludis:** At the *ludi* held to celebrate Augustus' dedication of the theatre, i.e. *quibus theatrum Marcelli dedicabat, euenit ut [Augustus] laxatis sellae curulis compagibus caderet supinus* (*Aug.* 43.5).

**Marcelliani theatri:** Dio records that Julius Caesar (in 44 BC) was 'anxious to build a theatre, as Pompey had done: he laid the foundations, but did not finish it; it was Augustus who later completed it and named it for his nephew, Marcus Marcellus' (43.49.2). The latter (43-23 BC) was Augustus' nephew (by his sister Octavia) and son-in-law (married to his daughter Julia). Then, in 11 BC (*NH* 8.65), Augustus 'dedicated the theatre named after Marcellus. In the course of the festival held for this purpose, the patrician boys, including his grandson Gaius, performed the equestrian exercise called "Troy", and six hundred wild beasts from Africa were slain. And to celebrate the birthday of Augustus, Iullus, the son of Antony, who was praetor, gave games in the Circus and a slaughter of wild beasts, and entertained both the emperor and the senate, in pursuance of a decree of that body, upon the Capitol' (Dio 54.26.1). There is a reference to it in the *Res Gestae* (*theatrum ad aedem Apollinis in solo magna ex parte a priuatis empto feci, quod sub nomine M. Marcelli generi mei esset: RG* 21.1) and in Suetonius' *Vita* (*quaedam etiam opera sub nomine alieno...fecit, ut...theatrum Marcelli: Aug.* 29.4). See also the article in Platner-Ashby, 1929: 513-15.

**acroamata:** The Greek form means 'a thing heard' and so it is especially applied to music, but it could be used of a performance or entertainment in general or of 'a turn' (*OLD* 29). It could also be applied to a performer – even, by Cicero, to Clodius: *ipse ille maxime ludius, non solum spectator sed actor et acroama qui in coetum mulierum pro psaltaria adducitur...* (*Sest.* 116).

**Apellae:** Apelles (if that be the correct reading) remains a mystery. The manuscripts give *appellari* (so Ihm) or *apellari* or *apelli*, for which editors have read *Apollinari* or *Apellari* or *Apellae*. But nothing is known of an Apollinaris or an Apellaris, whereas there was an Apelles prominent in Gaius' reign. It seems that the emperor 'always kept Apelles, the most famous of the tragedians of that day, with him even in public' (Dio 59.5.2) but he later humiliated him (*Calig.* 33). An Apelles was also mentioned by Petronius: *quando parem habui nisi unum Apelletem* (*Satyricon* 64), probably the same person and he could just possibly have still been on the stage some thirty-five years after Gaius' death.

**quadringenta:** *quadringenta sestertia.* Vespasian gave the same amount to the woman who *amore suo deperiret* (22).

**Terpno:** He was the most prominent lyre-player of Nero's reign (*citharoedum uigentem tunc praeter alios*: *Nero* 20.1), took part in the *peregrinatio Achaica inter comites Neronis* (4.4 above), but, in the musical contest, failed to defeat the emperor (Dio 63.8.3).

**Diodoro:** Diodorus also accompanied Nero on the musical tour of Greece and was also defeated by the emperor. But, on the latter's victorious return to Rome, 'by his side in the vehicle rode Diodorus the lyre-player' (Dio 63.20.3).

**coronas aureas:** Suetonius refers to the *coronae scaenicae* that Nero received for his victories on the stage (*Nero* 53) and Statius recalls how his wife embraced him *sancto indutum Caesaris auro* (*Silu.* 3.5.29). But rewarding actors with golden crowns was hardly novel, for Plutarch tells of the younger Cato's cost-cutting efforts as aedile – 'he gave the actors crowns, not of gold, but of wild olive as was done at Olympia' (*Cat. min.* 46.3); and the Elder Pliny refers to a variant of that practice, claiming that thin leaves of Cyprus copper *taurorum felle tinctum speciem auri in coronis histrionum praebet* (NH 34.94).

**conuiuabatur assidue ac saepius recta:** His dinner parties (*conuiuabatur*) were formal (*recta*) and frequent (*saepius*). The formal dinner (*recta cena*) consisted of at least three courses (*fercula* – though Juvenal mentions seven in *Sat.* 1.94), viz. *gustatio, cena* (that might be subdivided into *prima cena, altera cena...*) and *secunda mensa*. In this regard, Vespasian was once more following the example of Augustus who *conuiuabatur assidue nec umquam nisi recta*: *Aug.* 74). Despite Vespasian's alleged *auaritia*, Suetonius claims that he avoided the cheaper alternatives, the *publica cena* (one provided by the emperor in a public place such as the Forum) or the *sportula* (the term originally applied to the small portion of food provided by his *patronus* in return for some service). Nero had tried to limit expeniture by replacing the *publica cena* with the *sportula* (*adhibitus sumptibus modus, publicae cenae ad sportulas redactae*: *Nero* 16.2); for a time, Domitian was as generous as (according to Suetonius) his father (*promissa est nobis sportula, recta [cena] data est*: Martial 8.50.10), but later reversed the process and revived the cheaper option, the *sportula* – it appears in the later books of Martial (e.g. 9.100.1; 10.27.3).

These *cenae rectae* can hardly have endured for very long, given the financial problems facing Vespasian (e.g. 16.3 above); and that suggestion is reinforced by Suetonius' next statement – *et tamen ne sic quidem pristina cupiditatis infamia caruit*. On the *cenae* and *sportula*, see Friedländer *SG* 4.77-81 and Yavetz, 1987: 135-86.

**macellarios:** Stall-holders at the *macellum*. For attempts to regulate what was sold there and the prices charged, see *Iul.* 43.2 and *Tib.* 34.

**Saturnalibus:** The festival of the *Saturnalia* lasted from 17 to 23 December. It was a time of general enjoyment – law courts, schools and businesses were closed; there was a good deal of drinking, eating and gambling; slaves were allowed to behave as they liked and their masters wore leisure-wear instead of the *toga* (*synthesibus dum gaudet eques dominusque senator/dumque decent nostrum pillea sumpta Iovem*: Martial 14.1.1-2). It was also the custom for men to exchange gifts; see next item.

**apophoreta:** They were presents 'to be carried away' by guests, especially at the Saturnalia (see previous item). It is also the title of the fourteenth book of Martial's Epigrams, consisting of couplets intended to accompany such presents.

**Kal. Mart.:** The *matronalia* was celebrated on the Kalends of March, the first day of the religious year. The ancient festival in honour of Juno Lucina symbolised the sacredness of marriage and consisted of a procession of married women to her temple. Wives would receive gifts from their husbands – and from admirers. Hence Martial's *scis certe, puto, uestra iam uenire/Saturnalia, Martias Kalendas;/tunc reddam tibi, Galla, quod dedisti* (5.84.10-12); similarly, *munera femineis tractat secreta Kalendis* (Juv. 9.53).

19.2

**Alexandrini:** The Alexandrians displayed initial enthusiasm for Vespasian according to a papyrus fragment which purports to be an account of the moment when, early in 70, some months after being acclaimed emperor (on 1 July 69) by the prefect of Egypt, Tiberius Julius Alexander, Vespasian himself (accompanied by Josephus: *Vita* 415) came to Egypt and was greeted by the Alexandrians as he entered the Hippodrome. They shouted out his name and assigned him a number of titles: '[Tibe]rius Alexa[nder]...the emperor [into] the city...the crowds [coming out to meet him] throughout the entire Hippodrome [??gave a loud shout]...''In good health, lord Caesar, [may you come!] Vespasian, the one saviour and [benefactor!] Son of [Amm]o[n] rising up...Keep him for us [in good health. Lord] Augustus...Ser[apis (?)]...Son of Ammon and in a word [the one god (?)]. We thank Tiberius [Alexander]''...Tiberius [said...] ''god Caesar...in good health!...god Caesar Vespasian!...lord Augustus!''' (*MW* 41; see Montevecchi, 1981: 484-96).

Their enthusiasm did not last long. Dio discusses their attitude in some detail (66.8.2-6): 'The Alexandrians, far from delighting in Vespasian's presence, detested him so heartily that they were for ever mocking and reviling him. For they had expected to receive from him some great reward because they had been the first to make him emperor, but, instead of securing anything, they had additional contributions levied upon them... Hence the Alexandrians, both for these reasons and also because he had sold the greater part of the palace, were angry and hurled many taunts at him, this among others: "Six obols more you demand of us". Vespasian, consequently,...became angry and gave orders that six obols should be exacted from every man and he thought seriously about punishing them besides. For the words in themselves were insulting enough, and there was something about their unbroken anapaestic rhythm that roused his ire. Titus, however, begged that they might be forgiven and Vespasian spared them. Yet they would not let him alone, but in a crowded assembly all loudly shouted these words "We forgive him; for he knows not how to play the Caesar".'

Just when the demonstration occurred is unclear, but it was obviously before the middle of 70, when he left Alexandria for Rome. A papyrus fragment (*P. Graec. Vindob.* 25787 = *SB* 6. 9528) containing the opening lines of a speech addressed to the *Alexandrini* by a new emperor could be assigned to this period; it has been restored to read '[I am pleased to hear that you,] in accordance with the decrees of the most holy senate and the accord between myself and the most loyal armies, rejoice that I have succeeded to responsibility [for you]'. One interpretation could be that the speech was delivered, not at the same time as *MW* 41, but some months later, when the senate in Rome had formally ratified Vespasian's appointment and when the new emperor's financial plans were becoming known – plans that had to be explained to the people of Alexandria. Perhaps the result was the demonstration described by Dio.

On the other hand, it is possible that Vespasian reacted with vigour. Another part of the puzzle is a reference to Vespasian in a speech addressed to the emperor

Theodosius by Libanius (discussed by Jones, 1997: 249-53). Libanius refers to the riots in Antioch in 387 when portraits and statues of the emperor Theodosius were destroyed; ultimately, the emperor forgave the city and Libanius' speech is addressed to him. He compares former rulers who have shown clemency, one of whom is Vespasian and he adds 'Titus' father (had) undergone similar treatment with regard to his statues...and (had) meted out punishments... So many Alexandrians were slaughtered by the soldiers stationed in the city that the swords grew heavy in the hands of those who used them' (20.30-2). If this occurred in 70, then Suetonius has avoided mention of an incident that would, to some extent, contradict the version of the emperor's character given in 12 above, where Vespasian is described as *statim ab initio principatus usque ad exitum ciuilis et clemens*. A similar situation occurs in 15 above, where (s.u. *inlacrimauit...ingemuit*) Suetonius appears to have been selective in listing *exempla* of Vespasianic leniency.

However, it is more likely (on the assumption that Libanius' remarks are accurate) that Vespasian made a later visit to Alexandria. C.P. Jones has consistently argued (1973a: 302-9; 1978: 134 and 1997: 249-53) that Dio of Prusa's *Alexandrian Oration* should be dated to Vespasian's reign and refers to events ca 73 (or possibly earlier), an argument accepted by Moles (1983: 131 n.8) as 'plausible' but rejected by, e.g., Kindstrand (1978: 378-83) and Sidebottom (1992: 407-19 and 1996: 447-8). In *Or*. 32, the unnamed emperor is described as 'attentive to culture and reason' (32.60) and as one who had given the Alexandrians 'fountains and forecourts' (32.95). Presumably, the latter had not appreciated the emperor's generosity and had reacted accordingly. But even so, Vespasian's reported reaction ('so many Alexandrians were slaughtered...') sits ill with Suetonius' claim in 12 (*statim ab initio...clemens*) cited above.

Vespasian was not the only Roman official to experience their hostility. According to Seneca, *loquax et in contumelias praefectorum ingeniosa prouincia, in qua etiam qui uitauerunt culpam non effugerunt infamiam* (*Helu.* 19.6), a sentiment shared by Herodian – 'to a certain extent, it was a natural feature of the people to indulge in lampoons and repetition of many pungent caricatures and jokes belittling the authorities, since they are considered very witty by the Alexandrians, even if libellous to the victims' (4.9.2).

**Cybiosacten:** The *Cybiotanten* of the manuscripts has to be corrected to *Cybiosacten* in view of Strabo 17.796. The Alexandrians' enthusiastic greeting of the new emperor was soon replaced by unconcealed hostility at his imposition of new taxes (*MW* 41 and Dio 66.8.2-6: see previous item). In this instance, the reference was to the historical and extremely unpleasant Cybiosactes, who claimed to be descended from Syrian royalty, perhaps the son or illegitimate son of Antiochus X. After Ptolemy Auletes was expelled, the Alexandrians declared his daughter Queen (i.e. Berenice IV) and arranged a marriage for her with Cybiosactes (57 BC). The union was brief, for 'the Queen had him strangled to death within a few days (*sic.* of the marriage), being unable to bear his coarseness and vulgarity' (Strabo 17 c 796: see also Dio 39.57.1, where Berenice's husband is named Seleucus). No doubt the Alexandrians were also aware of the fact that, in Vespasian's retinue, was another Berenice, once married (or perhaps only betrothed) to Tiberius Julius Alexander's brother and now the mistress of Titus. But there was more to the insult. Since *cybium* means 'chopped and salted pieces of young tunny-fish' (*OLD* 480), *cybiosactes* can also refer to a 'dealer in salt-fish' (ibid.), an occupation that was traditionally despised; see *Vita Horat.* 1.

**Fauor:** The name occurs frequently on inscriptions, e.g. *CIL* 14.2408; nothing else is known of him (*PIR*² F 122).

**archimimus:** The mime was a loosely-constructed presentation of everyday life and a leading mime (*archimimus*) such as Favor would train his own company of performers. See *RE* 15.1727 and *OCD* 982-3.

**personam eius ferens:** Mooney (1930: 449) points out that this is the only reference to an actor wearing a mask of the deceased at the funeral, though waxen masks of distinguished ancestors (*maiorum imagines*: see 1.1 above, s.u. *sine... imaginibus*) were worn in funeral processions, e.g. of Tiberius' son Drusus (*funus imaginum pompa maxime inlustre fuit cum origo Iuliae gentis Aeneas...ceteraeque Claudiorum effigies longo ordine spectarentur*: *Ann.* 4.9).

**funus et pompa:** For a detailed description of the funeral rites, see Toynbee 1971: 56-61.

**exclamauit:** It would appear that behaviour of this nature was not regarded as unacceptable at Roman funerals. We have a number of examples (but none from funerals) of double-meaning references by *mimi* to an emperor's behaviour or activities, e.g., from Nero's reign, there is Datus' comment 'Farewell, Father! Farewell, Mother!' as he pretended to drink and swim, *exitum scilicet Claudi Aprippinaeque significans* (*Nero* 39.3).

***centum sibi sestertia darent:*** i.e. *centiens centena milia sestertium*. There is very little information on the cost of imperial funerals (Nero's cost 200,000 sesterces: *Nero* 50), but ten million sesterces is obviously excessive and intended to give more point to Vespasian's offer. According to Duncan-Jones (1974: 128), the highest tomb cost recorded in Italy was 500,000 sesterces, i.e. that of one Popillius

Theo...from Fabrateria (*CIL* 10.5624), with the median average cost for Italy being 10,000 sesterces and for Africa under 1,400 sesterces. On the other hand, the Elder Pliny mentions a freedman who died in 8 BC and requested that one million one hundred thousand sesterces from his substantial estate be spent on his burial (*NH* 33.135).

*in Tiberim*: Such was the fate of Tiberius' body: *morte eius ita laetatus est populus ut ad primum nuntium discurrentes...Tiberium in Tiberim clamitarent* (*Tib.* 75.1).

20

Some idea of Vespasian's physical appearance can be gleaned from his coins and from those few busts which survive; see Daltrop, 1966: 9-17; Breckenridge,1981: 492-6 and *MW* (facing p. 49). More detail could be expected from the literary sources, and every Suetonian *Vita* has some reference to the physical appearance of the *princeps*. The quantity of information provided varies enormously: compare the total of nine words to describe Vespasian's *statura, membra* and *uultus* with the extensive comments (*Aug.* 79-80) on such minutiae as the size of Augustus' ears and the problems he had with the forefinger of his right hand. For a summary of the descriptions in each of the *Vitae*, see Evans, 1935: 77-9 and 1969: 93-4; and, for their position within each *Vita* together with some comments on them, Baldwin, 1983: 494-501. Suetonius' usual practice is to cite such features as the *statura, uultus, membra* and *oculi*; sometimes, his descriptions can be usefully compared with the evidence of statues; see Wardman, 1967: 414-20.

Why did Suetonius bother to describe his subject's physical appearance? The most obvious explanation, that such details were of interest to his readers, has often been excluded and more recondite solutions sought. He may well have been following the Alexandrian biographical tradition of including every possible detail about his subject (Evans, 1969: 51-2) if he did indeed belong to that tradition (Bradley, 1978a: 281) and if he had included every physical detail in every *Vita* (which, as in the *Vespasianus*, he clearly did not).

Another explanation is based on Suetonius' concern with the character of his subjects and his proven interest in physiognomy, i.e. the 'science' of interpreting a man's character from his personal appearance. As early as the age of Pericles, a certain Zopyrus had claimed proficiency in this field (Evans, 1935: 47 n.5) and Latin authors before Suetonius were well aware of it (ibid. 51-7; Couissin, 1953: 239-40), especially Seneca (Evans, 1969: 28-33); so, by the second century AD, the practice had become well-established and fashionable. The major extant handbook on the topic available to Suetonius was the *Physiognomonica* (probably written by one of Aristotle's pupils), whilst the contemporary expert was Polemo of Laodicaea (88-144/5) who, like Suetonius, was a member of Hadrian's court;

see Wallace-Hadrill, 1995: 196-7.

Suetonius' interest in physiognomy can be assumed from the title of his lost work *On Physical Defects* and from some fragments from his *On Insults* that are apparently derived from the pseudo-Aristotle's *Physiognomonica*; see the discussion by Evans, 1935: 62-3. But the use he makes of it is in dispute. Why, for instance, are the descriptions of Vespasian and Titus so very brief? Evans has argued that, at times, Suetonius listed those physical characteristics 'which from the point of view of the physiognomists indicate either the virtuous or vicious nature of an emperor's character' (1935: 63; similarly 1969: 53). Couissin goes much further. He suggests that Suetonius does not try to describe his subject's personal appearance but uses the 'rules' of physiognomy to provide a description consistent with his character (1953: 234). Couissin's theory does at least explain why the personal descriptions in *Galba* 21, *Otho* 12.1, *Vit.* 17.2 and *Dom.* 16 are more substantial those in *Vesp.* 20 and *Titus* 3.1. Baldwin's summary is accurate – Suetonius 'avoided the major nonsenses of physiognomy' (1983: 500).

**statura fuit quadrata:** 'squarely-built, thickset, stocky' (*OLD* 1530).

**uultu ueluti nitentis...*dicam,* inquit, *cum uentrem exonerare desieris*:** Compare Martial's *utere lactucis et mollibus utere maluis:/nam faciem durum, Phoebe, cacantis habes* (3.89.1-2) with the explanation he gives of the effect of mallows in *exoneraturas uentrem mihi uilica maluas/adtulit* (10.48.7-8). Vespasian's own *dicacitas* tended towards the *scurrilis et sordida* (22) as appears in 22 s.u. *Vespasiano adamato*; 23.1 s.u. *improbiusque nato* and 23.3 s.u. *urinae uectigal*; and the comment attributed to *quidam urbanorum* is of that order and remarkably apt as is attested by, for example, the bust of Vespasian in *MW* (facing p. 49), the Florence bust from the Uffizi in Daltrop, 1969: Tafel 8d and the Copenhagen Vespasian in Southern, 1997 (facing p. 120). There may also be a reference to Vespasian's last actions; see 24, s.u. *dumque...nititur.*

**ualitudine prosperrima usus est:** However Dio does mention his 'accustomed gout' (66.17.1).

**in sphaeristerio:** The *sphaeristerium* was 'a court for ball games' (*OLD* 1804), on which see Harris, 1972: 84-5 and *OCD* 232. Such courts were part of the public baths and could be found in the more elaborate private homes and villas. For the *sphaeristerium* in each of Pliny's Laurentine (*Ep.* 2.17.12) and Tuscan (5.6.27) villas, see Sherwin-White, 1966: 193 and 326.

**defricaret:** The standard word for massage.

**inediam:** Celsus recommended fasting (*inedia* or *abstinentia*): *neque ulla res magis adiuuat laborantem quam tempestiua abstinentia* (2.16), but in moderation (*abstinentia unius diei*: 7.7.4), as was practised by Vespasian. Otherwise, it could become a means of suicide, e.g. *Gallum Cerrinium...captum repente oculis et ob id inedia mori destinantem...[Augustus] reuocauit ad uitam* (*Aug.* 53.3).

**interponeret:** This is the word Celsus uses when referring to changes of treatment: so *poterit a balneo etiam pinguius aut dulcius dari uinum; poterit semel aut bis interponi Graecum salsum* (3.6).

## 21

**ordinem uitae:** Vespasian's accessibility and the simplicity of his lifestyle is reported elsewhere, in Dio ('Vespasian's own style of living was very far from costly and he spent no more than was absolutely necessary... He lived but little in the palace, spending most of his time in the Gardens of Sallust. There he received anybody who desired to see him, not only senators but also people in general...The doors of his palace stood open all day long and no guard was stationed at them: 66.10.3-4); and in Tacitus (*sed praecipuus adstricti moris auctor Vespasianus fuit, antiquo ipse cultu uictuque*: *Ann.* 3.55). Similarly, in the *Epit. de Caes.*: *institutum uero uniforme omni imperio tenuit. uigilare de nocte, publicisque actibus absolutis caros admittere, dum salutatur, calciamenta sumens et regium uestitum. post autem negotiis, quaecumque aduenissent, auditis exerceri uectatione, deinde requiescere; postremo, ubi lauisset, remissiore animo conuiuium curabat* (9.15). For the similarity between Vespasian's working day and that of the Elder Pliny, see *Ep.* 3.5.9-10 (cited in the next item) and Crook, 1955: 27-8.

**maturius...uigilabat:** That he rose early appears also in Pliny, whose uncle *ante lucem ibat ad Vespasianum imperatorem, nam ille quoque noctibus utebatur* (*Ep.* 3.5.9), while Dio states that 'Vespasian would converse with his intimate friends even before dawn, while lying in bed' (66.10.4). According to Philostratus, 'when Apollonius came to the palace at daybreak and asked what the emperor was doing,...(he was told that) Vespasian had been up for a long time and was busy with his correspondence' (*V. Apoll.* 5.31). Millar (1977: 209) points out that this is the earliest description we have of an emperor's manner of life, the next being Dio's account (76.17.1-3) of Severus'.

**perlectis epistulis:** For the imperial correspondence, see Millar, 1977: 213-28.

**officiorum:** *officium* – 'a body of officials' (*OLD* 1243). It is used in the same concrete sense by Pliny in *Ep.* 3.12.2: *erunt officia antelucana* ('early-morning callers').

**breuiariis:** *breuiarium* – 'condensed report, brief account, summary' (*OLD* 241). Thus Eutropius' *Breuiarium Historiae Romanae* – but Seneca deprecated the use of the word: *uide ne plus profutura sit ratio ordinaria quam haec, quae nunc uulgo breuiarum dicitur, olim cum Latine loqueremur, summarium uocabatur* (*Ep.* 39.1).

**amicos admittebat:** Before coming to any important decision, an emperor would consult his *amici* (Millar, 1977: 110-22). Most scholars agree that there was no fixed list of *amici*, but that, usually, the same people were summoned for consultation. The majority would have been senators, but prominent equestrians (e.g. the Elder Pliny who may well have held the *praefectura uigilum* at that time: *Ep.* 3.5.9 and Sherwin-White, 1966: 223) were frequently included (discussed by Crook, 1955: 23-4 and Millar, 1977: 116). Helvidius Priscus (in 70) stated that *nullum maius boni imperii instrumentum quam bonos amicos esse* (*Hist.* 4.7); Suetonius thought that Titus' were *et sibi et rei publicae necessarii* (*Titus* 7.2) and the astute Vespasian was not adverse to giving two of his, Vibius Crispus and Eprius Marcellus, a completely free rein: *nunc principes in Caesaris amicitia agunt feruntque cuncta* (*Dial.* 8.3). For a list of probable Vespasianic *amici* and their retention by his sons, see Devreker, 1977: 223-43.

Before the *salutatio*, Vespasian had read his correspondence and any summarised reports from his officials while he was still in bed; it was then that his *amici* were consulted and decisions made. His accessibility was legendary, as Dio noted (66.10.3-4: quoted above, s.u. *ordinem uitae*).

**calciabat ipse se:** For those of high rank, this task was usually performed by the *calciatores* – so a neat detail to help round out Suetonius' portrait of Vespasian.

**gestationi:** *gestatio* is the 'action of riding or being carried on horseback or in a litter or other vehicle' (*OLD* 763). It was recommended as a form of exercise by Seneca: *gestatio et corpus concutit et studio non officit: possis legere, possis dictare, possis loqui, possis audire* (*Ep.* 15.7) or even, it seems, *possis aleam ludere* – Suetonius states that Claudius was *solitus etiam in gestatione [aleam] ludere, ita essedo alueoque adaptatis ne lusus confunderetur* (*Claud.* 33.2). Exercise was advocated by the medical experts of antiquity, e.g. *gestatio longis morbis aptissima est...genera autem gestationis plura sunt: lenissima est naui uel in portu uel in flumine, uehementior uel in alto, uel lectica, etiamnum acrior uehiculo* (*Cels.* 2.15.1).

**quieti:** the siesta (*meridiatio*).

**pallacarum:** *pallaca* – 'a concubine' (*OLD* 1284).

**defunctae Caenidis:** For Caenis, see 3 above. She died in the early seventies, according to Dio's 'chronology' (66.14.1).

**a secreto:** From the private section of the palace where he had been during and since the *gestatio*.

**balineum tricliniumque:** The usual time for bathing was the early afternoon, after the *prandium*, according to Martial (11.52.3) and Vitruvius (*maxime tempus lauandi a meridiano ad uesperum est constitutum*: 5.10.1). On the other hand, the Elder Pliny bathed before the *prandium* (*Ep.* 3.5.10), a practice that was deplored by military authorities as indicating the absence of *paterna disciplina*, especially when *tribuni medio die lauabant* (*HA, Pesc. Nig.* 3.10). It was customary to take the *prandium* around the sixth hour (*cibum meridianum: Aug.* 78.1; *meridie: Claud.* 34.2), between the *ientaculum* and the *cena*. For some, it tended to be a fairly substantial meal, as it was for Nero (*per uinum et epulas: Ann.* 14.2) and Vitellius (*Vit.* 13.1) as well as for Domitian (*prandebat ad satietatem: Dom.* 21), whereas Augustus confined himself to bread and dates (*Aug.* 76.1). Suetonius is completely silent on Vespasian's eating habits; what he found significant was the emperor's alleged availability at meals rather than the quantity of food he consumed and when he consumed it.

**domestici...captabant:** The influence of the freedmen residing in the palace was paramount and those seeking imperial favours needed the good offices of these *domestici*. As Epictetus put it, 'tyranny would be more tolerable if the *cubicularii* did not have to be approached as well as the emperor' (1.19.17-18). So Martial asked the *a cubiculo* Parthenius to ensure that Domitian saw his poems (5.6.2), he sent him a poem for the fifth birthday of his son Burrus (4.45) and even thought it politic to praise the gardens of the *a libellis* Entellus (8.68). Perhaps the seemingly easy-going Vespasian was easier to influence that his ever-suspicious younger son or perhaps he liked to be thought so.

## 22

**ioco:** Vespasian's sense of humour is further exemplified (*multa ioco transigebat; erat enim dicacitatis plurimae, esti scurrilis et sordidae*) in a carefully linked series of chapters (22-5) culminating in the death scene. We have eight instances (22-3.3) of Vespasian's *dicacitas*: (1) Mestrius Florus, (2) *Vespasiano adamato*, (3) the unnamed *procerae staturae improbiusque nato*, (4) Cerylus/Laches, (5) the pretended brother, (6) the *mulio*, (7) the *urinae uectigal*, and (8) the base of the statue – with two of them (2 and 3) in the latter category (*scurrilis et sordidae*). Reminding the reader that there will be more instances of imperial *dicacitas*, he introduces the last four (23.1-3.3) by harking back to his previous *exempla* (in 16 above) of Vespasianic *auaritia* (*maxime tamen dicacitatem adfectabat in deformibus lucris ut inuidiam aliqua cauillatione dilueret transferretque ad sales*: 23.1) and concludes (23.4) by linking this *dicacitas* to the omens portending Vespasian's death (*ac ne in metu quidem ac periculo mortis extremo abstinuit iocis. nam cum inter cetera prodigia...*).

In his discussion of the phrase *in metu quidem ac periculo mortis extremo*, Gorringe (1993: 436) points out that Suetonius is stressing the incongruity of Vespasian's sense of humour; death should be a source of *metus* and *periculum*, but seemingly not for Vespasian, who reacts to the threat of it (the omens) and the reality (the *accessio mortis*) with further jests – *multa ioco transigebat*.

**super:** 'over', 'during'.

**cenam:** After the *ientaculum* and the *prandium* came the *cena*, the last meal of the day. The usual time for the *cena* was the ninth (Cicero, *Ad Fam.* 9.26.1; Horace, *Ep.* 1.7.71; Martial 4.8.6) or tenth hour (Martial 1.108.9; 7.51.11) and it lasted for some time (Pliny, *Ep.* 3.1.9). See 21 above, s.u. *balineum tricliniumque*.

**comissimus:** The theory was that one showed *ciuilitas* to one's fellow citizens and *comitas* to one's friends. So Vespasian 'was looked upon as emperor only by reason of his oversight of public business whereas in all other respects...he lived on a footing of equality with his subjects' (Dio 66.11.1); see also 12, s.u. *ciuilis*. According to Seneca, a ruler whose qualities include being *adfabilis, aditu accessuque facilis...a tota ciuitate amatur, defenditur, colitur* (*Clem.* 1.13.4).

**multa ioco transigebat:** This was the standard view. 'Vespasian indulged in jests like a man of the people and enjoyed jokes at his own expense; and whenever any anonymous bulletins...were posted, if they contained scurrilous references to himself, he would simply post a reply in kind, without showing the least resentment' (Dio 66.11.1).

**scurrilis et sordidae:** Vespasian's occasional ribald sense of humour was part of what would now be dubbed 'a carefully cultivated image' and should not be interpreted as indicative of lowly birth or a 'peasant' upbringing. His father was extremely wealthy (see 1.3, s.u. *faenus...exercuit*), he was a welcome member of the courts of Gaius, Claudius and Nero (apart from an occasional lapse), his son was educated with the imperial prince Britannicus, he may have been granted patrician status as early as 47 (McAlindon, 1957: 260; but see 4.1 above, s.u. *Narcissi gratia*) – and he was inordinately ambitious, ever-ready (for instance) to accept both insults and rewards from Gaius. On the other hand, his sense of humour was one that would not be regarded as offensive in an ex-soldier and general who was, in just about every way, *antiquis ducibus par* (*Hist.* 2.5).

**praetextatis...uerbis:** *praetextatus* – 'characteristic of youth, i.e. unseemly, obscene' (*OLD* 1447): hence *impudica et praetextata uerba* (Macrobius, *Sat.* 2.1.9) and *non praetextatis sed puris honestisque uerbis* (Gell., *NA* 9.10.4).

**facetissima:** Vespasian's reputation for being witty is also noted in the *Epit. de Caes.: ferebat patienter amicorum motus, contumeliis eorum, ut erat facetissimus, iocularibus respondens* (9.3).

**Mestrium Florum consularem:** A friend of Plutarch (when Plutarch received Roman citizenship, he took the *nomen* 'Mestrius'), L. Mestrius Florus (*PIR*² M 531) appears frequently in his *Quaestiones Conuiuiales* and also in *Otho* 14.2, where he is described as a 'Roman of consular rank and one of those who then (i.e. 69, at the first battle of Bedriacum: see 5.7 above, s.u. *acie Betriacensi*) accompanied Otho by constraint and not of their own will'. But, despite Braithwaite (1927: 65), he was not of consular rank at that time. In fact, it was only in the middle of Vespasian's reign that he became suffect consul; then, some ten years later, he held the prestigious proconsulship of Asia; see Eck, 1970: 85-6 with n.48; Wellesley, 1975: 62, 68 and Chilver, 1979: 209.

***plaustra* potius quam *plostra*:** Suetonius attests that Vespasian's fondness for the older pronunciation was quite deliberate. Priscian's comment on the use of *plostrum* for *plaustrum* is '*frequentissime hoc faciebant antiqui*' (1.52). Perhaps Vespasian's pronunciation as well as his sense of humour could be added to Tacitus' list of the qualities that made him *antiquis ducibus par*: *Hist.* 2.5 (see above, s.u. *scurrilis et sordidae*).

***Flaurum*:** What Vespasian did was to avoid the form *Florus* (from *flos*) and use *Flaurus* which recalls the Greek equivalent meaning *uilis, inutilis* or *nequam*.

**sestertia quadringenta:** Vespasian gave the same amount to the actor of 19.1. Burman's argument that Vespasian was the payee and not the payer on the grounds that 'the penurious emperor would never have paid 400,000 sesterces for the favours of a lady who was only too anxious to grant them' (Mooney, 1930: 456) is not consistent with Suetonius' language in this section. Vespasian's *auaritia* (however extensive) did not go as far as that – witness the *plurimae pallacae* of 21 above.

**dispensatore:** The *dispensator*, usually a slave or a freedman, was 'an administrator concerned with finance and similar matters, treasurer, steward' (*OLD* 554).

**pro concubitu:** Zinn, 1951: 10 argues unconvincingly (see Hudson-Williams, 1952: 72-3) that *pro concubitu* means 'rather than lie with her' and *adamato* 'unseduced'.

***Vespasiano adamato:*** *adamo* – 'to conceive a sexual passion for, to love adulterously' (*OLD* 35). The phrase *Vespasiano adamato* has been discussed by Zinn, 1951: 10 and Hudson-Williams, 1952: 72-3 (see above), with the latter arguing that 'a straightforward entry in the emperor's expenditure account would specify the name of his inamorata. In the circumstances, Vespasian substitutes his own name, i.e. "to the loving of Vespasian"'.

### 23.1

**ut et de:** The manuscripts have *et de, et ut de* and *ut de*. Ihm's *et de* is unsatisfactory; the sense requires *ut et de*: see Mooney, 1930: 457.

**uersibus Graecis:** Vespasian's ambitious father (1.2-3 above) ensured not only that his sons were financially eligible to pursue a senatorial career but also that they were educated in an appropriate manner. Thus when he was serving in Ephesus, unwilling to expose the young Vespasian 'aux dangers d'une éducation à la grecque' (van Berchem, 1978: 269), he had arranged for him to be raised by his grandmother Tertulla, at Cosa (2.1). Similarly, the education of Vespasian's own sons was not neglected. Titus was educated at court and his poetry was praised by the Elder Pliny as being as good as his brother's (! *NH Praef.* 5); and Domitian, like his father, was also able to produce appropriate Greek quotations (see *Dom.* 12.3 and 18.2).

**improbiusque nato:** The sense is obvious. Note Braithwaite's delicate comment – *sensu obsceno* (1927: 65); but *nato* poses a problem. Its usual meaning ('a son': *OLD* 1160) is entirely inappropriate here and so scholars argued that Suetonius must have used *nato* in the sense of *natura* (i.e. 'the external organs of generation, the private parts': *OLD* 1159). On the other hand, earlier commentators were not convinced. Casaubon interpreted it as meaning *homo deformi et turpi proceritate corporis*; see Mooney, 1930: 457. A number of corrections have been suggested but the likeliest is *improbiusque uenato*, with the *ue* lost by haplography. *Vena* is often used of the penis (e.g. *rigida...uena*: Martial 6.49.2 from an epigram on a statue of Priapus: see *OLD* 2025) and, though *uenatus* is not attested elsewhere, Suetonius has several adjectives ending in *-atus* not found earlier, e.g. *sagulatus, tessellatus* and *pedatus* (*fuisse enim et modicae staturae et male pedatus* *scambusque [Otho] traditur*: *Otho* 12.1) in the sense of 'provided with feet' (*OLD* 1318).

Μακρά...εγχος: The quotation (*Iliad* 7.213) is from the description of Ajax about to fight Hector.

**Cerylo liberto:** Although this imperial freedman is not definitely mentioned elsewhere, he is probably the Cerylus of Martial 1.67: *Liber homo es nimium, dicis mihi, Ceryle, semper./In te quis dicit, Ceryle, liber homo es?*

**ob subterfugiendum...ius fisci:** The legal position is clear. In Roman law, the *patronus* was regarded as the heir of any of his childless freedmen or was entitled to a share in the estate if there were any legitimate children born after manumission. Cerylus must have been an imperial freedman and so, on his death, his estate (or part of it) would revert to his imperial patron. A change of name and a statement that he was freeborn would fool neither Vespasian nor the officials of the *fiscus* who, once Cerylus/Laches was dead, would soon claim whatever he had left.

**Lachetem:** Cerylus' choice of name was hardly appropriate as 'Laches' was one of the standard names for slaves in Greek comedy.

ὦ Λάχης, Λάχης: These words are from an unknown play of Menander (frag. 921: Kock).

επάν...εσει: This line is from the *Theophoroumene* ('Girl Possessed') of Menanander (frag. 223,2: Kock), with the last line added by Vespasian himself.

**dicacitatem:** For a comment on Vespasian's sense of humour and the eight anecdotes in these sections (from *dicacitatis* in 22 to and *iocis* in 23.4), see the introduction to 22 above.

**ut inuidiam...ad sales:** Vespasian's *auaritia* is the theme of the last four anecdotes.

23.2
**caris ministris:** One of his favourite freedmen; it is only very rarely that the literary sources provide information about the imperial court.

**dispensationem:** See 22, s.u. *dispensatore*.

**ordinauit:** 'appointed' as appears in *Iul.* 76.3 – *magistratus in plures annos ordinauit.*

**ad calciandas mulas:** Mooney (1930: 459) points out that, in antiquity, shoes were not usually put on horses or mules: when they were (e.g. on bad roads), they were never fastened by nails but by strings or straps. Shoes were generally of iron (*ferream ut soleam [derelinquit] tenaci in uoragine mula*: Catull. 17.26), but sometimes of silver (*soleis mularum argenteis: Nero* 30.3) or even gold (*NH* 33.140 and Dio 62.28.1: Poppaea's mules). See also 4.3 above, s.u. *mulio*.

23.3

**urinae uectigal...*lotio est*:** The same anecdote appears (more concisely) in Dio: 'When Titus expressed his indignation at the tax placed upon public urinals (one of the new taxes that had been established), Vespasian said, as he picked up some gold pieces that had been realised from this source and showed them to him: "See, my son, if they have any smell"' (66.14.5). Despite this public pose, Titus was as careful a financier as his father: 'In money matters, Titus was frugal and made no unnecessary expenditures' (Dio 66.19.3).

On one level, the anecdote could be said to exemplify Vespasian's *auaritia*: it also illustrates the fact that, for Suetonius, Titus was not co-ruler with Vespasian (but see Crook [1951: 164] who describes Titus as 'co-emperor' with Vespasian as does Rogers [1980: 90 – 'genuine co-ruler'], a view rejected by Jones [1984: 87]). So this was not a discussion between two partners, for Titus' role was that of apprentice (in money matters) to his master.

Urine was used by the fullers. The practice was for wool to be taken immediately from the loom to the fullers so that the grease and dirt could be removed, and this was done in a mixture of water, stale urine and fuller's earth; but now the fullers had to pay for the urine.

Although the procedure adopted by Vespasian in collecting this particular tax remains obscure, one explanation emerges from a phrase of C. Titius (ca 150 BC) as reported by Macrobius: *dum eunt, nulla est in angiporto amphora quam non impleant* (*Sat.* 3.16.15). So receptacles (*amphorae* or *dolia*) must have been placed in each alley (*angiportus*), but now the right to empty them was made subject to a tax. Vespasian's interest in such matters has been immortalised in French where the word for 'urinal' is 'une Vespasienne'.

**non mediocris summae:** According to Dio (see below), the sum was one million sesterces.

**iussit...ponere:** The manuscripts have either *poneret* or *ponerent*, but it is difficult to go beyond Bentley's *ponere*.

**cauam manum...dicens:** The money was to be the statue with Vespasian's hand as the base: compare Pliny's *iube basim fieri, ex quo uoles marmore, quae nomen meum honoresque capiat: Ep.* 3.6.5. For the beggar's 'hollow hand', note *stipem quotannis die certo emendicabat a populo cauam manum asses porrigentibus praebens*: *Aug.* 91.2. This is the last of the four anecdotes illustrating Vespasian's alleged *auaritia*, so firmly fixed in the literary tradition. Again, it appears in Dio – 'When some persons voted to erect to him a statue costing a million, he held out his hand and said: "Give me the money; this is its pedestal"' (66.14.5).

23.4

**ac ne in metu quidem...abstinuit iocis:** Similarly in the *Epit. de Caes.: seriis ioca, quibus delectabatur, admiscens interiit* (9.17). For a comment on this brief transition to the death scene, see the introduction to 22 above.

**prodigia:** Dio refers to the same two omens: 'Portents had occurred indicating his approaching end, such as the comet which was visible for a long time and the opening of the mausoleum of Augustus of its own accord' (Dio 66.17.2). Once again, Vespasian's reaction was, as Dio had put it, 'to indulge in jests' (66.11.1).

Vespasian's use of these omens is not without interest. Gorringe suggests that, by using Junia Calvina's descent from Augustus to dissociate the Mausoleum omen from himself, Vespasian 'implicitly draws attention to the success of his propaganda in establishing himself as (Augustus') legitimate heir and successor' (1993: 437). Again, there is the connection between *Calvina* and *caluus* – an adjective pointing unmistakably to Vespasian himself.

**inter cetera prodigia:** Suetonius gives no more detail on the nature of these *cetera prodigia*, an omission all the more noteworthy in view of the prominence ascribed to the omens that heralded his accession. Normally, they would be included in the death-narrative itself, but it would be inappropriate here, given the inclusion immediately before the death-narrative of two omens (the Mausoleum and the comet) as yet further examples of Vespasianic *dicacitas*; see further, Gorringe, 1993: 439.

**Mausoleum:** The opening of the doors of the Mausoleum also heralded the death of Nero (*de Mausoleo, sponte foribus patefactis, exaudita uox est nomine eum cientis: Nero* 46.2). In 28 BC, the *Mausoleum Augusti* (called the *tumulus Augusti* and *tumulus Iuliorum* by Tacitus, *Ann.* 3.4, 16.6) was built by Augustus in the northern part of the Campus Martius. This impressive circular building was about

87 metres in diameter and over 44 metres high with a statue of Augustus crowning its apex; see Toynbee, 1971: 148 for photographs (aerial view) and 153 (section and plan). Those whose ashes were placed there included Marcellus, Octavia, M. Agrippa, Tiberius' brother Drusus, Lucius Caesar, Gaius Caesar, Augustus, Germanicus, Livia, Tiberius, Agrippina the Elder and Gaius' brother Drusus. Claudius, Britannicus and Poppaea were probably buried there, as was (so Macciocca argues in Steinby, 1996: 239) Vespasian's wife, Domitilla. Laid to rest there also was the emperor Nerva, as were, for a time, both Vespasian and Julia Domna. No doubt Domitian had taken the ashes of Vespasian to the Templum Gentis Flaviae (Platner-Ashby, 1929: 247; Blake, 1959: 114 and Jones, 1996: 12) as well as those of Titus and Julia (*Dom.* 17.3), whilst his nurse, Phyllis, later placed his own there as well (*Dom.* 17.3). Further information is provided by Dio who reports that ' Hadrian was buried near the river itself, close to the Aelian bridge; for it was there that he had prepared his tomb, since the tomb of Augustus was full and from this time no body was deposited in it' (69.23.1). On the Mausoleum, see Toynbee, 1971: 144-54 (*passim*) and Steinby, 1996: 234-9.

**stella crinita:** The appearance of a comet heralded the death of a ruler, so it was thought – hence Shakespeare ('When beggars die there are no comets seen; the heavens themselves blaze forth the death of princes': *Julius Caesar* 2.2) and Suetonius (*stella crinita, quae summis potestatibus exitium portendere uulgo putatur, per continuas noctes oriri coeperat* : *Nero* 36.1). Claudius' death was also heralded by the same phenomenon: *praesagia mortis eius praecipua fuerunt: exortus crinitae stellae quam cometen uocant...* (*Claud.* 46).

**Iuniam Caluinam:** She was one of the four children of M. Junius Silanus Torquatus (*cos.* 19) and Aemilia Lepida; see Syme, 1989: 185-6, 197 and Table IV. The fate of her three brothers (Marcus, Decimus and Lucius) was determined by the fact that they were great-great-grandchildren of Augustus; see *OCD* 789-90. Calvina's brother Lucius was betrothed to Claudius' daughter Octavia, and, in order to remove this obstacle to Agrippina's dynastic plans for her son Nero, Lucius was accused of incest with his sister Calvina (his *decora et procax soror*: *Ann.* 12.4) who was at that time married to L. Vitellius (the future emperor's younger brother). The betrothal was cancelled; in 49, Lucius was forced to commit suicide and Calvina suffered *relegatio* (*Ann.* 12.8); ten years later, following Agrippina's death, she was recalled by Nero (*Ann.* 14.12).

**e gente Augusti:** She was Augustus' great-great-granddaughter. His daughter Julia married M. Agrippa, their daughter Julia married L. Aemilius Paullus and their daughter Aemilia Lepida married M. Junius Silanus Torquatus, on whom see the previous item.

**ad Parthorum regem qui capillatus esset:** The reference is to Vologaesus (*PIR*[1] V 630, successor to the king of the same name (*PIR*[1] V 629) discussed in 6.4 above, s.u. *e regibus Vologaesus Parthus*; and the Parthians, who succeeded the Persians, were *capillati* (see Hdt. 6.19), unlike the *caluus Vespasianus*. Vespasian's interpretation of the omen is reported both by Dio ('To those who said anything to him about the comet he said: "This is an omen, not for me, but for the Parthian king; for he has long hair, whereas I am bald"': 66.17.3) and in the *Epit. de Caes.* (*cum crinitum sidus apparuisset, 'Istud', inquit [Vespasianus], 'ad regem Persarum pertinet', cui capillus effusior*: 9.18). See also the discussion above, 23.4, s.u. *inter cetera prodigia*.

*puto deus fio*: Dio has the same report: 'When at last Vespasian was convinced that he was going to die, he said: "I am already becoming a god"' (66.17.3). This is the ultimate instance of Vespasian's *dicacitas*. Suetonius' use of Vespasian's comment is no doubt (see the argument of Schmidt, 1988: 83-9) intended to recall the last words attributed to Claudius: *ultima uox eius haec inter homines audita est, cum maiorem sonitum emississet illa parte qua facilius loquebatur: uae me, puto concacaui me (Apocol. 4.3)* and also, perhaps, to provide an ironical reminder of other links between Vespasian and Claudius (see 4 above). Gorringe aptly comments that 'not only does the joke...correspond with the rather earthy nature of Vespasian's preferences in humour, and also with his penchant for using literary quotations, but gains added impact from the fact that his own last illness was compounded by attacks of diarrhoea' (1993: 438).

However, Vespasian was not merely laughing at the concept of deification. As Fishwick notes, the remark should be interpreted as 'the ironic testament of a hard-headed administrator who realised that his eternal reward was to be posthumously "hoist with his own petard"'(1987: 300). For Vespasian was perfectly well aware of the political value of deification. In Rome and Italy, he was *ciuilis* (see 12 above) and made no claim to superhuman powers – but not so in Alexandria in 69/70 where he was indeed Serapis (so Henrichs, 1968: 68-70) and where he was addressed as 'Serapis, Son of Ammon, Saviour and Benefactor' (*P. Fouad* 8 = *MW* 41: see 19.2, s.u. *Alexandrini* for the complete text). In the provinces, he never discouraged those who proclaimed his divinity. Quite the contrary – in Spain, as Étienne (1974: 445-59) has shown, 'Vespasien renforce son autorité en étendant le culte impérial dans chaque catégorie de la hiérarchie administrative et en l'uniformisant: il fraie la voie à l'unité profonde de la péninsule' (1974: 454). In fact, throughout the western provinces of the empire, it was under

Vespasian that 'the extension of the ruler cult appears to have reached its climax' (Fishwick, 1987: 299); and, far from ridiculing the political value of deification, the evidence suggests that, in Lycia and Armenia, the person responsible for installing the provincial cult was Vespasian himself (see ibid. 300).

Vespasian's statement was more accurate than he imagined. At Ephesus, for instance, the cult of the Flavians remained in existence, even after Domitian's *damnatio memoriae*, but, by the end of the second century, was apparently referred to as that of Vespasian alone; see Friesen, 1993: 37 with n.27.

The honour of deification was decreed by the senate on a motion of the reigning emperor and the ceremony (*consecratio*) was normally held soon after his predecessor's death (see Clarke, 1966: 318-21). So it is usually assumed (e.g. by Weynand *RE* 6.2674; Braithwaite, 1927: 67; Scott, 1975: 20 and Hammond, 1959: 223) that Vespasian was deified not long after July 79. However, it seems that Titus delayed the ceremony for more than six months, finally holding it in the first part of 80 (Buttrey, 1976: 457).

Of Suetonius' twelve *Caesares*, only five (Julius Caesar, Augustus, Claudius, Vespasian and Titus) were deified and two of them were Flavians. For *diuus Vespasianus* on Titus' coins and inscriptions, see Scott, 1936: 40-5. Pliny also refers to Vespasian's *consecratio* in the *Panegyricus*, i.e. *dicauit caelo...Claudium Nero, sed ut irrideret; Vespasianum Titus, Domitianus Titum, sed ille ut dei filius, hic ut frater uideretur* (11.1).

For a detailed discussion of Vespasian's famous last words, see Fishwick, 1987: 295-300.

## 24

**consulatu suo nono:** He was in office until 13 January 79: see Gallivan, 1981: 215.

**in Campania motiunculis leuibus:** Celsus mentions the curative powers of the *aquae Cutiliae* in a discussion of why the stomach does not retain food (*cum cibi non tenax est*: *Med.* 4.12). So, when Vespasian was in Campania, he may not have been suffering from 'slight attacks of fever and ague' as Mooney (1930: 462) and Braithwaite (1927: 67) state, but from a stomach disorder that became even more serious with his visit to Cutiliae (a Sabine village about 12km from Reate).

**Cutilias:** That Vespasian died at Cutiliae is confirmed by Dio: 'Vespasian passed away at Aquae Cutiliae in the Sabine country' (66.17.1). The Elder Pliny refers to its lake, now the Lago di Contigliano (*in agro Reatino est Cutiliae lacum...Italiae umbilicum esse M. Varro tradit*: *NH* 3.10) and a number of ancient sources mention the curative powers of its springs, e.g. Pliny (*Cutiliae in Sabinis gelidissimae suctu quodam corpora inuadunt ut prope morsus uideri possit, aptissimae stomacho,* *neruis, uniuerso corpori: NH* 31.10) and Vitruvius (*est autem aquae frigidae genus nitrosum, uti Pinnae Vestinae, Cutiliis aliisque locis similibus, quae potionibus depurgat per aluumque transeundo etiam strumarum minuit tumores: De Arch.* 8.3.5) and Celsus (*consistere in frigidis medicatisque fontibus, quales Cutili-arum...sunt, salutare est: Med.* 4.12.7).

**Reatina rura:** See 1.2 above, s.u. *municeps Reatinus.*

**ubi aestiuare quotannis solebat:** During the extremely hot summer months, most (if not all) senators abandoned Rome, e.g. *Tusculum ubi [Galba] aestiuare consueuerat* (*Galba* 4.3). The Flavians must have regularly withdrawn to their Sabine retreat and it was here, and during much the same time of the year, that Titus died two years later – *excessit in eadem qua pater uilla Id. Sept. post bien-nium ac menses duos diesque XX quam successerat patri...* (*Titus* 11).

**frigidae aquae:** Similarly, Vitruvius (8.3.5), Celsus (*Med.* 4.12) and the Elder Pliny (*NH* 31.10); see above.

**legationes:** For a discussion of the significance of embassies to the emperor during the empire, see Millar, 1977: 375-85. In the late republic and the Julio-Claudian period, multi-member embassies were the norm. A change occurred after Nero's death – a limit of three representatives per embassy was imposed, as is clear from one of Vespasian's edicts, viz. *praecipitur autem edicto diui Vespasiani omnibus ciuitatibus, ne plures quam ternos legatos mittant* (*Digest* 50. 7.5.6). No doubt financial considerations swayed Vespasian, for this was an expensive practice both for Rome and for the provinces – see *Quaest. Rom.* 43 (Mor. 275c) and Pliny, *Ep.* 10. 43-4 (with Sherwin-White, 1966: 625) for some details of the costs involved. Only two embassies to Vespasian are attested (Vanacini and Sabora; see Millar, 1977: 235-6 and 435; Souris, 1982: 242); nonetheless, there is no reason to doubt his punctiliousness in performing his *munera imperatoria.*

**aluo...soluta:** Similar details appear in the *Epit. de Caes.* (*uentris eluuie fessus:* 9.18) and in Eutropius (*profluuio uentris extinctus est:* 7.20.2). Dio has a less precise and, it seems, less reliable report: 'Vespasian fell sick, not, if the truth be known, of his accustomed gout, but of a fever... Some, however, in the endeavour falsely to incriminate Titus, among them the emperor Hadrian, spread the report that he was poisoned at a banquet' (66.17.1). Dio's reference to Titus and a meal recalls what had happened to Caecina: *Aulum Caecinam consularem uocatum ad cenam ac uixdum triclinio egressum confodi [Titus] iussit* (*Titus* 6.2). On the other hand, the rumour may have had its origin in the fact that the administration

of poison is associated with gastric attacks – by Tacitus with diarrhoea (*Ann.*
12.67 and 13.15) and by Suetonius with vomiting (*Claud.* 44.3 and *Nero* 33.2);
in each case the victims were Claudius and Britannicus. However, Suetonius is
quite specific about the cause of death and has no hint whatsoever of foul play.
For further speculation, see Gorringe, 1993: 442-3.

**imperatorem...stantem mori**: Similarly, the *Epit. de Caes.* has Vespasian saying
*stantem imperatorem excedere terris decet* (9.18). Dio has the same anecdote: 'When
his physicians chided him for continuing his usual course of living during his
illness..., he answered "The emperor ought to die on his feet"' (66.17.2); and later
he repeats it, changing both its subject and the circumstances: 'Turbo was never
seen at home in the day-time, even when he was sick; and to Hadrian, who advised
him to remain quiet, he replied: "The prefect ought to die on his feet"' (69.18.4).

**dumque...nititur**: Perhaps Suetonius is deliberately harking back to the physical
description of Vespasian in 20: *statura fuit quadrata,...uultu ueluti nitentis; de
quo quidam urbanorum non infacete, siquidem petenti, ut et in se aliquid diceret:
dicam, inquit, cum uentrem exonerare desieris.*

**extinctus est VIIII Kal. Iul.**: 23 June 79. However, the date of his death is disputed,
e.g. by Homo (1949: 383) and Buttrey (1980: 7, 20) who nominate 24 June, on
the basis of Dio's inconsistent statement that 'he had lived for sixty-nine years
and eight months, and reigned for ten years less six days' (66.17.3); for a discussion of the possibilities posed by Dio's text, see Braithwaite, 1927: 68.

**annum agens aetatis sexagensimum ac nonum superque mensem ac diem
septimum**: Suetonius should have used *natus* rather than *agens* – Vespasian was in
(*agens*) his seventieth year. If *septimum* is taken with both *mensem* and *diem*, the
calculation is accurate: Vespasian was born 17 November 9 and died 23 June 79.
Dio, less precise, says that he lived sixty-nine years and eight months (66.17.3).

## 25

**genitura**: The reference is to Vespasian's horoscope. Despite Tacitus' well-
known comment that astrologers were a *genus hominum potentibus infidum,
sperantibus fallax, quod in ciuitate nostra et uetabitur semper et retinebitur* (*Hist.*
1.22), astrology was widely practised during the empire and its predictions often
accepted. As early as the second century BC, at a time when scientific astronomy
had come into its own thanks to Hipparchus of Rhodes, astrology had managed
to gain 'scientific precision' and intellectual respectability, especially when it
was taken over by the famous Stoic Posidonius (see Liebeschuetz, 1979: 121).

The Flavians and many others believed in this so-called science; Domitian, for instance, was convinced that the astrologers were able to predict his *annum diemque ultimum uitae...horam etiam nec non et genus mortis* (*Dom.* 14.1). That Vespasian consulted them on the subject of the succession is also mentioned by both Aurelius Victor (*De Caes.* 9.4) and Eutropius (7.20.3), both quoted below, s.u. *aut filios...aut neminem.* Dio also states that 'Vespasian banished the astrologers from Rome, even though he was in the habit of consulting all the best of them himself, and, by way of showing a favour to Barbillus, a man of that profession, had even permitted the Ephesians to celebrate some sacred games, a privilege that he granted to no other city' (Dio 66.9.2).

**assiduas in se coniurationes:** Not many can be identified. Just as vague are the versions of Aurelius Victor (*coniurationum multas scelere inulto abscedere patiebatur*: *De Caes.* 9.3) and Eutropius (*cum multae contra eum coniurationes fierent*: 7.20.3). Dio, however, refers to two incidents, both of which occurred in 79; for the date, see *Hist.* 4.67.

There was the execution of Julius Sabinus, his wife Epponina and their family (66.16.1). He had claimed to be descended from an illegitimate son of Julius Caesar and so, claiming the title *Caesar*, had taken part in Julius Classicus' unsuccessful uprising; see Wellesley, 1975: 183 for the details.

More important was the alleged conspiracy of Eprius Marcellus and Caecina Alienus. Suffect consul in 62, Ti. Clodius Eprius Marcellus (for a detailed discussion of his career, see Birley, 1980: 228-30) was one of the accusers of Thrasea Paetus and later emerged as a champion of the Flavians in the senate, engaging in fierce debate with Helvidius Priscus. For this, he was more than amply rewarded – with a three-year proconsulship of Asia and a second suffect consulship in 74 – and was rated as one of the two *principes in Caesaris amicitia* (*Dial.* 8.3). Aulus Caecina Alienus (*RE* 3.1238-40; *PIR*[2] C 95), on the other hand, had a more varied career. Outdoing even the Vicar of Bray, he had managed to be a supporter of Galba, then to hold a suffect consulship (from 1 Sept. 69) after commanding one of a Vitellius' armies and, ultimately, he became an *amicus* of Vespasian. His role in the seventies remains a mystery, apart from an isolated comment by the so-called epitomator of Aurelius Victor: *Caecinam consularem, adhibitum cenae, uixdum triclinio egressum, ob suspicionem stupratae Berenicis uxoris suae iugulari iussit* (10.4). Dio, however, believes that there was a conspiracy involving them both. According to him, Vespasian 'was the object of a conspiracy on the part of both Alienus and Marcellus.... But he did not die at their hands, for they were detected. Alienus was slain at once, in the imperial residence itself, as he rose from a meal with his intended victim. Titus issued this order, desiring to forestall any act of revolution that night, for Alienus had already got many of the soldiers in readiness. Marcellus was brought to trial before the senate and was condemned, whereupon he cut his own throat with a razor' (66.16.3). Suetonius, however, makes no mention of Marcellus and links the removal of Caecina with Titus' actions as the new regime's 'enforcer': *egitque [Titus] aliquanto inciuilius et uiolentius, siquidem suspectissimum quemque sibi summissis qui per theatra et castra quasi consensu ad poenam deposcerent, haud cunctanter oppressit. in his Aulum Caecinam...confodi iussit, sane urgente discrimine, cum etiam chirographum eius praeparatae apud milites contionis deprehendisset (Titus 6.1-2)*; and Titus was expert at copying others' handwriting, as Suetonius asserts: *e pluri- bus comperi...imitarique chirographa quaecumque uidisset ac saepe profiteri maximum falsarium esse potuisse (Titus 3.2)*.

Of course, the executions ordered by Titus may have been prompted by (or, on the other hand, have actually prompted) conspiracies real or imagined; but Vespasian was content to let the blame accrue to him, whereas *ceterum neque caede cuiusquam umquam iustis suppliciis inlacrimauit [Vespasianus] etiam et ingemuit* (15).

*aut filios sibi successuros aut neminem*: Aurelius Victor's version is similar (*simul diuinis deditus, quorum uera plerisque negotiis compererat, successores fidebat liberos Titum et Domitianum fore: Caes. 9.4*), as is that of Eutropius (*genituram filiorum ita cognitam habuit ut, cum multae contra eum coniurationes fierent, quas patefactas ingenti dissimulatione contempsit, in senatu dixerit aut filios sibi successuros aut neminem: 7.20.3*), whereas, in Dio, the anecdote has an entirely different setting: '(Helvidius Priscus) would not cease reviling Vespasian. Therefore the tribunes once arrested him and gave him in charge of their assistants, a procedure at which Vespasian was overcome by emotion and went out of the chamber in tears, saying merely: "*My* successor shall be my son or no one at all"' (66.12.1). Both versions, though incompatible, are internally consistent. According to Suetonius, Vespasian was provoked by *assiduas in se coniurationes* (two of which can be assigned to 79) and the general context of the remark suggests that it was made late in the reign. But the nature of Vespasian's dynastic policy was obvious as early as 70 and Dio's use of the singular ('son') is appropriate if Vespasian's outburst occurred after Helvidius had denounced the role assigned to Titus (see below) and advocated that the 'best man' (i.e. best senator) be the next emperor: after all; Titus' exceptional position, expressed publicly on coins and inscriptions, left no one in doubt as to Vespasian's intentions. On the other hand, Helvidius might have been objecting not to the principle of dynastic succession but to the character of the proposed successor (see 15 above, s.u. *Helvidio Prisco*) which would not have been quite as obvious if Vespasian's outburst had occurred in the early years of the reign.

127

Throughout the seventies, *Imp.* occurs in Titus' official titulature but in four different positions, viz. (*Imp.*) Titus (*imp.*) Caesar (*imp.*) Vespasianus (*imp.*); and whilst it never appears as a *praenomen* in documents from Rome, it does so on some coins and inscriptions from Asia; see Jones (1984) 102-3 and *MW* 86 (of 76 from Lesser Armenia, with *Imp. Tito Caesare Aug.f...*; but compare *MW* 93 of 72-3 from near Samosata, with *T. Caesar Vespasianus imp...*). However, the presence of *imperator* in any of these four positions implies some sort of *imperium* for Titus; its inconsistent location, though, as well as the absence of *Augustus*, leaves no doubt that it was secondary to Vespasian's.

Furthermore, within three years of his return to Rome, Titus was awarded, in conjunction with Vespasian, almost every imperial office and title – apart, that is, from *Augustus*, *pontifex maximus* and *pater patriae*, which, by their very nature, could be held by one person only. In view of Suetonius' statement that *neque ex eo destitit participem atque tutorem imperii agere* (*Titus* 6.1), he must have held proconsular *imperium*: we have epigraphic evidence for his *tribunicia potestas* and for his censorship (12 and 8.1 above). By the end of the reign, he had held seven ordinary consulships (in 74, for instance, he was already *cos. III ord.*) and was also praetorian prefect, appointed without a colleague, so it seems.

Particularly significant was the absence of a fresh salutation at the time of Titus' accession to the throne in June 79. He was already *imp. XIV* in 78 (Buttrey, 1980: 19) and remained so on Vespasian's death; *imp. XV* occurred later in 79 and is specifically attributed by Dio to the victory of Agricola in Britain (66.20.3). It would appear that, from the time of Claudius, the *praenomen* of *imperator* recorded the salutation an emperor received on his accession and that *imp. II* was reserved for the first victory won under his auspices. In addition, salutations were reserved for the emperor only and not available to his presumed heir. So Titus' first salutation so early in his father's reign proclaimed, for all to see, the extent of his power and the nature of his position. Hence he has been described as 'in practice, if not in theory, co-emperor' (Crook, 1951: 164); as 'quasi-equal colleague' of Vespasian (Hammond, 1956: 82); and even as 'genuine co-ruler' (Rogers, 1980: 90). Vespasian hardly needed to make another public statement about the succession and the role intended for Titus. His very first one had been made in June 71 a few days after Titus' arrival, i.e. at the time of the 'double' triumph'. Vespasian had rejected the senate's offer of separate triumphs (*BJ* 7.121) and so, in the procession, the dress and posture of Vespasian and his son were identical, as were their prayers and sacrifices (*BJ* 7.124 ff.).

Yet Suetonius' *filios* was accurate. Domitian's position was clearly inferior to Titus' and not unreasonably so, for Titus was just over thirty on Vespasian's accession and Domitian just under twenty; Titus had commanded a legion in his late twenties and was in overall control of four legions against Jerusalem immediately afterwards. But Domitian received six consulships (one of them ordinary, in 73) during Vespasian's reign – and three consulships was, according to the younger Pliny, the *summum fastigium* (*Ep.* 2.1.2) of an ordinary senator's ambition. Moreover, throughout Vespasian's reign, Titus always had two consulships fewer than Vespasian and Domitian one fewer than Titus; thus, in 76, Ves- pasian was *Cos. VII*, Titus *Cos. V* and Domitian *Cos. IV*, thereby reflecting exactly the relative status of each member of the family. His other honours included the titles *Caesar* and *Princeps Iuventutis*, various priesthoods (he is attested as *augur, frater arvalis, magister fratrum arvalium, pontifex* and *sacerdos collegiorum omnium*) and, from 72, he possessed the right to have coins issued theoretically under his own aegis (Jones, 1971: 269, notes 38 to 44). What he did not receive, either from Vespasian or from Titus, was *tribunicia potestas* and the title *Imperator*. Nevertheless, he was clearly designated by Vespasian as Titus' successor. Vespasian's dynastic intentions could not have been stated more clearly.

**media parte uestibuli Palatinae domus...Claudius et Nero:** This is in complete accord with Flavian propaganda that portrayed Vespasian as the legitimate successor of the Julio-Claudians and hence the scales are located, not in the *Horti Sallustiani* preferred by Vespasian, but in the official, imperial palace, the *domus Palatinus* or *Palatium*. Dio explains that the name originated from the fact that the emperor lived on the Palatine hill: 'if he resides anywhere else, his dwelling retains the name of *Palatium*' (53.16.6). This had long been the favoured residential area of the capital, but, under the empire, private homes gradually disappeared, with few surviving the fire of 64, and a complex of imperial residences, houses and gardens developed. Domitian's grandiose palace, for instance, covered the entire south-eastern half of the hill. By Suetonius' time, the terms *Palatium*/ *Palatinus* were regularly used of each emperor's official residence; so Tiberius starved Drusus to death *in ima parte Palatii* (*Tib.* 54.2), Gaius opened a *lupanar in Palatio* (*Gaius* 41.1) and Vitellius' 'abdication' was announced to his assembled troops *pro gradibus Palatii* (*Vit.* 15.2). Augustus had had a freedman in charge of the *Palatinae bibliothecae* (*De Gramm.* 20) and Domitian's *cubicularius* was described by Martial as *Palatinus Parthenius* (4.45).

**totidem annis:** i.e. twenty-seven – 41 to 68 for Claudius and Nero, 69 to 96 for the Flavians. See Mooney, 1930: 465 for the calculation in days, months and years.

**parique temporis...imperauerunt:** After the reference to Vespasian's insistence that his sons would succeed him and the fact that he was proven correct, Suetonius recalls the opening sentence of the *Diuus Vespasianus*, with its emphasis on the achievement of the Flavian dynasty: *incertum diu et quasi uagum imperium suscepit firmauitque tandem gens Flauia* (1.1).

129

# Bibliography

Ahl, F., 'The Art of Safe Criticism in Greece and Rome' *AJPh* 105 (1984) 174-208.

Anderson, J.C., 'A Topographical Tradition in the Fourth Century Chronicles. Domitian's Building Programme' *Historia* 32 (1983) 93-105.

——*The Historical Topography of the Imperial Fora* (*Collection Latomus* 182, 1984).

Anna, G.d', *Le Idee Letterarie di Suetonio* (La Nuova Italia, 1954).

Arnaud, P., 'L'Affaire Mettius Pompusianus ou le Crime de Cartographie' *MEFR* 95 (1983) 677-99.

Auguet, R., *Cruelty and Civilization: The Roman Games* (1972: repr. Routledge, 1994).

Baldwin, B., *Suetonius* (Hakkert, 1983).

Balsdon, J.P.V.D., *Roman Women: Their History and Habits* (Bodley Head, 1962: rev. 1974).

Bardon, H., 'Les Flaviens et la Littérature: Essai d'Autocritique' *Atti* (1981) 175-94.

Barrett, A.A., *Caligula: The Corruption of Power* (B.T. Batsford, 1989).

——*Agrippina: Mother of Nero* (B.T. Batsford, 1996).

Bastianini, G., 'Il Prefetto d' Egitto (30 a.C.-297 d.C.): Addenda 1973-1985' *ANRW* 2.10.1 (1988) 503-17.

Bauman, R.A., *Impietas in Principem. A Study of Treason against the Roman Emperor with Special Reference to the First Century AD* (C.H. Beck, 1974).

——'The Resumé of Legislation in Suetonius' *ZRG* 99 (1982) 81-127.

Benediktson, D.T., 'A Survey of Suetonius Scholarship, 1938-1987' *CW* 86 (1993) 377-447.

Bengstson, H., *Die Flavier. Vespasian, Titus, Domitian. Geschichte eines römischen Kaiserhauses* (C.H. Beck, 1979).

Bennett, J., *Trajan Optimus Princeps: A Life and Times* (Routledge, 1997).

Bérard, F., 'La Carrière de Plotius Grypus et le Ravitaillement de l'Armée Impériale en Campagne' *MEFR* 96 (1984) 259-324.

Berchem, D. van, *Les Distributions de Blé et d' Argent à la Plèbe Romaine sous l' Empire* (1939: repr. Arno Press, 1975).

——'Un Banquier chez les Helvètes' *Ktèma* 3 (1978) 267-74.

——'Une Inscription Flavienne du Musée d'Antioche' *MH* 40 (1983) 185-96.

——'Le Port de Séleucie de Piérie et l' Infrastructure Logistique des Guerres parthiques' *BJ* 185 (1985) 47-87.

Birley, A.R., 'Petillius Cerialis and the Conquest of Brigantia' *Britannia* 4 (1973) 179-90.

———'Agricola, the Flavian Dynasty and Tacitus' in *The Ancient Historian and His Materials* (Gregg International, 1978) 139-54.

———The Fasti of Roman Britain (Clarendon Press, 1981).

———'Hadrian and Greek Senators' *ZPE* 116 (1997) 209-45.

———Hadrian: The Restless Emperor (Routledge, 1997: repr. 1998).

Birley, E., 'The Adherence of Britain to Vespasian' *Britannia* 9 (1978) 256-8.

———'*Evocati Aug.*: A Review' *ZPE* 43 (1981) 25-9.

Blake, M.E., *Roman Construction in Italy from Tiberius through the Flavians* (Carnegie Institute of Washington, 1959).

Bosworth, A.B., 'Vespasian and the Provinces: some Problems of the Early 70's AD' *Athenaeum* 51 (1973) 49-78.

———'Vespasian's Reorganisation of the North-East Frontier' *Antichthon* 10 (1976) 63-78.

———'Arrian and the Alani' *HSCPh* 81 (1977) 217-55.

———'Firmus of Arretium', *ZPE* 39 (1980) 267-77.

Bradley, K.R., 'The Chronology of Nero's Visit to Greece' *Latomus* 37 (1978) 61-72.

———*Suetonius' 'Life of Nero': An Historical Commentary* (*Collection Latomus* 157, 1978a).

———'Nero's Retinue in Greece, AD 66/67' *Illinois Classical Studies* 4 (1979) 152-7.

———'The Imperial Ideal in Suetonius' *Caesares*' *ANRW* 2.33.5 (1991) 3701-32.

———*Suetonius Volume I* (Introduction): with an English Translation by J.C. Rolfe (Harvard University Press, 1998).

Braithwaite, A.W., *C. Suetonii Tranquilli Divus Vespasianus with an Introduction and Commentary* (Clarendon Press, 1927).

Branigan, K., 'Vespasian and the South-West' *Proceedings of the Dorset Natural History and Archaeological Society* 25 (1970) 50-7.

Branigan, K. and Fowler, J. P. (eds), *The Roman West Country: Classical Culture and Celtic Society* (David and Charles, 1976).

Braund, D.C., *Rome and the Friendly King: The Character of Client Kingship* (St Martin's Press, 1984).

Breckenridge, J.D., 'Imperial Portraits from Augustus to Gallienus' *ANRW* 2.12.2 (1981) 477-552.

Brown, F.E., 'History and Topography, Cosa I' *MAAR* 10 (1951) 73-5.

Brunt, P.A., 'Procuratorial Jurisdiction' *Latomus* 25 (1966) 461-87.

———*Italian Manpower: 225 BC – AD 14* (Clarendon Press, 1971).

———'Stoicism and the Principate' *PBSR* 43 (1975) 7-35.

Brunt, P.A., 'The Administrators of Roman Egypt' *JRS* 65 (1975a) 124-47.

——'The *Lex de Imperio Vespasiani*' *JRS* 67 (1977) 95-116.

——'Free Labour and Public Works at Rome' *JRS* 70 (1980) 81-98.

——*Roman Imperial Themes* (Clarendon Press, 1990).

Bureth, P., 'Le Préfet d' Égypte (30 av. J.C.-297 ap. J.C.): État Présent de la Documentation en 1973' *ANRW* 2.10.1 (1988) 471-502.

Burton, G.P., 'Provincial Procurators' *Chiron* 23 (1993) 13-28.

Buttrey, T.V., 'Vespasian's *Consecratio* and the Numismatic Evidence' *Historia* 25 (1976) 449-57.

——*Documentary Evidence for the Chronology of the Flavian Titulature* (*Beiträge zur Klassischen Philologie* 112, 1980).

Cadoux, T.J., Review of Vitucci, 1956. *JRS* 49 (1959) 152-60.

Campbell, B., 'Auxiliary Artillery Revisited' *BonnJhb* 186 (1986) 117-32.

Cantarella, E., *Bisexuality in the Roman World* (Yale University Press, 1992: Paperback, 1994).

Casson, L., 'Unemployment, the Building Trade and Suetonius *Vesp*. 18' *BASP* 15 (1978) 43-51.

Castagnoli, F., 'Politica Urbanistica di Vespasiano in Roma' *Atti* (1981) 261-73.

Castritius, H., 'Zu den Frauen der Flavier' *Historia* 18 (1969) 492-502.

Champlin, E., '*Figlinae Marcianae*' *Athenaeum* 61 (1983) 257-64.

Charlesworth, M.P., 'Flaviana' *JRS* 27 (1937) 54-62.

Chastagnol, A., '*Latus Clauus* et *Adlectio*: l' Accès des Hommes Nouveaux au Sénat Romain sous le Haut-Empire' *RHDFE* 53 (1975) 375-94.

——'Le Laticlave de Vespasien' *Historia* 25 (1976) 253-6.

Chilver, G.E.F., 'The War between Otho and Vitellius and the North Italian Towns' (*Atti: Centro Studi e Documentazione sull' Italia Romana*, 1970/71) 101-14.

——*A historical Commentary on Tacitus' Histories I and II* (Clarendon Press, 1979).

Chilver, G.E.F. and Townend, G., *An historical Commentary on Tacitus' Histories IV and V* (Clarendon Press, 1985).

Cizek, E., *Structures et Idéologie dans 'Les Vies des Douze Césars' de Suétone* (Les Belles Lettres, 1977).

Clarke, G.W., 'The Date of the *Consecratio* of Vespasian' *Historia* 15 (1966) 318-27.

Cohen, S.J.D., *Josephus in Galilee and Rome: His Vita and Development as a Historian* (E.J. Brill, 1979).

Coleman, K.M., 'The Emperor Domitian and Literature' *ANRW* 2.32.5 (1986) 3087-115.

Coninck, L. de, *Suetonius en de Archivalia* (Paleis der Academien, 1983).

——'Les Sources Documentaires de Suétone, "Les XII Césars": 1900-1990' *ANRW* 2.33.5 (1991) 3675-700.

Corte, F. della, *Suetonio: Eques Romanus* 2nd edn (La Nuova Italia, 1967).

Couissin, J., 'Suétone Physiognomoniste dans les *Vies Des XII Césars*' *REL* 31 (1953) 234-56.

Courtney, E., *A Commentary on the Satires of Juvenal* (Athlone Press, 1980).

Crawford, M.H., *Roman Statutes* (*BICS Suppl.* 64, 1996).

Creed, J.L., *Lactantius: De Mortibus Persecutorum* (Clarendon Press, 1984: repr. 1989).

Crook, J., 'Titus and Berenice' *AJPh* 72 (1951) 162-75.

———*Consilium Principis: Imperial Councils and Counsellors from Augustus to Diocletian* (Cambridge University Press, 1955).

Dabrowa, E., 'Le Limes Anatolien et la Frontière Caucasienne au Temps des Flaviens' *Klio* 62 (1980) 379-88.

———'Les Rapports entre Rome et les Parthes sous Vespasien' *Syria* 58 (1981) 187-204.

———'Roman Policy in Transcaucasia from Pompey to Domitian' *The Eastern Frontier of the Roman Empire: Proceedings of a Colloquium held at Ankara in September 1988* ed. by D.H. French and C.S. Lightfoot (*BAR International Series* 553 [1] 1989) 67-76.

———'Legio X Fretensis: A Prosopographical Study of its Officers [I-III c. AD]' (*Historia Einzelschriften* 66, 1993).

———'The Commanders of Syrian Legions (1st to 3rd c.AD)' *The Roman Army in the East*, ed. D.L. Kennedy (*JRA Suppl. Series* 18, 1996) 277-96.

Daltrop, G., Hausmann, U. and Wegner, M., *Die Flavier: Vespasian, Titus, Domitian, Nerva, Julia Titi, Domitilla, Domitia* (Gebr. Mann, 1966).

Daube, D., 'Did Macedo murder his Father?' *ZSS* 65 (1947) 261-311.

Davies, R.W., 'The Daily Life of a Roman Soldier under the Principate' *ANRW* 2.1 (1974) 299-338.

De Laet, S.J., *Portorium: Étude sur l' Organisation Douanière chez les Romains, surtout à l' Époque du Haut-Empire* (De Tempel, 1949: repr. Arno Press, 1975).

Derchain, Ph. and Hubaux, J., 'Vespasien au Sérapéum' *Latomus* 12 (1953) 38-52.

Derchain, Ph., 'La Visite de Vespasien au Sérapéum d' Alexandrie' *CE* 28 (1953) 261-79.

Devreker, J., 'La Continuité dans le *Consilium Principis* sous les Flaviens' *Anc. Soc.* 8 (1977) 223-43.

———'L' *Adlectio in Senatum* de Vespasien' *Latomus* 39 (1980) 70-87.

———'La Composition du Sénat Romain sous les Flaviens' *Studien zur antiken Sozialgeschichte: Festschrift Friedrich Vittinghoff* (ed. by W. Eck, H. Galsterer and H. Wolff: Kölner Hist. Abh. 28, 1980) 257-68.

———'Les Orientaux au Sénat Romain d'Auguste à Trajan' *Latomus* 41 (1982) 492-516.

Dilke, O.A.W., *The Roman Land Surveyors: An Introduction to the Agrimensores* (David and Charles, 1971).

———'Vespasian and Britain' *Atti* (1981) 393-8.

Dobson, B., 'The Significance of the Centurion and *Primipilaris* in the Roman Army and Administration' *ANRW* 2.1 (1974) 392-434.

Duff, J.W., *A Literary History of Rome in the Silver Age* 3rd edn (Ernest Benn Ltd., 1964).

Duncan-Jones, R., *The Economy of the Roman Empire* (Cambridge University Press, 1974).

Durry, M., *Les Cohortes Prétoriennes* 2nd edn (E. de Boccard, 1968).

Eck, W., *Senatoren von Vespasian bis Hadrian* (C.H. Beck, 1970).

———'Jahres-und Provinzialfasten der Senatorischen Statthalter von 69/70 bis 138/139 (I)' *Chiron* 12 (1982) 281-362.

———Caballos, A. and Fernandez, F. *Das Senatus Consultum de Cn. Pisone Patre* (C.H. Beck, 1996).

Engelmann, H., *The Delian Aretalogy of Sarapis* (E.J. Brill, 1975).

Étienne, R., *Le Culte Impérial dans la Péninsule Ibérique d'Auguste à Dioclétien* (E. de Boccard, 1974).

Evans, E.C., 'Roman Descriptions of Personal Appearance in History and Biography' *HSCPh* 46 (1935) 43-84.

———'The Study of Physiognomy in the Second Century AD' *TAPhA* 72 (1941) 96-108.

———'Physiognomics in the Ancient World' *Transactions of the American Philosophical Society* 59 (1969) 1-101.

Evans, J.K., 'The Role of *Suffragium* in Imperial Political Decision-Making: A Flavian Example' *Historia* 27 (1978) 102-28.

———'The Trial of P. Egnatius Celer' *CQ* 29 (1979) 198-202.

Fishwick, D., *The Imperial Cult in the Latin West. Studies in the Ruler Cult of the Western Provinces of the Roman Empire* (E.J. Brill, 1987).

Forni, G., *Il Reclutamento delle Legioni da Augusto a Diocleziano* (Università di Pavia: Facoltà di Lettere e Filosophia, 1953).

Forni, G., 'Estrazione Etnica e Sociale dei Soldati delle Legioni nei Primi Tre Secoli del Impero' *ANRW* 2.1 (1974) 339-91.

Frank, T., [ed], *An Economic Survey of Ancient Rome* Vols 1-5 (Johns Hopkins University Press, 1933-1940: repr. 1975).

Frassinetti, P., 'I Resconti dei Miracoli di Vespasiano' in *La Struttura della Fabulazione antica* (Univ. di Genova, Pubbl. dell' Istituto di Filologia Classica e Medioevale: 1979) 115-27.

French, D., 'Legio III Gallica' *The Roman and Byzantine Army in the East* (Krakow, 1994) 29-46.

Frere, S., *Britannia: A History of Roman Britain* 3rd edn (Pimlico, 1991).

Friedländer, L., *Darstellungen aus der Sittengeschichte Roms in der Zeit von Augustus bis zum Ausgang der Antonine* (ed. 7) English tr. *Roman Life and Manners under the Early Empire* by L.A. Magnus (George Routledge and Sons, 1907: repr. Routledge and Kegan Paul, 1968).

Friesen, S.J., *Twice Neokoros: Ephesus, Asia and the Cult of the Flavian Imperial Family* (E.J. Brill, 1993).

Gagé, J., 'Vespasien et la Mémoire de Galba' *REA* 54 (1952) 290-315.

———'L'Empereur Romain devant Sérapis' *Ktema* 1 (1976) 145-66.

Galand-Hallyn, P., 'Bibliographie Suétonienne (Les "Vies des XII Césars") 1950-1988. Vers Une Réhabilitation' *ANRW* 2.33.5 (1991) 3576-622.

Gallivan, P.A., 'Nero's Liberation of Greece' *Hermes* 101 (1973) 230-4.

———'The *Fasti* for the Reign of Claudius' *CQ* 28 (1978) 407-26.

———'The Fasti for AD 70-96' *CQ* 31 (1981) 186-220.

Garzetti, A., *From Tiberius to the Antonines: A History of the Roman Empire, AD 14-192* tr. J.R. Foster (Methuen, 1974).

Gascou, J., *Suétone Historien* (École Française de Rome, 1984).

Gichon, M., 'Cestius Gallus's Campaign in Judaea' *PEQ* 113 (1981) 39-62.

Goodman, M., *The Ruling Class of Judaea: The Origins of the Jewish Revolt against Rome AD 66-70* (Cambridge University Press, 1987: repr., Paperback, 1995).

Gordon, R., *et al.*, 'Roman Inscriptions 1991-1995' *JRS* 87 (1997) 203-40.

Gorringe, C.F., *A Study of the Death-Narratives in Suetonius'* De Vita Caesarum (Diss. Queensland, 1993).

Graf, H.R., *Kaiser Vespasian. Untersuchungen zu Suetons* Vita Divi Vespasiani (Kohlhammer, 1937).

Greenhalgh, P.A.L., *The Year of the Four Emperors* (Weidenfeld and Nicolson, 1975).

Griffin, M., *Seneca: A Philosopher in Politics* (Clarendon Press, 1976).

Gugel, H., *Studien zur Biographischen Technik Suetons* (Wein Böhlau, 1977).

Gwatkin, W.E. Jr., 'Cappadocia as a Roman Procuratorial Province' *University of Missouri Studies 5* (University of Missouri Press, 1930).

Hammond, M., 'The Transmission of the Imperial Powers of the Roman Emperor from the Death of Nero in AD 68 to that of Alexander Severus in AD 235' *MAAR* 24 (1956) 63-133.

———*The Antonine Monarchy* (American Academy in Rome, 1959).

Harris, H.A., *Sport in Greece and Rome* (Thames and Hudson, 1972).

Henrichs, A., 'Vespasian's Visit to Alexandria' *ZPE* 3 (1968) 51-80.

Herrmann, L., 'Basilides' *Latomus* 12 (1953) 312-15.

Hind, J.G.F., 'The Invasion of Britain in AD 43 – An Alternative Strategy for Aulus Plautius' *Britannia* 20 (1989) 1-21.

Hoffman-Lewis, M.W., *The Official Priests of Rome under the Julio-Claudians: A Study of the Nobility from 44 BC to 68 AD* (Papers and Monographs of the American Academy in Rome: Vol. 16, 1955).

Homo, L., 'Une Leçon d'Outre-Tombe: Vespasien Financier' *REA* 42 (1940) 453-65.

———*Vespasien, L' Empereur du bon Sens* (Albin Michel, 1949).

Hopkins, K., *Death and Renewal: Sociological Studies in Roman History 2* (Cambridge University Press, 1983).

Houston, G.W., *Roman Imperial Administrative Personnel during the Principates of Vespasian and Titus* (Diss. North Carolina, 1971).

———'Adlection of Men *in Senatum*' *AJPh* 98 (1977) 35-63.

Howell, P., 'The Colossus of Nero' *Athenaeum* 46 (1968) 292-9.

Hudson-Williams, A., 'Suetonius, *Vesp.* 22' *CR* 2 (1952) 72-3.

Isaac, B., 'Vespasian's Titulature in AD 69' *ZPE* 55 (1984) 143-4.

Jones, A.H.M., *The Cities of the Eastern Roman Provinces* 2nd edn (Clarendon Press, 1971).

Jones, B.W., *The Emperor Titus* (Croom Helm, 1984).

———'Agrippina and Vespasian' *Latomus* 43 (1984a) 581-3.

———*The Emperor Domitian* (Routledge, 1992).

———*Suetonius Domitian: Edited with Introduction, Commentary and Bibliography* (Bristol Classical Press, 1996).

Jones, C.P., Review of Eck, 1970; *Gnomon* 45 (1973) 688-91.

———'The Date of Dio of Prusa's Alexandrian Oration' *Historia* 22 (1973a) 302-9.

———*The Roman World of Dio Chrysostom* (Harvard University Press, 1978).

———Egypt and Judaea under Vespasian' *Historia* 46 (1997) 249-53.

Keaveney, A., 'Vespasian's Gesture (Suet. *Vesp.* 8.5 and Dio 65.10.2)' *GIF* 39 (1987) 213-16.

Kennedy, D., 'C. Velius Rufus' *Britannia* 14 (1983) 183-96.

———'Syria' in *CAH* X, 2nd edn (Cambridge University Press, 1996) 703-36.

Keppie, L., 'Legions in the East from Augustus to Trajan' *The Defence of the Roman and Byzantine East* (*BAR International Series* 297: 1986) 411-29.

Keppie, L., 'The Changing Face of the Roman Legions' *PBSR* 65 (1997) 89-101.

Kienast, D., 'Diva Domitilla' *ZPE* 76 (1989) 141-7.

Kindstrand, J.F., 'The Date of Dio of Prusa's Alexandrian Oration – A Reply' *Historia* 27 (1978) 378-83.

Kleiner, F.S., 'A Vespasianic Monument to the Senate and Roman People' *SNR* 68 (1989) 85-91.

———'The Arches of Vespasian in Rome' *MDAIR* 97 (1990) 127-36.

Kokkinos, N.K, *Antonia Augusta: Portrait of a Great Roman Lady* (Routledge, 1992).

Kokkinos, N.K, *The Herodian Dynasty: Origins, Role in Society and Eclipse. Journal for the Study of the Pseudepigrapha Suppl. Series* 30 (1998).

Le Glay, M., 'Les *Censitores Provinciae Thraciae*' *ZPE* 42 (1981) 175-84.

Levick, B., *Claudius* (B.T. Batsford, 1990).

——*Vespasian* (Routledge, 1999).

Lewis, N., and Reinhold, M., *Roman Civilization Sourcebook II: The Empire* (Harper Torchbooks, 1955: repr. 1966).

Lewis, R.G., 'Suetonius' "Caesares" and their Literary Antecedents' *ANRW* 2.33.5 (1991) 3623-74.

Liebeschuetz, J.H.W.G., *Continuity and Change in Roman Religion* (Clarendon Press, 1979).

Lindsay, H.M., *Suetonius Caligula: Edited with Introduction, Commentary and Bibliography* (Bristol Classical Press, 1993).

——'Suetonius as *Ab Epistulis* to Hadrian and the Early History of the imperial Correspondence' *Historia* 43 (1994) 454-68.

Loane, H.J., 'Vespasian's Spice Trade and Tribute in Kind' *CPh* 39 (1944) 10-21.

Lounsbury, R.C., *The Arts of Suetonius – An Introduction* (American University Studies 17, Vol. 3: Lang, 1987).

Luttwak, E.N., *The Grand Strategy of the Roman Empire from the First Century to the Third* (Johns Hopkins University Press, 1976).

Magie, D., *Roman Rule in Asia Minor to the End of the Third Century after Christ* (Princeton University Press, 1950: repr. Arno Press, 1975).

Malitz, J., 'Helvidius Priscus und Vespasian: zur Geschichte der "Stoischen" Senatsopposition' *Hermes* 113 (1985) 231-46.

Marrou, H.I., *Histoire de l'Éducation dans l' Antiquité* 3rd. edn, tr. G. Lamb (Sheed and Ward, 1956).

Martinet, H., *C. Suetonius Tranquillus, Divus Titus: Kommentar* (Beiträge zur Klassischen Philologie 123, 1981).

Mason S., *Flavius Josephus on the Pharisees: a Composition-Critical Study* (E.J. Brill, 1991).

Maxfield, V.A., *The military Decorations of the Roman Army* (B.T. Batsford, 1981).

May, G., 'L' Activité Juridique de l' Empereur Claude' *RHDFE* 15 (1936) 213-54.

McAlindon, D., 'Senatorial Advancement in the Age of Claudius' *Latomus* 16 (1957) 252-62.

McDermott, W.C., 'Flavius Silva and Salvius Liberalis' *CW* 66 (1973) 335-51.

McDermott, W.C. and Orentzel, A.E., *Roman Portraits: The Flavian-Trajanic Period* (University of Missouri Press, 1979).

McGuire, M.E., *A Historical Commentary on Suetonius' Life of Titus* (Diss. Johns Hopkins, 1980).

McLaren, J.S., *Power and Politics in Palestine: the Jews and the Government of their Land, 100 BC – AD 70. Journal for the Study of the New Testament Suppl. Series* 63 (1991).

MacMullen, R., *Enemies of the Roman Order: Treason, Unrest and Alienation in the Empire* (Harvard University Press, 1966).

Meyer, E.M., Review of Eck and others, 1996: *CJ* 93 (1998) 315-24.

Millar, F., 'The *Fiscus* in the First Two Centuries' *JRS* 53 (1963) 29-42.

————*The Emperor in the Roman World (31 BC – AD 337)* (Duckworth, 1977).

————*The Roman Near East 31 BC – AD 337* (Harvard University Press, 1993).

Mitchell, S., 'Imperial Building in the Eastern Roman Provinces' *HSCPh* 92 (1987) 333-65.

Mitford, Terence B., 'Roman Rough Cilicia' *ANRW* 2.7.2 (1980) 1230-61.

————'Cappadocia and Armenia Minor: Historical Setting of the *Limes*' *ANRW* 2.7.2 (1980) 1169-228.

Moles, J.L., 'Dio Chrysostom: Exile, Tarsus, Nero and Domitian' *LCM* 8 (1983) 130-4.

Momigliano, A., *The Development of Greek Biography* (Harvard University Press, 1971).

Montevecchi, O., 'Vespasiano Acclamato dagli Alessandrini' *Atti* (1981) 483-96.

Mooney, G.W., *C. Suetonii Tranquilli De Vita Caesarum. Libri VII-VIII* (Longmans, Green and Co., 1930).

Morgan, M.G., 'Vespasian and the Omens in Tacitus *Histories* 2.78' *Phoenix* 50 (1996) 41-55.

————'Two Omens in Tacitus' *Histories*' *RhM* 136 (1993) 321-9.

————'Vespasian's Fears of Assassination' *Philologus* 138 (1994) 118-28.

————'Tacitus, *Hist.* 2.83-84: Content and Positioning' *CP* 89 (1994) 166-75.

————'Vespasian and the Omens in Tacitus, *Histories* 2.78' *Phoenix* 50 (1996) 41-55.

Mottershead, J., *Suetonius: Claudius* (Bristol Classical Press, 1986).

Mouchova, B., *Studie zu Kaiserbiographien Suetons* (Praha Universita Karlova, 1968).

Murison, C.L., *Suetonius: Galba, Otho, Vitellius: Edited with Introduction and Notes* (Bristol Classical Press, 1992).

Murphy, J.P., 'The Anecdote in Suetonius' Flavian "Lives"' *ANRW* 2.33.5 (1991) 3780-93.

Musurillo, H.A., *The Acts of the Pagan Martyrs: Acta Alexandrinorum* (Clarendon Press, 1954).

Nash, E., *Pictorial Dictionary of Ancient Rome* 2 vols (Zwemmer, 1961-62).

Nicols, J., *Vespasian and the Partes Flavianae* (*Historia Einzelschriften* 28, 1978).

Paltiel, E., *Vassals and Rebels in the Roman Empire: Julio-Claudian Policies in Judaea and the Kingdoms of the East* (*Collection Latomus* 212, 1991).

Parker, H.M.D., *The Roman Legions* (Clarendon Press, 1928).

Pflaum, H.-G., *Les Procurateurs Équestres sous le Haut-Empire Romain* (A. Maisonneuve, 1950).

———*Les Carrières Procuratoriennes Équestres sous le Haut-Empire Romain* (P. Geuthner, 1960).

Pigon, J., 'Helvidius Priscus, Eprius Marcellus and *Iudicium Senatus*' *CQ* 42 (1992) 235-46.

Platner, S.B. and Ashby, T., *A Topographical Dictionary of Ancient Rome* (Oxford University Press, 1929).

Pollini, J., '*Damnatio Memoriae* in Stone: Two Portraits of Nero recut to Vespasian' *AJA* 88 (1984) 547-55.

Potter, D., Review of Eck and others, 1996: *JRA* 11 (1998) 437-57.

Price, H., *C. Suetonii Tranquilli de Vita Caesarum Liber VIII: Diuus Titus* (Diss. Pennsylvania, 1919).

Price, J.J., *Jerusalem under Siege: The Collapse of the Jewish State 66-70 C.E.* (E.J. Brill, 1992).

Raepsaet-Charlier, M.Th., *Prosopographie des Femmes de l'Ordre Sénatorial (Ier-IIème Siècles)* (Aedibus Peeters, 1987).

Rajak, T., *Josephus: The Historian and His Society* (Duckworth, 1983).

Reekmans, T., 'Verbal Humour in Plutarch and Suetonius' *Lives*' *Anc Soc* 23 (1992) 189-232.

Richardson, L. Jr., *A New Topographical Dictionary of Ancient Rome* (Johns Hopkins University Press, 1992).

Rickman, G., *The Corn Supply of Ancient Rome* (Clarendon Press, 1980).

Ritter, H.W., 'Zur Lebensgeschichte der Flavia Domitilla, der Frau Vespasians' *Historia* 21 (1972) 759-61.

Rogers, P.M., 'Titus, Berenice and Mucianus' *Historia* 29 (1980) 86-95.

Roxan, M.M., 'An Emperor Rewards his Supporters: the Earliest Extant Diploma Issued by Vespasian' *JRA* 9 (1996) 248-56.

Saddington, D.B., 'Early Imperial *Praefecti Castrorum*' *Historia* 45 (1996) 244-52.

Salomies, O., *Adoptive and Polyonymous Nomenclature in the Roman Empire* (*Societas Scientiarum Fennica*, 1992).

Salway, P., *The Oxford Illustrated History of Roman Britain* (Oxford University Press, 1993).

Schalit, A., 'Die Erhebung Vespasians nach Flavius Josephus, Talmud und Midrasch: zur Geschichte einer Messianischen Prophetie' *ANRW* 2.2 (1975) 208-327.

Schieber, A.S., *The Flavian Eastern Policy* (Diss. Florida State University, 1975).

Schmidt, M.G., 'Claudius und Vespasian. Eine Neue Interpretation des Wortes "vae, puto, deus fio" (Suet., *Vesp.* 23.4)' *Chiron* 18 (1988) 83-9.

Schwartz, S., *Josephus and Judaean Politics* (*Columbia Studies in the Classical Tradition* Vol. 18: E.J. Brill, 1990).

Scott, K., *The Imperial Cult under the Flavians* (Kohlhammer, 1936: repr. Arno Press, 1975).

Scullard, H.H., *Festivals and Ceremonies of the Roman Republic* (Thames and Hudson, 1981).

Shatzman, I., 'Artillery in Judaea from Hasmonaean to Roman Times' *The Eastern Frontier of the Roman Empire: Proceedings of a Colloquium Held at Ankara in September 1988* ed. by D.H. French and C.S. Lightfoot (*BAR International Series* 553 [ii] 1989) 461-84.

Sherk, R.K., 'Roman Galatia: the Governors from 25 BC to AD 114' *ANRW* 2.7.2 (1980) 954-1052.

———*The Roman Empire: Augustus to Hadrian* (Cambridge University Press, 1988).

Sherwin-White, A.N., *The Roman Citizenship* (Clarendon Press, 1973).

———*The Letters of Pliny. A Historical and Social Commentary* (Clarendon Press, 1966).

Sidebottom, H., 'The Date of Dio of Prusa's Rhodian and Alexandrian Orations' *Historia* 41 (1992) 407-19.

———'Dio of Prusa and the Flavian Dynasty' *CQ* 46 (1996) 447-56.

Simpson, C.J., 'The "Conspiracy" of AD 39' *Collection Latomus* 168 (1980) 347-66.

Smallwood, E.M., *Documents illustrating the Principates of Gaius, Claudius and Nero* (Cambridge University Press, 1967).

———*The Jews under Roman Rule from Pompey to Diocletian* (E.J. Brill, 1976).

Sordi, M., *The Christians and the Roman Empire* tr. A. Bedini (Editoriale Jaca Book Sp A, 1983: repr. Routledge, 1994).

Souris, G.A., 'The Size of Provincial Embassies to the Emperor under the Principate' *ZPE* 48 (1982) 235-44.

Southern, P., *Domitian: Tragic Tyrant* (Routledge, 1997).

Speidel, M. A., 'Roman Army Pay Scales' *JRS* 82 1992) 87-106.

Stambaugh, J.E., *Sarapis under the Early Ptolemies* (E.J. Brill, 1972).

Steinby, E.M. (ed.), *Lexicon Topographicum Urbis Romae* (Quasar, 1993 [I] and 1996 [III]).

Strobel, K., 'Zur Rekonstruktion der Laufbahn des C. Velius Rufus' *ZPE* 64 (1986) 265-86.

Suceveanu, A., 'M. Arruntius Claudianus et l' Annexion Romaine de la Do-
broudja' *Anc Soc* 22 (1991) 255-76.

Sullivan, R.D., 'The Dynasty of Cappadocia' *ANRW* 2.7.2 (1980) 1147-68.

Syme, R., *Tacitus* (Clarendon Press, 1958).

———'The March of Mucianus' *Antichthon* 11 (1977) 78-92.

———*The Augustan Aristocracy* (Clarendon Press, 1986: Paperback, 1989).

———*Roman Papers* Vols 1-2 ed. E. Badian; 3-7 ed. A.R. Birley (Clarendon
Press, 1977-1991).

———*Anatolica: Studies in Strabo* ed. A.R. Birley (Clarendon Press, 1995).

Takacs, S.A., *Isis and Sarapis in the Roman World* (E.J. Brill, 1995).

Talbert, R.J.A., *The Senate of Imperial Rome* (Princeton University Press, 1984).

Thompson, L., 'Domitian and the Jewish Tax' *Historia* 31 (1982) 329-42.

Thulin, C., *Corpus Agrimensorum Romanorum* (Teubner, 1913: repr. 1971).

Townend, G.B., 'The Date of Composition of Suetonius' *Caesares*' *CQ* 9 (1959)
285-93.

———'Some Flavian Connections' *JRS* 51 (1961) 54-62.

———'The Hippo Inscription and the Career of Suetonius' *Historia* 10 (1961a)
99-109.

———'The Restoration of the Capitol in AD 70' *Historia* 36 (1987) 243-8.

Toynbee, J.M.C. *Death and Burial in the Roman World* (Thames and Hudson, 1971).

Turner, E.G., 'Tiberius Julius Alexander' *JRS* 44 (1954) 54-64.

Vacher, M.-C., *Suétone: Grammariens et Rhéteurs* (Les Belles Lettres, 1993).

Versnel, H.S., *Triumphus: An Inquiry into the Origin. Development and Meaning
of the Roman Triumph* (E.J. Brill, 1970).

Wallace, K.G., 'The Flavii Sabini in Tacitus' *Historia* 36 (1987) 343-58.

Wallace-Hadrill, A., *Suetonius: The Scholar and His Caesars* (Duckworth, 1983:
2nd edn, Bristol Classical Press, 1995).

———'The Imperial Court' in *CAH* XI, 2nd edn (Cambridge University Press,
1996).

Wardle, D., 'Vespasian, Helvidius Priscus and the Restoration of the Capitol'
*Historia* 45 (1996) 208-22.

Wardman, A.E., 'Description of Personal Appearance in Plutarch and Suetonius:
The Use of Statues as Evidence' *CQ* 17 (1967) 414-20.

Watkins, T.H., 'Vespasian and the Italic Right' *CJ* 84 (1988/89) 117-36.

Watson, A., '*Adsertor Libertatis Publicae*' *CQ* 23 (1973) 127-8.

Watson, G.R., *The Roman Soldier* (Thames and Hudson, 1969: repr. 1970).

Weaver, P.R.C., 'Where Have all the Junian Latins Gone? Nomenclature and
Status in the Early Empire' *Chiron* 20 (1990) 275-305.

Webster, G., *Rome against Caratacus: The Roman Campaigns in Britain AD
48-58* (B.T. Batsford, 1980).

Wellesley, K., *The Histories, Book III* (Sydney University Press, 1972).

———*The Long Year AD 69* (Elek, 1975).

———'What Happened on the Capitol in December AD 69' *AJAH* 6 (1981) 166-90.

Williams, M.H., 'Domitian, the Jews and the "Judaizers" – A Simple Matter of *cupiditas* and *maiestas*?' *Historia* 39 (1990) 196-211.

Wiseman, T.P., 'Flavians on the Capitol' *AJAH* 3 (1978) 163-78.

Woodside, M.S., 'Vespasian's Patronage of Education and the Arts' *TAPhA* 73 (1942) 123-9.

Yavetz, Z., *The Urban Plebs: Flavians, Nerva, Trajan* in *Opposition et Résistances à l' Empire d' Auguste à Trajan* (*Entretiens sur l' Antiquité classique* 33, 1987) 135-86.

Zinn, T.L., 'To Keeping Vespasian a Virgin' *CR* 1 (1951) 10.